For my
big sister

George

LIFE'S DATA STACKERS

GEORGE JONES

LIFE'S
DATA
STACKERS

LIFE'S DATA STACKERS

Copyright © 2008 by George D. Jones
All rights reserved
Printed in the United States of America
Designed by Eric T. Jones

ISBN 978-0-557-20940-8

For my family

LIFE'S DATA STACKERS

CONTENTS

THE BOSS'S WORST NIGHTMARE -------------- 1

THE HUMAN COMPUTER --------------------- 26

WHAT'S REAL IS REAL -------------------- 54

PREDICTABILITY ------------------------- 87

THE FAMILY - FOR BETTER OR WORSE ------ 128

LOVE AND WAR WITH THE HOI POLLOI ------ 155

TIME TO GO TO WORK -------------------- 183

A FEW IDEAS FOR MANAGERS -------------- 216

IMPROVING LABOR (PEOPLE) RELATIONS ---- 251

RESOLVING PROBLEMS AND GRIEVANCES ----- 283

THOSE UNPREDICTABLE POLITICIANS
LARGE AND SMALL ----------------------- 317

CODA ---------------------------------- 358

CHAPTER ONE

THE BOSS'S WORST NIGHTMARE

"I seldom, if ever, make a mistake!" Looking up at Ted Bailey, my handsome, well dressed and self assured new assistant in the Human Resource Department, I saw from the expression on his face that, unfortunately, he was quite serious and meant what he had said. Not an iota of doubt clouded the face of the young Adonis. As I later discovered, what he really meant, was that he NEVER made a mistake. He sincerely believed that he never made an error in judgment, a false assumption, a screw-up, a slip of the lip, or exhibited any of the frailties that beset the rest of we more humble human beings. He was absolutely secure in his knowledge of how to handle delicate interpersonal relations at home and at work. Clear of eye, chin out, he spoke with complete confidence in his correctness and

LIFE'S DATA STACKERS

infallibility. If he had been Catholic, they might have made him Pope.

Yet standing there, comfortably wrapped in his invisible cloak of perfection, Ted failed to notice that he had just made a large and serious error. Before his fellow employees, and his boss, he had made a public proclamation that could only lead to trouble in his business and personal life. For instance, do you know anyone who really likes to associate with a person who claims to be at least almost perfect? After hearing such an intemperate and self serving remark, any boss (and I was no exception) would be forced to consider firing someone like Ted before he could seriously damage the Company's relationship with its employees.

By the time I first met Ted Bailey, I had spent seven years dealing with all kinds of people as a sales representative for a major steel company. Now, after an equal number of years as a Human Resource Manager, I had met Ted. And he was to be a severe test of my accumulated human relations skills, not to mention my temper. This was a test where failure could lead to serious labor relations problems. It was not a problem that could be solved by a three martini lunch or taking two aspirin and going to bed.

As you will learn, Bailey was the type of manager who might well inspire our white collar employees to form a union, and our steel mill United Steelworkers union to file grievances.

THE BOSS'S WORST NIGHTMARE

His lack of consideration for the ordinary working person and his or her opinions was exceeded only by his confidence in himself and his presumed knowledge of how the world should REALLY be run.

The plant already had a union representing the production employees. Almost immediately, Ted's manner and statements began to cause excessive friction between the union and Management. And now, with Ted's "assistance", the white collar employees were becoming dissatisfied and "restless" as well. As Ted strode through the plant and offices, talking to the employees, there was a chin-up superior manner about him. He seldom listened to what others, whom he perceived to be of a lower social and/or intellectual level, had to say. If he listened at all, he quickly refuted whatever opinion they may have expressed and then proceeded to tell them why they were wrong. The subject matter was unimportant. If it disagreed with his viewpoint, it wasn't worth considering. His superior manner, his unwillingness to listen with an open mind to the opinion of another person, his always putting the blame on someone else, and his arbitrary decisions all combined to make him a totally unacceptable Human Resource manager. As the old saying goes, "it is hard to be humble when you are as great as I am". And Ted was anything but humble.

QUICK ASIDE: I realize that this description of Ted Bailey also describes many Chief Executive Officers - which reminds us that holding a title does not necessarily make one a truly effective manager or a leader. This type of executive tyrant seldom, if ever gets the best out of his subordinates. Fear is very limited in its power to motivate people, except to quit their jobs. In too many cases, it isn't what you know that lands a position or takes you up the corporate ladder. It may, instead, be who you know, or even what you know about who you know. (And it doesn't hurt if you marry the boss' daughter, are a "silver tongued devil", or related to a major stockholder.)

WHERE WE ARE GOING, AND 9 IMPORTANT RULES

In this book I hope to give you some clues that will help you understand why people like Ted Bailey manage to become their own worst enemies, and why people, in general, behave the way they do. I will also suggest ways that you can use that understanding to improve your relationships with others both at home and at work. While the knowledge necessary to gain such understanding is readily available, simply possessing the requisite knowledge doesn't necessarily lead to understanding. Understanding requires that you either spend years gaining experience on your own – or learn from someone else, like me, who's had decades of practical experience in the everyday world dealing with people from all walks of life. The experience I've gained over six decades includes blue collar work in sweltering steel mills, participation in local, state and national politics, a Northwestern University education, U.S. Naval officer training, professional seminars, countless union negotiations, consulting, and holding management positions in the steel, appliance manufacturing, brewing, computer, and mining industries.

Over all those years I've come to realize how each of us – yes, even YOU, and Ted Bailey, is molded, influenced and controlled by a large group of people, things, and events that I call DATA STACKERS. You may not be fully aware of how these data stackers have, with or without your intent or knowledge, shaped your personality and the ways you interact with others. We are all both victims and beneficiaries of the data stackers' actions, over which we at least seem to have too little control. Just who and what are these life shaping forces that have made us into what we are today? In the following chapters I'll describe these sometimes obvious, but usually ignored forces. In addition I'll discuss nine basic rules you can use to improve your personal relationships with others at home and at work - rules that will help YOU become a positive DATA STACKER.

The nine rules are as follows:

1. To listen is divine.

2. Every decision you make is 100% correct.

3. Each action will normally result in a similar and equal reaction (apologies to Sir Isaac Newton).

4. An absence of communication will always result in negative rumors and/or assumptions.

LIFE'S DATA STACKERS

5. All grievances/complaints are caused by a breakdown in predictability.

6. What's real is real, or, perception is reality.

7. Each person desires and deserves recognition.

8. As the computer is stacked, the person will act.

9. Beware the arrogance of the incompetent and/or ignorant.

NOW BACK TO GOOD OLD TED

After Ted was hired, it didn't take long for the complaints to start coming in. As the months passed, Ted's depredations became more and more obvious and intolerable, and the number of formal grievances filed began to increase. And now, after having made his public proclamation of infallibility, he proceeded to confirm my worst fears. Ted himself was totally oblivious to the problems he was causing. His mind was so attuned to the idea that he never made a mistake, that he simply could not perceive one when it did occur. Such blind arrogance! He also failed to realize that none of us has any interest in hearing someone tell us that he or she is perfect. We know that he or she isn't - no one is.

Displays of truly superior talent; whether a difficult dunk by a basketball player, a faultless piano concerto performed by a pianist, or a young computer whiz confounding his parents with his skill; may tend to make us feel a bit inferior. This is an uncomfortable and unwelcome sensation that usually results in our feeling some degree of jealousy or even sadness over our lack of skill. However, we can appreciate and enjoy such displays if the talented performer displays <u>sincere</u> humility and modesty. In fact, it's a great disappointment to us when we see a truly gifted person begin to bray like the proverbial jackass or behave in an uncivil or unsportsmanlike manner: such as the athlete who takes steroids, the hacker who creates a computer virus, or the CEO who acts only for his own benefit while his company crumbles or stockholders and pensioners suffer.

In about the length of time it took him to find the outhouse and the coffee pot, Ted started alienating everyone in the plant. He had never worked in an industrial situation, but this did not prevent him from freely offering his "expert" opinion to just about everyone. It wasn't so much the opinion, but the way he delivered it. Standing erect, radiating supreme self-confidence, using an authoritative tone, and perhaps with just a wee bit of a condescending smile on his face, he would deign to bless his listener with his words of wisdom. There was no need for him to waste time listening to the other person who was, after all, obviously of inferior intelligence and/or position. ***Ted firmly believed the saying "there is no one more ignorant than the person who disagrees with me".*** And conversely, to him, the only ***smart*** people were those who ***did*** agree with his viewpoint. This approach promised to cause considerable dissension in a

LIFE'S DATA STACKERS

unionized plant where management's goal was to prevent grievances, not cause them. We had achieved excellent relations with our hourly employees by spending many hours in the plant talking one-on-one with the workers. Our goal was to resolve problems before they blew up into major union-management hassles.

As the situation with Ted got worse and worse, I spent more and more of my time correcting his mistakes and patching up relationships with disgruntled employees. Every time I would sit down with Ted to counsel him and discuss his mistakes, he would pass the blame off on some other person. After all, if you seldom (if ever) make a mistake, then it **must** be the other guy's fault. This illusion of being "almost nearly perfect" (like Mary Poppins) was not unique to Ted. Many others (perhaps you know some of them) share his affliction.

For instance, we have all seen the distasteful actions of temperamental overpaid sports figures and petulant movie stars who demand that we listen to their opinions on subjects about which they know very little. At this point, the "gifted" persons change, in our eyes, from role models whom we can look up to and admire, to simple braggarts - insufferable jerks with whom we do not wish to associate.

COUNTRY SINGERS ARE NOT ALWAYS GOOD

I once had the misfortune to attend a performance by one of the country's best known and most talented country singers.

THE BOSS'S WORST NIGHTMARE

The huge 4000 seat auditorium darkened, multi-hued spotlights reflected off the sparkling Christmas scenery, and the band announced the arrival of "the legend". His lack of modesty (and interest) became quite evident as he strolled casually out on to the stage. A bored expression heralded the lukewarm attitude he was to exhibit throughout the concert. When he did acknowledge our presence, it seemed to be with reluctance. In the course of his perfunctory presentation of the elaborate Christmas show, he continued to treat his audience with indifference and apparent disdain. His lack of preparation was quite obvious, and he often turned his back on the audience. Worse yet, he further disgusted the audience as he several times forgot the words to his songs. The members of the audience, who had paid a considerable amount of their hard-earned money to see the show, were not amused, and many vowed never to attend another of his concerts. Talent: good but ill-used. Manners: lousy. Result: disappointment and resentment. I for one will never "gamble" on one of his performances again.

Ted and the country singer shared some of the same dubious attributes. A person's first impression would lead him to believe that both Ted and the country singer were conceited and cared little about the opinions of others. I am sure you have encountered similar persons. Have you ever wondered why people like that behave the way they do?

For a few minutes put your natural revulsion and disdain for conceited people on the shelf and consider two possibilities:

LIFE'S DATA STACKERS

First, a person who appears to you to be conceited may instead be suffering from feelings of inferiority. Often such a person will try to compensate for or try to hide his or her failings by acting in a superior manner. Second, it's possible that the person really is as conceited as he or she appears to be. In either case, the source of conceited behavior may be traced back as far as the day of the person's birth and the lifelong input and stacking-up of incorrect and/or poor "data" into their individual and very personal internal "computers". (You may call it a brain - and hopefully we all have at least one.) This "data stacking" occurs in everyone one of us.

I suspect the country singer had done so many successful concerts over so many years that his "data" told him it was not necessary for him to knock himself out. After all, each concert was only a brief appearance in a town to which he would not return for several years. Then there was the input from his adoring fans who tended to overlook his transgressions. He had probably been sloppy and unprepared in previous performances and gotten away with it. Each time he "got away with" some kind of negative behavior, his internal computer told him it would continue to work the next time in a similar situation. There is an old show business axiom that, despite problems, "the show must go on". Too bad the bearded country singer had learned that it needn't be a *good* show.

THE BOSS'S WORST NIGHTMARE

THE "ARROW COLLAR MAN"

My memory of an event that had happened some years earlier when I was a college student, gave me some insight into Ted's problem. In those years my *alma mater* actually had a good football team and even won a Rose Bowl game. On the team was a second or third string quarterback with more good looks than talent. He would strut about the campus trying to impress the young women with his handsome visage, trim body, and position on the football team. Behind his back he was referred to as the "Arrow Collar man". This was an allusion to the perfectly groomed young men, with classic Greek profiles, who were then being used in Arrow Shirt advertisements. Chin held high, the quarterback could present a very haughty godlike look, a veritable model of classic beauty. From time to time some "fortunate" young lady might even be blessed with the opportunity to go out with him. Although he appeared to believe he was immensely popular, he was, in fact, thoroughly disliked. What talent he did have was not accompanied by any degree of modesty. Then, suddenly, he was gone - no longer in school. Eventually the story came out. He was actually suffering from a severe inferiority complex that had been well-hidden by a tremendous amount of overcompensation. He wanted to seem perfect and in control at all times. It was unfortunate that none of us around him were then mature or experienced enough to see beyond his surface actions, and were unable or unwilling to help or befriend him. Eventually, when he could no longer carry the burden, he broke down and cried in his advisor's office. Shortly thereafter, he dropped out of school and left for home. Several semesters later, as a much more normal and likeable person, he returned and finished his education. The thought that Ted Bailey might have the same problem as the "Arrow Collar man", and knowing that, at times, Ted could be quite sociable and charming, caused me to delve deeper.

As I will describe in later chapters, we are all largely the products of the constant flow of "data" that pours into and stacks up in our own personal internal computing machines. Almost every decision we make is based upon the totality of the information that the "data stackers" have poured into our ever receptive "computers" since birth. Each of us can only hope that our own personal data flow cannot be described as a case of GIGO - that is, "garbage in, garbage out".

Now to return once again to our talented and tormented friend, Ted Bailey. His story will give you an introduction to a common type of Data Stacker.

So, was Ted Bailey's data stacked in such a way as to have made him into a truly conceited person, or was he the victim of the kind of mental warping and poor data stacking that only caused him to *appear* conceited? After all, there were clues if one knew what to look for: On the whole, Ted was a pleasant and friendly fellow, so his casual and matter-of-fact comments

THE BOSS'S WORST NIGHTMARE

about his errorless ways just didn't fit. Indeed, as I was to later confirm, despite all outward appearances, Ted did not have a true superiority complex, but was, instead, trying to overcome overwhelming feelings of inferiority engendered by his relationship with his father. And, as is so often the case, in his efforts to avoid revealing his inferiority he tried to emulate the traits of his presumed perfect father. Ted was simply the product of his home. Those closest to Ted had stacked his mental computer with harmful and incorrect data. To a considerable degree, his was a case of "monkey see, monkey do".

How did he come to conclude he was perfection embodied? To learn the answer required that I discover a good bit more about his earlier years and family life. It required that I recall and consider what I'd already learned about Ted's childhood, and that I learn more by engaging Ted in many, many hours in intense one-on-one discussions.

I started by considering how I had first been introduced to him. One day the President of our company telephoned and asked that I come to his office to meet my new assistant. This was my first inkling of trouble. Was I suffering from a lapse of memory? Was I suffering from "Earlyheimers"? I did not recall asking for additional help and was not aware of any pressing need for an assistant. Upper management is normally intent upon cutting staff - so why was the personnel department being given a "freebie"? Upon arrival at the Big Boss's inner sanctum I was introduced to Ted. It seems that Ted's father was the autocratic

LIFE'S DATA STACKERS

and wealthy President of a small airline. "Fortunately" (NOT!) for me, "Father" was also an old friend of the Chairman of the Board of my company, and his darling son needed a job. Since Ted wasn't educated in any particular field and was something short of earning a degree in anything, the President immediately thought of putting him somewhere HE wouldn't have to deal with him. Lucky me! The Human Resource Department is the "obvious" place to put someone with no experience. Where else would you put someone with such a charming personality? Like too many top executives, even among the members of today's "enlightened managements", the President failed to realize the irreparable damage that can be caused by using the Human Resource Department as a dumping ground for the incompetent and/or unqualified. The litany of this type of corporate folly would fill a sizeable book.

As we noted earlier, in about the length of time it took him to find the outhouse and the coffee pot, Ted started alienating everyone in the plant. Time after time I tried to correct his actions using conventional counseling techniques, but failed. Eventually, the situation became intolerable - but he could not be fired. Remember, he came strongly recommended by the Chairman of the Board and the President.

The final straw was Ted's behavior during a meeting with a salesman. As part of our safety program, we required all employees to wear safety glasses. A salesman for a safety supply company had convinced us to undertake an extensive vision

THE BOSS'S WORST NIGHTMARE

testing program. Given the average age of our employees, he told us we could expect to find that at least 25% of them would require prescription lenses. We bought the testing machine and began our program. Ted did much of the testing - during which he freely gave people the benefit of his "extensive" knowledge in the field of optometry. Upon completion, of the program, the salesman returned to see how we had done. The meeting was held in my office with Ted present. I reported to the salesman that we had been surprised to find that almost 33% of our employees appeared to need prescription glasses - many more than he had predicted. At this point, Ted spoke up to tell me that I was wrong, that it was some other slightly lower number. No, I said, I think it is 33% and tried to continue the discussion. But Ted would not let it go - he again insisted that I was wrong. I told him that the exact number was not critical. The point was that either number was high and the problem needed to be dealt with. As we went on with the discussion, Ted quietly left the office and returned shortly with a sheet of paper. He then interrupted the discussion to point out, once more, that my numbers were not exactly correct (though indeed, the percentage was very close to the number I had cited, and more to the point, significantly higher than the salesman's predicted number). He was eager to prove me wrong, and that he was once more perfectly accurate. After all, he truly believed that *he* never made even minor errors. Oh vanity - how it does clog up the ears and the thinking process!

LIFE'S DATA STACKERS

Embarrassing your boss in front of anyone, especially visitors, does not make you a hero. One might even consider it an ERROR in judgment. For me, it conjured up visions of a firing squad with good aim. The inevitable confrontation could not be delayed any longer.

Firing "politically connected" Ted would be difficult, and might well put my own job in jeopardy. Truly a situation in which I, as a young married man with a wife and three children to support, should proceed with considerable caution. I would have to try to find out what was going on inside his well-groomed head. The only way to find the answer was to ask the right questions. Questions designed to reveal the basis for Ted's thoughts and actions. What had happened to Ted to cause him to act the way he did? Where did he get the idea that he should never make a mistake? Who had twisted his thinking so badly and given him his unacceptable philosophy? What was **his** view of the world around him? HOW WAS HIS DATA STACKED? It was time for me to take my own advice and do a lot of listening.

And so dear readers, here is rule number one - **TO LISTEN IS DIVINE!** So please, LISTEN, LISTEN, LISTEN. Even if you can't bring yourself to go in with an open mind to listen to the other person's stupid, uninformed, illogical opinion - do try to at least listen. When you least expect it, the other person may just, purely by accident of course, say something of interest.

THE BOSS'S WORST NIGHTMARE

As an old saying has it, "even a broken clock is right twice a day".

There was one thing I had learned in several years of working with people of all kinds: If you hope to truly understand other people, it is imperative that you learn all you can about their backgrounds. You have only to listen to any one of the many current television talk shows to learn how past events usually influence peoples' actions. The abused child, the family of an alcoholic, people who were raised in poverty etc. etc. However, the results of hardship are not always bad. The great depression of the thirties taught many people the value of saving money and being careful with their expenditures. Virtues (and vices) are only partially acquired from parents - generally among the first of our data stackers. All of our information comes from using the five senses while reading books, going to church and school, exposure to the multitude of things that happen around us, and the people with whom we associate in our day to day living. Like it or not, it is the sum total of all our experiences, from the day of our birth to the present that largely determines our personalities, our decision making and our actions. Research suggests that genetic factors play a role, but the environment also provides very powerful inputs to each person's internal computer. Unfortunately, as in Ted Bailey's case, the flow of data appeared to be - as stated earlier – a case of GIGO. (garbage in, garbage out)

E'S DATA STACKERS

UNSTACKING TED'S DATA

Shortly after the episode with the salesman, Ted and I had an "after work" conference - a serious multi-hour meeting during which we both expressed our feelings and answered each other's questions. I will not try to relate all of those questions and answers, but will confine this report to the more pertinent portions of the discussion.

A short time into our discussion, it became fairly obvious that Ted sincerely wanted to be liked by others and had dreams of becoming a respected and successful business man *like his father*. Ted felt that he had put his talents to good use in his new job and that he had been effective. Surely his fellow employees appreciated his generous suggestions and obvious intelligence. As I began to reveal to him what his fellow employees actually thought of him, he was forced to reconsider: Was it possible that all of those long hours he had spent in the plant talking to employees about their problems had been wasted? Didn't they realize he was trying to help them? Why would they say unkind things about him behind his back? However, as most people eventually come to realize, even your closest friends will seldom, if ever, tell you face to face about your shortcomings - even when you ask them to level with you. They do not want to run the risk of offending you and losing your friendship. So they keep silent, avoid the subject, or tell those little "white lies". And so it was in Ted's case. The more he learned about what others *really* thought about him and the adverse effect it was having on

THE BOSS'S WORST NIGHTMARE

his work, the worse he felt. Delivering the "bad news" was not pleasant, but it was necessary. A problem had to be defined and recognized before a solution could be found. Ted needed to acknowledge his mistakes and decide to do something about them. It's easy for counselors to provide suggestions, but nothing will happen unless the "problem child" makes a conscious decision to change. This is a well-known principle used by most treatment groups. The individual <u>must</u> recognize that a problem exists and <u>must</u> be the one to decide to take more appropriate action.

After the first hour we had pretty well outlined his problem. I had become convinced that Ted was not truly conceited, but he certainly had many unacceptable beliefs and traits. I was happy to see that he could possibly be salvaged and become a productive manager. Ted, on the other hand, was unhappy and thoroughly confused. He had worked hard and tried his best, but had failed for reasons he did not understand. My next step was to learn more about his basic philosophies and, especially, who or what had created them. I knew from previous counseling experience that once people have been forced to consider enough information about their problems, the solutions quite often will "tumble out" of them or at least become obvious to them. To get to the information, though, you must ask questions – and, more importantly, listen very carefully to the answers.

LIFE'S DATA STACKERS

In Ted's case, the most important person and role model throughout his life was his Father – a man who, to anyone else, appeared to be a gross and unfeeling person. Still, here was a man who was in full control of his business, his finances, his employees, his life, and his family. He ran, as they say, a "tight ship" with a firm hand. He fit the stereotype of the "corporate bully" - of which there are far too many. Some of his more endearing qualities included smoking big cigars, pounding on the desk, never allowing opposing viewpoints, and abusing subordinates. And, big surprise, *he was always right*!!! How could anyone possibly dislike him? However, in spite of all his loveable qualities, Mrs. Bailey Senior had finally gotten a divorce. (Remember this – it's important.)

Poor Ted had spent his childhood trying to live up to his Father's unrealistic expectations. There was constant pressure to excel and no excuse for doing things wrong. This led Ted to undertake many unusual actions. At least at first, Ted's desperate goal was to prove that his Father was sometimes wrong. Ted told me of midnight forays during which he ransacked his Father's office and desk, searching every room of their home, doing things to his car etc. etc. All these efforts were directed at Ted trying to prove himself right - and his Father wrong. Of course, there was no way he could win. No matter what Ted found to support his position, the omniscient parent always made the final judgment about who was correct. As you can well imagine, it wasn't poor Ted. There was no way the know-it-all Father in a position of power was going to allow his offspring to win. One might expect that these constant defeats would drive Ted into despondency or feelings of inadequacy, but do not forget that Bailey Senior was Ted's idol and the subject of his admiration. So it wasn't too surprising when our discussion eventually evolved into the following exchange:

Q. Ted, what is your goal in life?

A. I would like to be a successful businessman.

Q. Any particular type of businessman?

A. Well, like my Dad. He is certainly successful.

Q. Why do you seem to feel that you must never make a mistake?

A. That is necessary if I want to reach my goal.

Q. Do you believe that successful businessmen never make mistakes?

A. Of course, they can't afford to be wrong.

Q. **Ted, can you name <u>any</u> businessman who has never made a mistake?**

A. **Yes, my Dad**

The logic was really quite simple. Dad was a successful businessman. Dad never made a mistake. Ted wanted to be a successful businessman. Therefore: Ted must never make a mistake. The senior Bailey was obviously the major data stacker in Ted's life.

LIFE'S DATA STACKERS

When Ted did screw up, as we all inevitably do, he had to blame it on others. This was the only way in which he could maintain his record of "perfection". Harmful and inaccurate input to his "human computer" caused him to decide to act in this manner.

Having acquired extensive background information, I was now able to start another and very necessary line of questioning. It was also time to provide Ted's "computer" with new data.

Several days earlier, Bailey Senior had telephoned the Company and asked the switchboard operator to connect him with "young Teddy". When this was related to Ted, he was terribly embarrassed. It was enough to make any young man's ego flop on the floor like a dying fish.

Q. Ted, do you consider your Father's approach to be the proper way for a businessman to ask for someone on the telephone?

A. No

Q. Would you say that your Father made a mistake when he did so?

A. Yes he did.

Q. Ted, is your Father still a successful businessman, in spite of his mistake?

A. Yes

Then followed several more questions and illustrations of mistakes made by the Father. Eventually the knowledge

THE BOSS'S WORST NIGHTMARE

of family background paid off with a final critical question.

Q. Ted, does your Mother (remember, she had divorced Bailey Senior) feel that your Father has made mistakes?

The answer to that question could be seen in Ted's eyes and his stunned open-mouthed look. He sat perfectly still for several minutes. It looked as though his past life must have been flashing through his brain, but this time it was being illuminated by flashes of new knowledge and understanding. Finally he looked up and said, "I can see how this has affected my whole life - and my marriage". Now the words began to flow more and more rapidly as Ted recounted other imperfections in his Father that he had previously excused. He was able to see how he had become a victim of his Father's warped personality. All of this made it easy for him to now understand why his fellow employees, not to mention his boss - and probably his wife, had come to dislike the way he dealt with them.

From that day forward, Ted would admit his mistakes and began to give credit to others when deserved. Not everything could be changed overnight, but he was on his way. The internal computer now had new, and correct, data that would guide him in his future relations with others. He now knew that he, as well as his Father, could be successful in spite of occasional mistakes. Of course it did take some time before the other employees were convinced that the new Ted was for real - they had to get their

LIFE'S DATA STACKERS

"computer" data changed, or unstacked. Their first impressions of him had been slammed into their skulls pretty hard and it would take awhile to change all that internalized information.

Although we eventually parted ways, I did see Ted again sometime later and am happy to report that he was doing quite well and appeared cheerful and happy.

Well, that's the legend of Ted Bailey. Like in any good Saturday afternoon movie, I hope Ted continued to ride happily into the sunset. Let's now let Ted's story serve as a springboard into the next chapter, which concerns "the Human Computer". We've already discussed it generally in this chapter, so let's get on with a further explanation of what it is and how it works.

THE BOSS'S WORST NIGHTMARE

CHAPTER TWO

THE
HUMAN
COMPUTER

Well folks, guess what? Strangely enough, good old Ted Bailey was right about being right, but for all the wrong reasons. All his decisions, and all of YOUR decisions, are 100% correct. Not just once in awhile - all of the time. Hard to believe isn't it? Each and every time you decide to take an action or say something to anybody it is, in your mind, the right thing to do. This is due to the second of the nine rules you need to remember:

EVERY DECISION YOU MAKE IS 100% CORRECT.

But what does this mean? Can it possibly be? If it's true, how should you act? Obviously, you shouldn't strut around thinking that you rarely or never make a mistake - as Ted Bailey did. That would drive people away from you, and it's no fun to be right if it means being oh so lonely. Sure, the good news is that you never make an incorrect decision. But the really bad

THE HUMAN COMPUTER

news is: Every decision you make is 100% correct **only in relation to what you know at the moment.** Your 100% correct decision is only as good as the data it's based on - the data that has been accumulating in your brain since the day you were born.

Your challenge, then, is to recognize that what appears to be the correct decision to you, may not be a **good** or correct decision in the eyes of others – that your personal database....that is, all the information upon which you base your decisions....is not, and never can be, complete. You don't want to resemble that caricature of a boss who brooks no argument: "Don't confuse me with the facts; I've already made up my mind!" Once you become aware that, despite all your experience, you may yet benefit from the opinions of others, or may need to ask more questions, you improve your odds of making objectively good decisions. Note here that this means you must be listening - listening so that you can learn new facts.

You will recall that, in Ted's case, he needed his decisions to be correct 100% of the time in relation not only to his own accumulated data, but in relation to everyone else's as well. This required that Ted, instead of listening, make a conscious effort to insure that others also recognized his decisions as being error free. In his mind, this was necessary if he were to become a successful businessman. Remember, Ted learned from his father that hot shot executives never make mistakes. So, although he <u>was</u>, in a sense, 100% correct in his

LIFE'S DATA STACKERS

decisions, based on what he had learned since he was a child, he failed to anticipate that none of his associates would agree - since they had been brought up in a different manner and with entirely different "facts" in their computer/brains.

In Ted's mind, since it was always the other guy who was wrong, it didn't matter that the other guy wasn't operating on the same information base he was. Ted just wasn't interested in what others had to say or what was in THEIR computers. He didn't listen.

Like Ted, most of us don't stop to question whether what we are doing is the "right" thing - we just assume we are. Given what we know, we take the path that appears most correct. From small everyday decisions, to life changing events, we never, at the deciding moment, see ourselves as making a mistake. No one in his or her right mind will consciously set out to fail or to do something wrong. When was the last time you sat down and said to yourself, "today I think I will make an error in judgment"?

At this point you might want to respond "wait just a darn minute! Many people knowingly decide to break the law – they intentionally exceed the speed limit, commit murder, and do drugs, etc. entirely on a voluntary basis". You would be correct, but the question is whether, in their own minds, their decisions to engage in illegal behavior were correct under the circumstances. How about a few examples?

THE HUMAN COMPUTER

IS THE DECISION RIGHT OR WRONG?

In my hometown there was a pervasive illegal numbers racket involving much of the community. People would wager their money on what numbers would appear on the closing quotes from the stock market. Sellers were everywhere: on street corners, in mom and pop grocery stores, and even in little old ladies' homes. I must be mistaken about the little old ladies you say? (Surely little old ladies would not knowingly engage in such an illegal activity?) Oh yes they would! Although basically honest, these elderly outlaws were poor, with little or no Social Security benefits, no other pensions or way to earn a living. Their data stacks told them it was illegal, but they had to eat and pay the rent. To them there was no alternative: Sell the illegal numbers or starve. Under those conditions both you and I might have done the same thing, and figured that it was a 100% correct decision. To those little old ladies it was the correct thing to do despite being illegal.

Next, try to picture yourself as a soldier in the jungles of Viet Nam or the streets of Iraq, or perhaps as a policeman in Israel. You are confronted by a 10 year old child with either a gun or what appears to be a bomb. Do you shoot the child or wait to see whether he'll kill you? How do you know whether or not the child will detonate an explosive or shoot you? If your data bank has been stacked with many instances of children killing your fellow soldiers, what would you do? In modern warfare it

LIFE'S DATA STACKERS

has not been unusual for soldiers to be killed by children carrying guns or explosives. What is the "correct" decision?

Similar situations often occur with respect to suicide bombers in the Middle East. Much closer to home are the incidents that take place, on an almost daily basis, in our own inner cities. Teen and sub-teen killers and muggers using guns and knives threaten other people's lives with little regard for the consequences. Most people's data banks have been properly stacked to regard the killing of children as cruel, immoral, and unnecessary. But perhaps it is, on rare occasion, the correct thing to do. If your life were on the line, what would you decide?

What if it's not just your own life that's at risk? Suppose, for example, that you're driving down a narrow mountain road in an Army truck carrying 25 other soldiers. Rounding a curve you see two refugees ahead: an old man and an old woman. Unable to stop in time to avoid hitting them, will you drive off the cliff killing yourself and the 25 soldiers?

Now expand the number of potential victims even further: would you have decided to use atomic weapons against Japan, killing 100,000 to save the 500,000 or more lives that would likely have been lost in an invasion? These are all very hard decisions that someone has to make - from Presidents to hungry widows.

How is it possible to claim that a burglar or bank robber is making a correct decision when he undertakes an illegal action? First you must remember that they were probably raised under different circumstances than you. Somewhere, at home, from peers or older role models, they learned that it was OK to steal from others. Take from the rich (that is anyone with more money than the bandito has) and give it to me, who is more deserving. Society owes it to me. Nobody will give me a chance. Why should I work for minimum wage, and why should I work at all when stealing is so much easier? The robber knows, in fact, that it's wrong - at least according to the law and to honest people, but the robber's logic and input from his peers tell him it pays to be an outlaw. Believe me. There is a lot of negative irrational thinking going on in this world, and too many have been taught that this illegal behavior is really the right thing to do. Again, as I mentioned before: garbage in garbage out.

HOW ABOUT YOUR OWN INTERNAL DATA?

Now then, what kinds of information have YOU been tucking away in that skull of yours since the day you were born? Some of it is bound to be somewhat crumby. When it comes time to make a decision, without even knowing we are doing it, we summon up everything we have ever learned from the day of our birth, and take action. Memories of how you enjoyed sucking your thumb are right up there with how you felt when the school bully punched you in the nose, or how you reacted to your first kiss - all combine with everything else you have done to provide the raw data for your ever-faithful and compliant internal computer. The information you need is furnished in a

LIFE'S DATA STACKERS

nanosecond. Unfortunately, the data is sometimes insufficient or is unacceptable to others - and then we make what other people see as mistakes.

"What's that" you say? That it's impossible? Considering all the goofs you've made during your life, you couldn't possibly be correct all the time? "After all", you say, "some of those decisions were real bummers - had really bad results - cost mucho dinero - caused a divorce!" To learn how to distinguish a subjectively "correct" decision from an objectively "good" one, maybe it will help if we look at a few examples.

SOME CASE HISTORIES (MOSTLY TRUE)

Case #1 – Low on gas.

You're driving down a lonely highway in Nevada. You're halfway to your favorite "guest ranch", and notice your gas tank is almost empty. You quickly take stock:

- It's 4:30 and the "Ranch" closes at 5:00.
- The hostesses do not accept late arrivals.
- There's gasoline available at the "Ranch" for the return trip.
- You're eager to arrive as soon as you can.
- The last time the "idiot light" came on at this location you were able to stretch it and arrive safely.

Your internal computer quite logically tells you to go ahead.

THE HUMAN COMPUTER

You decide to pass up a nearby gas station and happily put the pedal to the metal..... subsequently running out of gas 25 miles from the nearest pit stop/gas station. **Your decision not to buy gas was 100% correct.** After all, it paid-off the last time.

It may be difficult to convince you of this while you are trudging through the sagebrush with only coyotes and prairie dogs for company, but under the above circumstances, it's understandable that your internal computer would quickly tell you to go ahead. A decision that's reasonable and correct - as far as it goes. The only difference this time, however, was that, in your haste to arrive before closing time, you went 70mph instead of 50mph. This, of course, caused your engine to consume more gasoline per mile traveled - something you should have learned a long time ago. But being a "let's turn the key and go" type of nimnal you (and your internal computer) were ignorant of that fact, and you, despite your subjectively correct decision, are now blessed with a long stroll through the cacti.

Luckily, or unluckily in this case, unexpectedly high fuel consumption rates have never caused you to run out of gas before. Therefore, this simple relationship between speed and fuel consumption was not in your computer as a factor to consider. Or maybe you would have swallowed the story the lady told the State Trooper who stopped her for speeding: She said she had to drive that fast so that she could reach the gas station before she ran out of gas.

33

See how obvious it is? One plus one equals two. Or, in the case of your ill-fated trip to the ranch, all the factors you knew of added up to a go-ahead signal. Your decision to proceed was 100% correct based on your accumulated data. There was no negative information in the old data bank. Well, cheer up ... the next time you head for the "Ranch" your computer will direct you to make a different 100% correct decision: to either buy gas or drive more slowly!

Case #2 – The job offer.

A young department head, who we'll call Joe, was debating an attractive job offer from another company. Almost simultaneously, a large corporation bought out his current employer. The acquiring company wanted to retain Joe's services and move him to the corporate office. It was an extremely attractive offer, both financially and professionally, so Joe decided to turn down the first company's offer and take the job with the new owners. A few years later Joe was let go from his job with no pension benefits and a bleak future. Meanwhile, the person who took the other job Joe had been offered became a Vice President within six months. Did Joe make a mistake? In retrospect, yes. Based on what he knew at the time of the decision, no. What did the takeover company have to offer that sounded so attractive?

A higher salary.

An office in a more desirable part of the country.

THE HUMAN COMPUTER

An opportunity to build a whole new department.

An opportunity to work with an exceptionally good boss.

Generous capital accumulation and profit sharing plans.

It was a much more profitable company

It seemed like a no-brainer. However, in this case, a combination of lies and misrepresentations rendered this subjectively good decision objectively bad. Joe didn't know that the acquiring company, which was aware of his other job offer, wanted his talents just long enough to insure a smooth takeover. They had no intention of moving him up. Also, Joe didn't know – until too late - that the company's management had a long history of prejudice against Joe's religion. As a final blow, the really good boss was also fired and replaced with an incompetent who wanted to bring in his own people. The moral: sometimes you can't win for losing. But again, note that Joe's decision was correct - based on what Joe knew at the time. Poor naive Joe had never been in this type of situation before and his limited experience with selfish corporate liars allowed Joe to make a 100% correct decision that would lead him down the wrong path. It's situations like this that give rise to expressions like "hindsight always has 20-20 vision".

Case #3 – Improper advances.

A high ranking Company official makes improper advances toward one of his female employees. His persistence

35

LIFE'S DATA STACKERS

finally drives the woman to file damaging charges against him with the Equal Employment Opportunity Commission.

Unfortunately this is not an unusual scenario, and it's one that often ends with the offender and his Company paying a substantial price for his improprieties. Why did he do it in this case? How could he possibly believe, especially these days, that his actions were acceptable? Were his decisions really 100% correct? Obviously not in the eyes of the female employee, the company and the courts. So why was it right in his mind? How was his data stacked?

This man had moved up the corporate ladder and held many jobs in which he exercised considerable control over the lives and fortunes of his employees. They had to "butter him up" to get pay raises or promotions. His internal computer had been well-stacked with the information that his underlings would do whatever was necessary to please him. He had also been taught from childhood that women were there to serve men and they should expect and accept sexual advances as normal and reasonable - even in the office. To help this impression along, some women had intentionally used sex appeal and favors to improve their relationship with him. No one had ever complained in the past! So there he sat: fat, dumb and out-of-date with the modern world and, in **HIS** mind, 100% correct in the actions he had taken.

This type of person can often be brought around to acting in a proper manner if someone will reach into his "computer",

THE HUMAN COMPUTER

pull out the bad stuff, and cram in some new and more proper data, or, as our psychologist friends might say, if someone will help him bring the past events up to the present for reexamination in light of current knowledge. When individuals understand what has been affecting their decision making (it's usually well hidden in the subconscious) they can make permanent changes in their future decisions. This type of reexamination is what helped Ted Bailey.

Case #4 - The Case of the Frustrated Usher.

One of the biggest tourist attractions in the United States is the so-called new "country music capital", Branson, Missouri. Tour buses loaded with the "over 50" crowd flood daily into this small Ozark Mountain community. One day, a bus containing 45 "seasoned citizens" pulled up to the theater of country comedian Ray Stevens. Those 45 senior citizens had traveled over a thousand miles crammed into narrow seats separated by a narrow aisle that was overhung with baggage racks, carry-on baggage, and television sets. The theater employed "Greeters" whose job it was to meet the bus, instruct the passengers, and then lead them into the theater to their seats. The Greeter who met this particular bus was experienced and had long ago learned that every person on the bus would want an aisle seat in the theater. (The entire tour group would be lucky to get two.) The Greeter knew he would hear all the usual reasons - "I want to take a lot of pictures", "I have a weak bladder", "I can't bend my right (or

37

LIFE'S DATA STACKERS

left) leg", "I can't see around the person in front", "I want to get out early", etc. etc. etc. The Greeter's computer was well stacked with a large store of these persuasive excuses. With this background, and not wanting to have to deal with all of these worn-out, predictable reasons, the Greeter climbed on the aging bus to meet the tour. To forestall any such problems he told the tour group, up front, that these old excuses wouldn't cut it and there were only two aisle seats available for the group. His internal computer told him this would do the trick - the cordial but firm speech had always worked before. Feeling confident in his handling of the situation, he off-loaded his charges and headed for the front door.

All went well until they got inside the theater. The seating capacity was over 2000 people - it had an entirely open area with the ceiling at least 50 feet high - there was ample space between rows. As the group reached their seats, the Greeter heard a nice polite voice behind him say, "I must have an aisle seat. I have claustrophobia". The Greeter could not believe what he had heard. This woman who had traveled a long distance for many hours in a bus with narrow seats, a narrow aisle, and baggage rack immediately overhead, and now was suddenly afflicted with claustrophobia in this huge open expanse of the theater. The Greeter had to admit to himself that he really hadn't yet heard everything after all. The lady got her aisle seat, not for her claustrophobia, but really as a reward for the day's most original excuse. The Greeter's data stack had not included that particular excuse, leaving him unprepared to politely deflect the request. He'd thought he could predict the outcome based on his previous experience, and took the correct preventive action relative to his accumulated data, but because of the limitations of his data stack, it failed to help him politely deflect a novel, unanticipated excuse.

Case #5 - The Military Mentality

Anyone who has been in a military organization is well aware of the fact that orders from higher ranking officers are meant to be obeyed. You're undoubtedly familiar with military expressions such as "ours is not to reason why, ours is but to do and die", or "yes sir, no excuse sir", and of course "Mister, that is an order". The level of discipline that these expressions assume is very important – at least when troops are engaged in or preparing for an activity as hazardous as combat. It's essential that the cohesive nature of a military unit be preserved and that soldiers not attempt to execute their own self-directed, uncoordinated, personal battle plans. For a military commander to accommodate disobedience or dissent in the heat of combat would create chaos and result in lost battles. However, once a war has been won and the fighters have returned home, another battle begins - especially for higher ranking commissioned officers and non-commissioned officers (sergeants). These are the veterans who have the most difficult time adjusting their command techniques to the civilian workplace because they have

LIFE'S DATA STACKERS

spent the most years operating with the expectation that subordinates will simply obey their commands.

Consequently, I have seen many highly qualified and intelligent senior officers become near-pariahs in the work place because of their inability to adjust. For years they've taken the principle of unquestioned obedience for granted. To give a clear and direct order to a subordinate is the way to get things done. However, in today's work place, assuming you want a good human relations atmosphere, that technique can be counterproductive. Without additional training, the retired officer who is placed in a civilian managerial position runs a great risk of failure. Subordinates are not accustomed to, and will resent, military-style orders. Unless someone counsels the retired officer, he may well fail in his new job.

The point, once again, is that a retired military officer's decision to obtain prompt obedience by giving direct orders is 100% correct - in the proper context. However, it's obviously a mistake to operate in the civilian setting to take actions based on old "computer" data acquired in the military. The retired officer's "computer" needs new data - data that tells him to make requests, give reasons, and heaven forbid - listen to other opinions. My intent here is not to insult all military officers. The comments above really pertain to individuals in any calling who are too inflexible to adapt to new circumstances.

As I understand it, our armed forces are now doing a much better job of developing leaders rather than "drivers". I'm

THE HUMAN COMPUTER

told that in today's military leadership schools they teach commanders to use different leadership styles depending on the situation and on the type of people being led. The authoritarian leadership styles I have described above are now taught as generally being appropriate only in basic training and in combat or simulated combat situations. More relational and motivational styles of leadership are taught as being appropriate when directing professional officers or self-motivated and highly disciplined enlisted people.

However, while they may now be less common, there are still military commanders and business leaders who insist on using an authoritarian leadership style in all situations. It seems that we may always have these types with us whose acquired data has been corrupted either by sleeping through human relations and leadership lectures during their leadership training, or, as with Ted Bailey, by an unfortunate role model.

LEADERSHIP DATA STACKING

A good leader does not need shoulder or collar insignia or a CEO title to motivate subordinates. Those who do, are the ones most in need of having their data re-stacked. Unhappily, there are too many company officials who are sold on the "military mind set" and an authoritarian leadership style - much to the detriment of their companies. When you see these types in high positions, you have to wonder how much more successful their organizations could be with better leadership.

LIFE'S DATA STACKERS

Hopefully, by now you've been able to spot the common thread that runs through all of these little stories. In every case the individual reacted almost automatically, based on past experiences and teachings. The DATA STACKERS, (parents, employers, friends, enemies, teachers, books, religion, etc. etc.) all contributed their input. The type and quality of "correct" decisions you make will be largely influenced by which of the stackers have had the most influence on you. A person raised in a very religious family might look to a future life as a member of the clergy. A child from an abusive family, unless someone teaches him otherwise, will also often become an abuser of his children and/or wife. Almost without fail, a person's characteristic behavior can be traced back to the person's early formative years - the years in which the young mind was most susceptible to new information. The famous expert on child behavior, Dr. Jaime Ginott, put it very well when he said "children are like wet cement. Whatever falls on them makes an impression".

Perhaps the most important thing an education can do for a child is to make sure that as much "good" data as possible is stacked in the child's brain. Even the negative effects of a poor home environment can be counteracted by exposing a child to sources of information and guidance such as schools, youth groups, churches, and books. With this "outside" help, children can be taught the information necessary to make better

THE HUMAN COMPUTER

judgments and techniques to improve their logic and decision making abilities.

Speaking of the value of an education, I'm reminded of the story of a Democrat politician from Arkansas who stopped off at the farm of a constituent. "Well Jake", he said, "I suppose you and the boys are all going to be voting for me in the coming election". "Well sir, me and Luke will be votin' for you, but Lem's votin' Republican". "Jake, what happened? Why is Lem voting Republican after all these years"? "Well, Jake said, you know that Lem, he always was one to take to readin'". (Switch the parties if you prefer – but this is the way the story was originally told.)

MEMORY, THE FIVE SENSES AND THE HUMAN COMPUTER

What is this human computer I'm talking about? Where does it get its information (data) and how does it operate? One can discuss these questions in either technical or layman's terms. For those of you who are more scientifically inclined, I will quote from a November 29, 1993 article in U.S. News & World Report:

> Memories are stored, scientists believe, as electrical patterns in neurons deep in the brain's hippocampal region. Over time, these patterns are translated into new neural circuitry in different brain areas, creating a permanent record of events. Intensely traumatic events, says Yale University psychiatry professor Michael Davis, "produce

LIFE'S DATA STACKERS

unusually strong nerve connections that serve as long-lasting memories". Years later, the right stimulus can set those nerve circuits firing and trigger the fear, with no immediate understanding of its source.

As increasing numbers of researchers delve into the mysteries of human memory, it becomes clearer that the brain is a *permanent* storehouse for all of our past experiences. True, those memories are not always readily available when we want them - such as during a final exam - but that is called forgetfulness, or the inability to *recall* information. It's not memory loss. According to Dr. David Salmon of the University of California at San Diego School of Medicine, "people do develop forgetfulness. It's not a loss of information; it's a difficulty in retrieving information".

Researchers have confirmed this by surgically exposing portions of subjects' brains and then using electrical probes to stimulate various points in the exposed brain regions. The subjects are kept fully conscious so that they can describe their responses to signal inputs from the probes. When researchers contact various points of the surfaces of subjects' brains, the subjects suddenly recall memories of long "forgotten" events - and with perfect clarity and detail. They remember not only facts, but sights, sounds, odors, etc. as clearly as if they were present at the moment the memory was being created.

There are also less invasive techniques that psychologists use, such as regression therapy, to find out what went on in a

THE HUMAN COMPUTER

subject's past. For example, regression therapy may be used to help a patient recall events that occurred early in the patient's life, i.e., the proverbial trip back to the subject's childhood. (Hey folks, this is where Ted Bailey went astray.) Another example is the use of hypnosis to drag out an individual's secrets. (Sorry, I don't buy the "past lives" theory to explain peoples' actions - one life is about all most of us can handle.)

On a day-to-day basis, though, we poor laymen have to rely more on good oral and written communications, books, photographs, friends and relatives, and finally, our own miserably inadequate ability to recall. Knowing what went on in the past, i.e., how your computer data has been stacked, helps you, your therapist, and your acquaintances to better understand the reasons for your present actions. Conversely, the more you know about others' experiences and training, the better you can predict and understand their actions. Good communications are not a passing fad; they are the basis for a happier and more productive life.

Now then, shall we continue to discuss scientific experiments and talk in a very learned manner about axon systems, calcium channels, synaptic plasticity, the hippocampus, or neural circuitry? No? Well how about mossy fibers, granule cells or monoclonal antibodies? I think not. Let's leave all that good stuff to the psychologists, the neurobiologist, and other similar folks. After all, this book is not a scientific treatise. I am writing it for ordinary people like you and me.

LIFE'S DATA STACKERS

Suffice it to say that research data strongly supports the day-to-day "real life" observations of the author: namely, that *everything* you have ever experienced remains firmly implanted in your brain. You need not know how the brain operates to make use of its powers. It's somewhat like driving a car. You can make it go where you want when you want without knowing one blessed thing about the operation of an internal combustion engine. Accordingly, I will continue to use the computer analogy to help you further understand how people use those wonderful organs we call our brains. And in so doing, I hope to provide you with an even better understanding of what controls your actions and why other people do what they do. Perhaps you will at least consider these things when you need to make an important decision. After gathering all the actual facts that you can, make sure your decision is based on "good data" and not emotion or dubious information from unreliable sources.

So now that we have the academic stuff out of the way, it's time to remind you that I am neither a psychologist nor a psychiatrist. Fortunately for you, however, more than thirty-five years in the human relations field has taught me a few things. I will attempt to present my findings in a manner that will not require you to earn a PhD before you can understand what I am saying.

Start by thinking of your brain as a phenomenally complex and efficient computer with umpteen gigabytes of storage capacity. The biggest "hard drive" you can begin to

THE HUMAN COMPUTER

imagine. Somewhere along the line, either before or immediately after your birth, the "fantastic five" (the first and most important of the DATA STACKERS) begin to pump information into your internal computer's "data bank". (Brain, to those of you who haven't figured it out yet.) The "fantastic five", which are the five senses: touch, sight, smell, sound, and taste; pour a steady stream of information (data) into a brain that seems to have no limit to its storage capacity. Among newborns, touch is the first sense to develop. Newborn babies cannot see very well, but they certainly seem able to sense a dirty wet diaper or a mother's touch. And, much to the delight of their new parents, their little hands are quick to grasp their parents' fingers.

From infancy forward there is no stopping the torrent of information into our brains. You cannot stop the flow - not even while you are asleep. You can, however, do a lot to control the quality of data input by exposing yourself to good books, beautiful music, intelligent friends, and even people with opposing viewpoints. Wherever you go, and whatever you do, you are constantly absorbing new experiences and information. All of it providing additional data for your limitless "computer" - data upon which your computer will make future decisions - all of them 100% correct!

Most people will acknowledge the probability of being influenced by the "fantastic five" while they are awake, but might argue that these senses shut off when they are asleep. So let's consider that argument. I'm not sure if it's feasible to learn a

LIFE'S DATA STACKERS

foreign language by slipping a small loudspeaker under your pillow as some have suggested, but I am certain that external inputs do have some effect on a sleeping brain. Do you remember, or have you perhaps heard of, that old camper's trick of placing a fellow camper's hand in a pan of warm water while the person is asleep? The intent, and often successful result, is a wet bed - much to the embarrassment of the victim. The feel of the warm water obviously percolates into the subconscious, in the midst of a deep sleep, and triggers the unpleasant result. It's also quite common for sleeping brains to sense sounds and smells and incorporate them into dreams. If your spouse gets up early and fixes coffee or fries up some bacon, you may well start dreaming of a breakfast at Brennans. How much or how little a sleeper may be affected is certainly a matter of debate, but it does appear that those five senses do continue to do their job, and continue to stack data in our brains, twenty-four hours a day. While the quality and type of data that we acquire while sleeping may not be of any significant value in future decision making. The inputs that we allow our brains to be exposed to as we sleep can affect our decision making ability by affecting the quality of our sleep.

Recall, of course, is something we all wish we could improve. And as far as data stacking is concerned, improved recall obviously correlates well with improved decision making ability. How nice it would be if we could retrieve any memory we wanted at any time. Just think of how it would improve our

THE HUMAN COMPUTER

decision making ability – not to mention all the money we could win on TV quiz shows. Too bad it doesn't work that way. We often struggle to remember a word, fact or a name with little success. Some purveyors of "memory systems" will have you use a system of associating the item to be remembered with one or more other objects or thoughts. (I haven't yet become comfortable with the idea that I have to recall a whole chain of things in order to recall one simple name or fact, but it seems to work for many people.) Sometimes, while vainly trying to remember a word, a person will recall the first letter and perhaps the number of syllables but not the word itself. Other information may be remembered only under conditions similar to those under which it was learned. The smell of a lovely perfume may many years later trigger memories of a pleasant evening. While most folks wrinkle their noses at the smell of sulfuric coal smoke, I get a positive reaction. It reminds me of a happy childhood in a steel town that reeked of smoke from coal burning locomotives and the steel plant coke ovens. One whiff of that aroma and my mind automatically responds in a positive manner.

Most people have had a feeling that a particular event has occurred before or they have seen a person or place at an earlier time. The French use the phrase déjà vu, which means "already seen", to describe this condition. This feeling most probably results from our "computer" recognizing parts of some forgotten memory. A small bit of the data in your "human computer" is jostled from the subconscious to the conscious by a smell, a

LIFE'S DATA STACKERS

word, an action, a face or a situation. However, since we don't recall the complete situation, it leaves us with only a vague feeling of having experienced something at an earlier date. Once again, we see that inputs from years ago are still safely ensconced in our brains - now if only we could get it all back out on demand – and improve the quality of our decisions.

So how can you use this knowledge of how your brain works to adjust your data stack and improve your relations with others? Consider this example: Suppose you meet a stranger and take an immediate dislike to that person. Instead of just writing the person off, ask yourself why. What caused your brain to produce that reaction? To find the answer, search your data stack (your memory) to see if you can recall anyone else you might have known who had an appearance or mannerisms similar to the stranger you've just met. If you disliked the first person, it could explain your negative reaction to the stranger. At least recognize that your feelings are based on how you felt about an entirely different person and withhold making a hasty judgment about the new acquaintance, as we usually do, based on your first impression! Ask questions and LISTEN to the person you've just met! As you learn more, you will form new and hopefully more positive associations.

Employment interviewers, for example, have to be particularly careful regarding the effects of negative first impressions. They talk to thousands of people, each of whom helps stack the interviewer's data by leaving some type of impression upon them - whether good or bad - and each applicant thus has at least a minor effect on each of the interviewer's decisions to hire other applicants.

Another common misuse of acquired data that personnel men fall victim to is the "halo effect": If an applicant has interests and experiences in common with the personnel man doing the interview, a "halo effect" may well be created giving the applicant much better standing in the interviewer's mind than the applicant deserves. For the rest of the interview the interviewer may tend to overlook the applicant's shortcomings because of the "good feeling" he or she is experiencing.

Less well recognized data stacking problems are subconscious reactions to something as simple as an applicant's mannerisms, perfume, or accent. The interviewer can guard against the effects of obvious factors such as common interests, but may be completely unaware of the more subtle responses that have been aroused within his "computer". His decisions may still be "100% correct", but unless the interviewer can get his internal computer straightened out, he's likely to hire applicants who turn out to be problem employees, and reject applicants that would have turned out to be highly-valued employees.

Incidentally, some of you may have wondered why interviewers ask so many probing questions - some that seem to be overly personal - about all facets of your background. The likely reason is that they've been trained well enough to know that it's important for them to find out how **your** data is stacked.

LIFE'S DATA STACKERS

Therefore, if you're the one being interviewed, before going into your interview, make sure you do know how your own data is stacked and how to affect what your interviewer's impression of it will be. More on this later.

One final note, **speech** is <u>NOT</u> one of the five senses. We learn by hearing, tasting, smelling, feeling, and seeing. When we are talking, we are NOT learning how other people's data is stacked. That may be why people who talk the most sometimes seem to know the least. (Perhaps it's a ploy to keep you from asking them questions and thereby learning that they are not all that smart.) To help convince yourself of the value of studying how others' data is stacked, try an experiment: Go for one entire day using your voice ONLY to ask questions. After asking the questions, make sure you listen carefully to the answers. By the end of the day, I can guarantee you that you will know a lot more than you did that morning - and your personal and very human computer will have considerably more useful information. In addition, your friends will appreciate your attention!

Understanding a human computer is just the beginning. It is of critical importance that you learn how to make it operate to your advantage. You need not know all that technical stuff described above, but you do need to know that this great brain of yours is constantly acquiring and using information. Some of that information is bad and some is good - your job is to sort it out. The nine rules will help you in that regard.

THE HUMAN COMPUTER

CHAPTER THREE

WHAT'S
REAL
IS
REAL

Well there you are! It's right smack dab in front of you! The next important rule for you to know and remember:

WHAT'S REAL, IS REAL

Remember all of that good stuff we talked about in the last chapter? All about the fantastic five constantly loading your internal computer? This vast accumulation of facts, theories, myths, outright lies, good and bad experiences etc., results in each one of us having our own private, personal, confidential, and individualized view of the world around us. It's an all encompassing view of all our relationships to people, places, and things. It's OUR PERSONAL REALITY. And that, in turn, creates our personalities. Like fingerprints, there are no two exactly alike. Even twins, raised in apparently identical circumstances, will have different experiences and will have unique outlooks on life.

It's impossible for any two people to have matching perceptions - even of virtually identical events. For instance: Two people in a reception line shake hands with the same person. That person uses exactly the same amount of pressure when shaking the hands of the two people as they pass by in the reception line. The first person in line might perceive the handshake to be firm while the other thinks of it as limp. Why? Because each of the two people in line will compare this handshake with perhaps hundreds of previous handshakes. If one of the two people had, a moment before, met and shaken hands with the San Francisco Forty-niners football team, and the other with Miss Lovejoy's Junior Dance Class, the contrast between the two people's perceptions of a subsequent person's handshake would be quite extreme.

Another way to express this is to say that "perception is reality". All of your actions with regard to the people in your life, the house you live in, your job or whatever else, are governed by your perception of those things.

Some people, for example, hate military service with its disciplined, structured life and the way so many day-to-day decisions are made for them by superiors. For these folks, military life can seem like life in a prison. On the other hand, others seem to thrive on the lifestyle. To them, it's a relief not to have to decide when, where, or what to do. In either case, it's

LIFE'S DATA STACKERS

often previous life experiences that determine whether one's experience in the military will be tolerable or not. I recall from my own days in the Navy, actually enjoying the infamous S.O.S., or creamed chipped beef on toast. While my buddies were gagging on it, I was enjoying a breakfast that I was used to eating at home. (Ok, so it wasn't like Mom's cooking, but I was used to eating the basic ingredients) Yes indeed, we all had different perceptions of what constituted a good breakfast. Of course when it came to beans and powdered eggs for breakfast, we all seemed to have the same "reality".

Go to any auction or garage sale and you see how true it is that "one person's junk, is another's treasure". What you may consider an old ugly chair, someone else will be more than willing to buy as an antique. My wife and I attended an auction in which a large collection of mostly costume jewelry was offered for sale. Everyone passed-over the plain looking ring with its lone blue stone as just another piece of "junk" jewelry. Their "reality" predicted that, as they'd experienced at other such sales, there would only be cheap "dime store" baubles available. My wife took a closer look and decided to bid. She was the successful bidder at $35. The ring that was perceived as "junk" by others turned out to be a star sapphire worth hundreds of dollars. Why such a difference of opinion? Again - and I'll keep saying it until it really sinks in - because each person's internal computer has been stacked in a different manner, and each person's reality, based on that data stacking, is different. Lucky

WHAT IS REAL, IS REAL

for us, all the other folks at that auction had their realities tuned to believe that you never find anything really valuable at a household auction.

Hooray for all of our individual differences!! Imagine what a boring world it would be if we all thought exactly alike, looked exactly alike, acted exactly alike, or perceived everything exactly alike. As it is, each person's perceptions of the world around them - based on the information in their internal computers - will determine how they'll act and make decisions. What's real to them (not you) will set the stage for their actions.

You may object and say that what I refer to as a person's "reality" is, in fact, only that person's perception of reality. After all, a native of the Ozarks might perceive a pile of dirt and rocks as a mountain while a Westerner would call it a hill, but an objective standard exists for determining whether the pile is, in reality, a mountain or a mere hill. However, such an objective standard is irrelevant when seeking to understand and influence behavior. So I refer to people's perceptions as their "realities" to emphasize that their personal perceptions are the only REAL realities to them.

The next time someone tells you they know where you're coming from, ask them, "where"? They may think they know, but they can never know fully and completely. When trying to understand others, it certainly helps to learn as much as possible

LIFE'S DATA STACKERS

about them, but never assume you know or comprehend all of another person's experiences. Even experienced psychologists using regression techniques are unable to learn everything about a patient. If you have ever attended a funeral you may have said or have been tempted to say to the "next of kin" something to the effect of, "I know how you must feel". No you don't! Not unless you've recently lost a loved one. And even then, you couldn't really perceive the depth of the other person's grief at that moment. And, it may even be that the other person has been looking forward to this event thinking "I'll be glad when you are gone you rascal you!" Be careful what you assume you understand about others until you've done what's necessary to really know how their data's stacked.

However, if, after having attempted to understand another's reality, you end up acting on a misperception of that reality and embarrassing yourself, don't let that negative experience deter you from continuing to try to understand people – from continuing to ask questions and listen closely to the answers. The road to understanding is seldom smooth. In the process, you will learn more about those around you. At the very least they're likely to be flattered by your interest and attention - and you'll know just a bit more about where they're "coming from".

WHAT IS REAL, IS REAL

GREAT VARIETY IN ORDINARY PEOPLE

There are countless examples of how people differ in their outlook on various aspects of everyday life. What do you say we whip through some examples of how ordinary people live their lives in worlds that they perceive in ways that may be entirely different from the way you and I perceive them? At the risk of sounding overly negative, I would also like to illustrate how some people, in various professions, can go astray - or at least project a bad image that causes others to get negative "data" into their internal computers.

First, let's consider those in the Accounting field. The old stereotypical picture of the accountant included the garter on the sleeve, the green eyeshade and a firm grip on every dollar. These days the image includes an MBA, a business suit (with power tie) and a presidency before age 40. Unfortunately, the fancy suit and education have failed to remove the too often narrow view held by many financial people. (Yes I know they aren't all bad - one of my best friends is an accountant!)

One of my first experiences with this mentality occurred while I was a salesman for a major steel company. Contrary to the popular view of some sales departments, ours spent very little money on frills, and we were not allowed the infamous three martini lunches or fancy gifts to purchasing agents. At one point, sales began to falter due to the slowing of the national economy. What was the financial Vice President's solution? Stop spending any money at all on ordinary lunches and reduce visits to the

LIFE'S DATA STACKERS

customers. Bummer!! All salesmen know that the only time you make sales, and money, is while you are in front of the customer. Consequently a good salesman will get in as many calls as possible each day - and usually use the lunch hour to make one more call. Needless to say, this practice did not help our sales. The sales people knew this would happen, but the number crunchers could only think of reducing expenses - THEIR reality said they should only worry about making the books balance. Too often they were unable to envision the likely consequences. Do you suppose it was this type of attitude that created the expression "penny wise and pound foolish"?

During a television talk show interview, the famous comedienne Carol Burnett was asked about her early years in the business. She pointed out how, despite poor initial ratings, her show was kept on the air because network executives felt it was good and would eventually succeed. It did, magnificently. Now, however, ratings are all-important and shows that start slowly are quickly dumped. As Miss Burnett put it, "networks used to be in **SHOW** business - now they are in show **BUSINESS"**. Getting the emphasis on the right word makes all the difference - and those with the "bean counter" mentality still just don't get it. That is not their reality. Perhaps if television network executives would learn a bit more about what really makes show business tick, they would understand and become more useful and productive in their jobs.

WHAT IS REAL, IS REAL

In another case, a large multinational mining company came close to losing its future. This type of company spends large amounts of money and years of time searching out new ore bodies all over the world. It's a slow and costly process. Once an ore body is found, land must be acquired, environmental permits obtained, roads built, equipment bought, buildings erected, and sometimes whole towns constructed to provide for labor imported from miles away. All of this takes years of planning and foresight. In this particular case, the Company had located a veritable mountain of ore within a reasonable (100 miles) distance of some of its other operations. The financial people looked at the expenditures required and the years that would pass before the mine could become operational, and voted NO. They could not see any immediate return on the investment. If this mining company had been one of those unfortunate enough to have been staffed clear to the top with Ivy League MBAs the project might have stopped right there. Instead, the Corporate office had a good combination of not only financial people, but also capable staff from such departments as Sales, Production, Human Resources, Exploration, and others - a well-rounded team that was free to discuss the problem from each department's particular point of view. Do I dare say it? Each had their own "reality" based on years of data input to their "personal computers". Conferring together and sharing their realities enabled them to reach a consensus decision. The end result was a decision to go ahead with the multimillion dollar purchase - over

LIFE'S DATA STACKERS

the objections of the financial staff. As the President put it, "we must protect our future by ensuring our ore supply. The Accounting Department's function is to keep track of our money. It does not decide where or when we will spend it".

The inability to assess value other than in dollars and cents has traditionally been one of the biggest shortcomings of financial people. This can be seen in the negative influence that accounting departments often have on decisions that companies make with regard to safety programs. The National Safety Council learned, years ago, that for every dollar spent on a safety program, a company could expect four dollars in savings. Now that is a fairly straightforward number. But too many Accounting Departments can't seem to understand. They don't see the four dollars actually coming into the company's coffers. The problem that accountants face in attempting to take such phenomena into account is that the savings, and the success of any safety program, are based on the things that don't happen. It's the broken leg that doesn't happen, the cut wrist that doesn't occur, or the life that is not lost. The savings are in NOT having to pay out large sums of money for medical and lost time benefits. Not to mention a few other intangibles such as employee morale etc. I guess the business schools don't teach methods of evaluating such things - which leaves their graduates with an incomplete data bank for making decisions. Theirs is an incomplete and "unreal" reality.

WHAT IS REAL, IS REAL

To help decision-makers learn to appreciate factors that their respective disciplines haven't taught them to quantify, many companies undertake extensive cross training of their management people. One approach is to have all new management trainees undergo a lengthy program during which they work in a variety of departments. In this way they can learn each area's needs and concerns, and the peculiar problems that they each face. Other organizations will move higher level experienced department heads into new positions to achieve a similar understanding - and not coincidentally, as a way of training them for the President's job.

Bringing a variety of "realities" together can also be advantageous when hiring managerial prospects. A number of people, each from a different department or specialty, are brought together to interview each candidate. They each hear all the questions and all of the answers in a common environment. Each person brings his or her own set of standards, beliefs etc. to the meeting. After the interview they get together and express their opinions. Each person's unique background will result in viewing the applicant in many different ways. The sum of these viewpoints will usually be quite accurate and reliable.

NUMBERS CAN BE MISLEADING

I could go on and on with examples of this type, but let's take a gander, instead, at just one particularly noteworthy example of a financial man's inadequate reality. This case

LIFE'S DATA STACKERS

involves a Comptroller who had considerable influence with not only the Division President, but with the Corporate office as well. Strangely enough, his rise to the top was not based on his financial acumen so much as his ability to make a speech - but that is another story for another time. His reality seemed to be that EVERYTHING could be learned by looking at the numbers. Why get new typewriters that cost so much money when the typists can get along with the old ones? They still work don't they?? Eventually the Personnel Manager, who had been busy listening to employee complaints and conducting too many exit interviews, pointed out to the President that those typewriters were, on average, twenty years old and much slower than modern equipment. With great reluctance, and only on direct order from the President, the Comptroller ordered new machines. The number of exit interviews immediately took a downward turn.

The same Personnel Manager was also having a terrible time trying to hire people to work for this Comptroller. The Comptroller would turn down one applicant after another for what seemed like irrational reasons. After the Comptroller had rejected a large number of what appeared to be well-qualified people, the Personnel Manager finally discovered that the Comptroller was basing his hiring decisions solely on intelligence test scores. And we all know that there is nothing more reliable, trustworthy, and illegal than basing a hiring decision on a single test score number. What did it matter that no

WHAT IS REAL, IS REAL

test yet devised could really measure such things as motivation, common sense, or ability to deal with others? That one test score told the Comptroller all he needed to know. Somewhere along the line he must have hired an individual with a great test score who turned out to be a real whiz bang. And from then on, the Comptroller's reality was that high scores meant good employees. It's also a lot easier to make a decision based on a simple number rather than taking the time to evaluate an applicant's personal characteristics.

Then, one day, the frustrated Personnel Manager came across an applicant who tested extremely high on general intelligence. With that kind of a score, the Comptroller would perceive this person as being qualified for just about any job in his department. The Comptroller granted the applicant an immediate interview even though there were no job openings at that time. Shortly after the interview, the Comptroller, full of smiles and enthusiasm, came to the Personnel Manager's office. "We have to hire this young man. If necessary, we'll *make* a job for him". It was only then, as Paul Harvey would say, that he learned "the rest of the story". The brainy applicant had been causing trouble since high school days. Fired from one job after another for insubordination, laziness, fighting, and embezzlement, his jobs were interspersed with years spent in prison. Most of it was right there on the application blank, but the Comptroller had focused only on the test score. To obtain an

LIFE'S DATA STACKERS

employee with that kind of a test score, the Comptroller would have hired the devil himself.

By this time you may think that you have every right to conclude that I'm prejudiced against the financial folks. But actually, I'm not - because I have not "prejudged" them. What I have is a well-considered <u>bias</u> against the "bean-counter" type of financial person.

Further, I am appalled by those corporations that put the Human Resource department under any type of financial vice-president since their data is so narrowly stacked. Too often the Human Resource function is crippled by supervision from those who are unable to understand the many intangible but powerful benefits of a good employee relations program.

A good Human Resource Manager will try hard to prove how his or her department provides monetary benefits to the company. But as previously noted, as in a safety program, some of the best savings come from bad things not happening. For example, what price do you put on a company's **NOT** getting a bad reputation? To be known as a good place to work decreases turnover and saves a lot of money due to reduced recruitment needs. The public relations and sales budgets become smaller as the word gets out that yours is "a good company and a good place to work". That is why large sums of money are often spent to purchase the "blue sky" (goodwill) assets of a company. In many cases the reputation is more important than the buildings and inventory. In other words, the public's perception (reality) of any organization (or you) should be a major consideration at all times. Incidentally, I have personally worked under both financial and non-financial types and know whereof I speak. With that, let us quit delineating the fiscal follies and get on with other types of reality conflicts.

GOOD AND BAD REALITIES

Reality Check: You are driving down the highway and find yourself stalled behind an older couple's car that's moving very slowly and exhibiting evidence of indecision on the part of the driver. Do you get angry, or do you try to put yourself in their place? Too often it's Maalox time, and you indulge in intemperate horn honking. Hopefully, the next time this happens you will try to consider their "reality". At an advanced age they very probably have slower reaction times, perhaps poor hearing, and sometimes failing eyesight and often are a bit slower in making decisions. Their internal computers, taking these factors into consideration, are telling them to slow down, think it over, and be cautious. Instead of flapping your lips with obscene remarks, say thank you for taking care and not causing a wreck. Some day you may be in their predicament.

Did you know that the wrong kind of reality can kill you? Back in 1929, at the time of the great stock market crash, a number of people committed suicide by jumping out of windows. Men who had previously made millions of dollars in the market saw the value of their investments tumble drastically.

LIFE'S DATA STACKERS

Despondent, they leaped from tall buildings to a messy end. Yet many of those unfortunates had not been reduced to poverty at all - at least not by most people's standards. Many still had what an average person would call a fortune. But in their minds, they had become impoverished. Their reality told them that it took a multimillion dollar fortune to live a "proper" or "reasonable" life style. Rather than face the difficulties, and perhaps more important, the humiliation of having to endure an ordinary standard of living, they ended their lives.

This same twisted view of reality persists today. Have you ever watched one of those TV shows where some "poor" soul, who is up to his eyeballs in credit card debt, explains how impossible it is for him to live on only eighty or ninety thousand dollars a year? Don't let him get near a window in a tall building! Other times it may be a couple that just knows it would be impossible for them to exist without two incomes. Surely you can't expect one of them to stay home to take care of their juvenile delinquents - no, not even if one of them is earning over $200,000 a year. It's all a matter of perspective (reality), sometimes encouraged by simple greed, selfishness, or data and expectations they've accumulated from their moneyed past.

These differences in how we view our lives are all around us. Sometimes it's funny, and at other times it makes your heart ache for those whose realities are less than pleasant. I recently listened to a medical doctor describing his experiences working with Washington, D.C. high school students. He had volunteered to visit inner city schools to provide the students with health information. During a question and answer period a young girl, being perfectly serious, asked this question: "If a pregnant girl gets shot, does the baby die"? The doctor, who practiced in a more affluent neighborhood, could hardly believe his ears. Why would anyone ask such a seemingly bizarre question? The reason is quite obvious. When you live in an area where drive-by shootings and murder for trivial reasons are common, it's a reasonable concern. Obviously the girl and the doctor lived under completely different circumstances. With that one question, the doctor acquired a much broader view of life in the real world of the inner city. For a moment, he had a glimpse of the young girl's reality.

Reality Check: A prospective factory employee was filling out an application form. On the form it asked the applicant to list and explain any periods of unemployment longer than thirty days. His answer: "So many I can't remember, and my mind was so numb with starvation I couldn't remember how many days". That was his reality - probably quite different from yours. For a few minutes sit back and try to imagine how you would view life from his perspective.

There is a lot of talk these days about crime and cold hearted criminals. Have you ever noticed how often those who lie or steal assume everyone else lies and steals too? They assume this to help them rationalize their bad behavior and feel less guilty. "Don't censure me for something you all do" they say.

LIFE'S DATA STACKERS

Teenagers will commonly use a similar line on their parents when they want something. Over and over and over again the phrase tumbles from the poor persecuted child: "but everyone else has one, is doing it, can go, has a license, etc".

When people make statements like this, they may very well feel that they're telling the truth. They want the world to be a certain way, so they call upon their internal computers to perceive the incoming messages in a particular manner. They tell their brains to emphasize, and even exaggerate, the favored viewpoint while discounting any opposing information.

Naturally, when "everyone else" is doing something, it must be OK. Right? No, wrong! If more people would only learn to confront this type of misguided reasoning by asking pointed and specific questions, something closer to the true facts would probably emerge: "You say ALL of your friends have nose rings? Tell me specifically who. John has one? Who else? Oh - Lucinder has one also! Anyone else? So, two of your friends have nose rings? Now, tell me how many other friends you have? Twenty-five or thirty? Well, what you are really telling me is that only two of your thirty friends have nose rings – that's not all of them, is it"? It really helps to ask questions and learn more about why and how other people have arrived at their conclusions and formed their realities. After acquiring sufficient information, you are then in a position to provide them with other viewpoints or possible answers - thereby changing their, and possibly your, perception of the subject.

WHAT IS REAL, IS REAL

TEACHERS ALSO HAVE REALITIES

Now, just for a moment, let's take a look at primary and secondary school teachers. (Another subject, along with politics and religion, where most mortals are supposed to tread lightly.) Disputes often arise between teachers, school boards, and parents about what and how to teach. Too many teachers seem to resent any questioning by parents about what and how subjects are taught in their classrooms. Teachers acquire this attitude during their college years when professors begin indoctrinating them to accept all the latest educational techniques as scientific fact – techniques based on "theories" having little or no empirical support, but promoted nonetheless by academics who are more interested in advancing certain social agendas or political views than they are in teaching children. The closest many of these "experts" get to real live children is often in on-campus laboratory schools where, despite the application of the latest educational techniques, chaos and lack of learning are too often the rule.

Thus, teachers start their careers with the firm belief (perception) that they've been endowed with a higher knowledge that far exceeds that of parents. Some parents, perhaps blinded by the teacher's education degree, will go along with the scam. Others, who may hold degrees in much more difficult disciplines, and who have not been brainwashed by collegiate educators, will rightly question the techniques and subjects to which their

LIFE'S DATA STACKERS

children are being exposed. The teachers' realities tell them that they, as teachers, know far more than parents about how to educate children. Some parents' realities tell them that it's perfectly all right to question those assumptions, as they would any other professional's claims to superior knowledge. A good solid exchange of ideas will generally help to improve perceptions and update the realities of both parties.

Those academics who mislead student teachers and other students in our colleges often haven't a clue about how the real world operates. The proverbial "ivory tower" is not an illusion - it exists. Oh how the esoteric and flawless theories float about its crenellated parapets! Academics know the tower is not really made of ivory. Rather it seems to be an ever growing pile of inconsequential research papers, often ghost-written by anonymous graduate students, waiting to be published. I recall a cocktail party where a "learned" much published professor was arguing the merits of socialized medicine (which he favored) with a physician who had practiced under a Communist regime in Eastern Europe. Talk about a difference in realities! After many minutes of argument, during which neither could comprehend the position of the other, the physician finally got in a final telling comment: "Professor, why do you continue to talk so much about those things about which you know so little"? As someone who had administered medical programs for thousands of employees, I could only say aloud, "AMEN!"

WHAT IS REAL, IS REAL

Another time I was taking a graduate level labor relations class at the University of Minnesota. A young graduate student who was working on his PhD taught the course. It wasn't long before it became obvious that the students were in a different world from that of their instructor. We all read our textbooks (written by other "academics") and listened to the lectures on the history and theories of labor relations. The history part was fine, but things fell apart as we began to deal with the current problems of handling real grievances and real contract negotiations. When the University assigned the young instructor to teach this class, they forgot an important fact: As a night class often is, it was composed mostly of people who had worked for some years in industry. Among the "students" were a union President, a Maintenance Department Superintendent, a Labor Relations Manager, and others with similar backgrounds. On the other hand, the instructor had never worked a single day in business/industry. All of his knowledge of Labor Relations had come from textbooks he'd read as he worked to earn his Master's degree and during his PhD studies. Even more disheartening was the fact that he had been earning money on the side teaching supervision techniques to Managers. Where do you suppose he learned them? From a textbook of course.

It did not take long - pretty soon the student "animals" were running the "zoo". The real learning occurred when the "students" shared their personal practical experiences and knowledge with each other, and with the instructor. In this case,

LIFE'S DATA STACKERS

the instructor was smart enough to allow us to share realities - the practical and the theoretical. As a result, we all gained new input to our "computers" and altered our personal realities.

All of this should hopefully serve as a warning to those of you who are considering hiring a consultant. Make sure that you choose someone with real practical experience. If the consultant hasn't served his time "in the trenches", he doesn't know the answers. A solid education PLUS practical experience is your best bet.

This reminds me of the time I hired a new graduate having a degree in Labor Relations from a well-known university in Oregon. He was assigned the task of keeping the minutes of a grievance meeting with the local United Steelworkers Grievance Committee. After the meeting he walked down the hall with a puzzled look on his face. "What's wrong Bruce" I asked? His reply illustrates what I have been pointing out: "That wasn't like the books and professors said - they don't want to bargain, they just want it!" That was lesson number one for Bruce in the real world of labor relations.

Regrettably, Human Relations people are also susceptible to relying on unproven academic theories. In one mining company the Vice President of Industrial Relations decided to expose all supervisors to an extensive course in decision making. It was a well known and highly touted system that is still on the market. The supervisors were taken to a motel where they labored hard through several days and late into the nights. No

WHAT IS REAL, IS REAL

interruptions by business associates or family were allowed. During this time they were taught a system of decision making. Approximately a year later a survey of the participants was undertaken. Almost without exception, they agreed it had been a fine course and they had learned a lot. However, only one out of over a hundred supervisors was using the system. The universal response was something like, "it's a good system, but I don't have time to use it. I have to make my decision right now". It seems the system required extensive charting, list making, brainstorming and considerable time mulling the alternatives. Here again, the academic approach in the book sounded quite good and was fine for long term planning, but the average supervisor, confronted with an urgent problem, did not have the luxury of taking hours to make a decision. The system developer's perception of the work place was obviously quite different from the actual environments in which the system was to be implemented. To be fair, the developer may have simply gotten his experience in a field where they did have plenty of time to make decisions. Pursuit of too many of these useless programs finally got the Vice President (known behind his back as Freddy Fudpucker) fired.

All of this is not to say that all persons in Academia are incompetent or uninformed. After all, they have earned lots of college degrees. We all know what B.S. stands for. Well, M.S. is simply "More of the Same", and PhD stands for "Piled Higher and Deeper". For university faculties, lack of real-world

LIFE'S DATA STACKERS

applicability is, perhaps, an inevitable occupational hazard that they, and their theories, may seldom if ever overcome. To them the world of the campus is the real world – real to them, but quite different from the world in which most of the rest of us live and work.

Listed below are a few more people who also had unique perceptions of the world they lived in. Remember, what is real, is real!

MINISTERS AND BUREAUCRATS

Once upon a time there was a minister who lived in a large city where he was the leader of a large, well-established downtown church. Contrary to his denomination's usual practice he had held this position for some twenty years. His sermons, which were commonly quite good, reflected his high intellect and extensive knowledge of his subject matter. So why, after twenty years, was he removed from his post? Why had a large group of parishioners gotten together and asked the church hierarchy to end his service to their church?

It turns out that there was growing disagreement over how the minister was "tending his flock" - yes, different perceptions of the same endeavor. The pastor was determined to build a new large church - one more appropriate for a man of his talent - and needed large amounts of money. Therefore, as the years went by, the minister spent more and more of his time with

WHAT IS REAL, IS REAL

the wealthier members of his congregation. If a wealthy constituent so much as sneezed, he was there. Thus, the wealthier and generally older members of the congregation perceived him as doing a wonderful job and tended to support him wholeheartedly.

It was a different story for others. Members of more modest means he almost totally ignored. After church one morning the minister was shaking hands with members of the congregation. He greeted one couple warmly, asked their names, and with some enthusiasm suggested they join one of the church's couples clubs. Good idea, if a little late. The husband and wife were at that time the Co-Presidents of the oldest and largest couples club in the church. An even worse example of his indifference was what happened to a young couple of modest means. The husband had served as the head usher at both morning services for several years. After years of trying, the couple, in their late thirties, were blessed with the arrival of a baby. The minister never noticed. About a year later the baby died - still the minister showed no interest and offered no comfort.

This attitude eventually caused a split in the church and the end of the minister's career. He had forgotten that his real job was to serve the spiritual needs of his congregation, not collecting money to build an edifice for his own self glorification. Somewhere his internal computer had acquired poor information that led him down the wrong path. Perhaps it

LIFE'S DATA STACKERS

was some professional fund raiser that had pumped practical but uncompassionate data into his internal computer.

At another time I attended a conference where the deliberations were centered on the working woman. The United States Secretary of Labor was the keynote speaker, followed by a series of panel discussions led by experts in various fields. A husband and wife team, both psychologists, extolled the virtues of a two-income family. They had two or three children in their early teens and felt they had not suffered due to both parents working. There were the usual platitudes about "quality time", a secure home environment, loving parents etc. That at least was their perception. In their view (reality) everything at home was going smoothly. However, the reality of the man sitting next to me was quite different. He was their next door neighbor. The truth of the matter was that the psychologists' kiddies were completely undisciplined and wild. Their behavior was so bad that the neighbors had literally gotten together and signed a petition encouraging the family to please move out of the area. Perhaps the psychologists were simply lying to us at the conference, but it's just as likely that their reality was out of sync with their neighbors'.

I've already discoursed about how many in academic occupations are out of touch with the realities of the "working" world. However, academics are not the greatest sinners in this flight from the truth and fact. That dubious honor must go to the

WHAT IS REAL, IS REAL

legions of blinded bumbling bureaucrats in our Federal and State governments. While most academics simply haven't allowed themselves to be exposed to real world facts, and therefore their computers do not have the necessary data to make sensible judgments. On the other hand, governmental gauchos constantly ignore the data when it's presented and ride roughshod over the bodies of "We the People" - for our own "good" of course. The professor's rush to publish is nothing compared to a government clerk's eagerness to promulgate more and more administrative law. What a feeling of power it must give them - to know that with a few strokes of their keyboard they can control the lives of thousands of people.

Administrative laws are those innumerable, usually confusing and onerous regulations that government bureaucrats add to "administer" basic legislation passed by Congress or a State Legislature. The results may be completely contrary to what the legislature intended or even considered. However, unless successfully challenged by an individual or corporation in a lengthy law suit, the bureaucratic bumbling remains law. What chance do you or I have to fight the resources of the government? It costs mucho dinero to go all the way to the Supreme Court.

The point of this little lesson is that those who write these costly and stifling rules do not live in the real world. Oh yes, they set up their little industry "committees" (which I have served on)

LIFE'S DATA STACKERS

to advise them, but THEY make the final decisions and pay too little attention to the input of others. Their perception of our world is quite different from those of us who have to live and work in it.

I hearken back to the time the steel company I was working for bought five old World War II Liberty ships. They were towed to a nearby dock where they were to be cut up and melted in the plant's furnaces. The federales, seeing that we now owned five ships, assumed we must have lots of longshoremen working for us and decided we were covered by the Longshoreman and Harbor Workers Act. As such, we would be required to file forms showing how many longshoremen we had, how many injuries, hours worked, first aid cases etc. etc. etc. Knowing that we had zero people covered by the Act, I returned the form saying we did not employ any longshoremen. The second identical request for information, I threw into the waste basket. Then followed a number of requests to send in the report and finally a somewhat threatening letter. Feeling a bit silly, I filled out the report with row upon row of zeros (the truth), explained again that we had no covered employees, and sent it back. That was A-OK with the government - until the next quarterly report was due. When it came in I treated it the same way and got the same result. Sending back more zeros since that was apparently acceptable to the bureaucrats. After going through this charade a number of times I wrote them a letter in which I pointed out in detail the ridiculous routine we were being

WHAT IS REAL, IS REAL

forced to follow. It took almost a year, and long after the last ship had been turned into molten steel, before we won the battle.

The administrators blotted out the real world, or at best, ignored it. They could not understand our reality anymore than I could comprehend theirs.

SOME BUSINESS AND CORPORATE REALITIES

There is another large group of people who have unique realities. They are those independent business owners who are the backbone of our nation. These entrepreneurs work long hard hours to make their organizations successful. Starting small, learning from their mistakes, often close to financial disaster, they persevere until they achieve their goals.

It should not come as any big surprise that these folks have developed some rather firm ideas about how to run a company. After all, it was their initiative and business techniques that allowed them to reach their goals. Now, they obviously did not all use exactly the same methods - in fact each has his or her own unique approach based on their individual judgments and circumstances.

One thing many of them do too often have in common, however, is an unwillingness to listen to outside business consultants. As one put it, "I wouldn't be where I am today if I didn't know how to run my business". However, those around them often know that the success came in spite of the owner's

LIFE'S DATA STACKERS

efforts and not because of them. But, you know the old saying, "You can't argue with success".

On the other hand, good consultants (not academics) have usually had the benefit of seeing many business operations. It has been possible for them to glean from each experience the most useful and effective problem solving techniques. However, it isn't easy to convince a business man who is grossing $1,000,000 a year, that by changing his ways he might gross $10,000,000. The many years of struggle have firmly implanted many memories into the owner's internal computer - memories that have shaped the realities and decisions.

Too few of these people are open to considering even an expert consultant's more objective view of reality. If you count yourself a successful entrepreneur, don't allow yourself to fall into that category.

Reality check: If someone talks about sauerkraut what do you think of? Careful now, it depends on where you come from or how you were raised. In Bavaria it's sweeter than the standard more sour type and is made with caraway seeds. Also, note the difference between the traditional American potato salad and German potato salad. Make sure you know whose reality is defining the potato salad before you order it. Then again, if you are from the East Coast, don't go to South Texas and order the "hot salsa" - it ain't the same as what you get in Maine.

WHAT IS REAL, IS REAL

Now let's jump from individuals to a couple of "corporate realities". In the late 70s and early 80s many oil companies decided to expand their operations into other basic natural resources such as coal, copper, gold etc. They reasoned that these types of resources were in limited supply and could be expected to increase in value as ore bodies around the world became depleted. So far their logic was fine. Next you must be made aware of a basic fact: Oil companies, due to the nature of their business, are capital intensive, while mining companies are labor intensive. Which is to say, that oil companies get their production with large amounts of money and only a few employees, while the mining companies must have large numbers of hourly paid human beings to extract their minerals.

It's a small wonder then that many of those corporate "marriages" failed. The profit margins of oil companies are far greater than those of mining companies, which gives oil companies the luxury of having large salaried staffs - overhead that is. Most mining companies are much more conservative in their spending habits and tend to have very "lean" office staffs.

A friend in a major international copper company confided to me one day that he couldn't keep track of all the new employees who had been hired since an oil company had taken over. Extra staff had been added to a level similar to that of the oil companies, but the copper company's budget could not sustain that excessive level of expenditure. As the next few years

LIFE'S DATA STACKERS

went by the copper company closed more and more of its properties, and finally shut down entirely.

This was not an isolated incident. I know of at least two other similar cases. In each case the oil companies were used to having steady predictable production rates from their wells and little trouble from labor unions. If a union did strike, the refineries could often be operated by supervisors.

In the mining companies, labor relations are a major concern. Large groups of hourly employees, belonging to powerful national unions, were not averse to calling a long strike every few years. The tremendous difference in these corporate realities doomed many of these mergers to failure.

Once again, a little more investigation would have saved much trouble and many, many jobs. Uh oh, there is that financial bean counter mind set again! Like the man says, they sometimes seem to have a "froze brain".

Now a few quick final examples: Time and time again, otherwise happily married couples can find themselves at odds with one another due to different perceptions of how to behave, or due to conflicts in lifestyles. A spouse who is used to roast turkey with all the trimming for Christmas, may get in trouble if the "other half" - a pure Norwegian from Minnesota - is expecting lutefisk and lefsa. Take my word for it; those are really two widely disparate realities.

WHAT IS REAL, IS REAL

Also, have you noticed how some folks simply "air kiss" while other expect a kiss on the lips? That can sometimes lead to trouble if the person being kissed is a good-looking member of the opposite sex.

I'm sure you have also heard some families referred to as "straight laced" or "proper". Obviously that family's perception of how to behave in public is quite different from some families described as "Bohemian". It's not my place to say which is more desirable. I simply want to call your attention to the obvious dissimilarities in life styles and what people call a "normal" way to live.

Couples who come from different religions, political views, and/or life styles often get in trouble once the "honeymoon" is over. Too often, it seems, the biological urges overcome the more rational approach of sharing "realities" before marriage. I suspect it will continue to be that way.

Well, by now you may think that I either hate everyone or at least think of them as incompetents. No, I am simply trying to illustrate that we all have our data stacked in very personal and individual ways. We each have our own uncommon realities that guide us as we make everyday decisions. Each person is unique, and it's up to you to learn more about them if you wish to relate well to one another.

Yes, I know. My own realities are showing - but at least I know they exist!

LIFE'S DATA STACKERS

CHAPTER FOUR

PREDICTABILITY

A MAJOR KEY TO SUCCESSFUL INTERPERSONAL RELATIONS

In the three previous chapters you've learned how your "human computer" stores data and that it never makes a mistake. You've also seen how the sum total of that stored data determines an individual's "reality" - or, their perception of the world around them. And, of equal, or greater, importance, you've learned the value of listening. The more we can gain access to all of those billions and billions of bits of stored data in our own and others' heads, the easier it will be for us to understand our own, and others' "reality". With that understanding we can hope to improve our ability to predict what their, and our, actions will or should be. If I'd known more about Ted Bailey's background at first, my earlier predictions about his behavior would have been better and I would have taken action sooner. That ability, to know in advance how a person will react to different situations, is one of the most essential ingredients in achieving good relations with other people.

LIFE'S DATA STACKERS

Conversely, it's the unexpected that causes many of our problems. When something happens that we do not expect or understand, we become upset, confused, and maybe a bit angry. The difference between what does happen and what we expected to happen determines, in large part, the extent to which we become unhappy about a situation or occurrence and how we react to it. Occasionally, if the difference is great enough, we may even become violent. If the difference is lesser, or our demeanor more level headed, we may instead simply protest or file a formal complaint of some kind. But rather than becoming upset or immediately reacting by retaliating, we should first start asking questions so that we can reload our internal computers. With additional information comes increased understanding. It will help to review how this works:

We know that in some respects each individual is like **ALL** other people in that all people have bones on the inside of their bodies, get tired when they work too hard, breath oxygen and require food and sleep. Each individual is in some respects like **SOME** other people in that he or she may be blue-eyed, black, white, Indian, Japanese or belong to a special team or club. Every individual however, is also different in some way from **ALL** other people. This is because each individual's experiences, while similar in some degree to the experiences of others, are unique to that individual. Each internal computer is programmed differently from that of any other person on the

PREDICTABILITY

planet. Like fingerprints and snowflakes, no two persons can have absolutely identical experiences - or reactions.

You will recall that using the "fantastic five" DATA STACKERS (sight, sound, taste, touch and smell), individuals record all of the information, experience and sensations to which they have been subjected during their lifetimes. Whether they like it or not, it is all stored in that wonderful organ we call the brain. The data is in permanent storage waiting for them to put it to good, or bad, use. In general, we would call this their "stored data" about the world in which they live. The stored data of any particular individual will be different from that of any other individual. Remember, no two persons can possibly have the exact same emotions, perceptions, and experiences.

As we have seen, each person uses the total relevant stored data (in his human computer) about each particular thing on which he has acquired information. This he does to compute and predict the result of, or his answer or reaction to any given situation. It has been definitively established that individuals do not make a mistake in executing the actual physiological brain functions involved in computing what their reaction or response to a situation should be. If, however, such an individual has a lot of incorrect data on which he bases his computation, then he will obviously compute an answer with some degree of incorrectness in it. Wrong data is all too easy to acquire. Your son becomes involved with a street gang. A student attends a course taught by a professor from a slanted viewpoint. Citizens of a country hear

LIFE'S DATA STACKERS

only the propaganda of the local Dictator. Or, your spouse hears only PART of a conversation about you at a cocktail party. All these experiences provide incorrect or incomplete data, upon which, these people may subsequently make incorrect decisions. Good luck in dealing with them!

The computational machinery that man uses (man's brain) is so fast (at a rate of millions of computations per second) that if a person is unable to immediately understand something, a lot of so-called "thinking" will probably not make it more understandable. What an inability to understand generally indicates is that the person simply needs more information! That's why it's often said that, when taking a multiple choice exam, your first reaction is probably the right one. When someone has a "gut feeling" about what action to take, it's their human computer telling them what to do after having processed all available and relevant stored data. The brain has already assimilated and processed all the relevant information available in the brain cells and has come up with an answer. Many things we ascribe to "instinct" or actions that are "second nature" come from this same phenomenon. The information available for decision-making has already been stored away and our brains simply retrieve and process that information in a millisecond. At least when dealing with problems that are generally unrelated to human actions, it generally isn't necessary or productive to sit and ponder at great length all of the possibilities and ramifications of your response. Your internal computer already

PREDICTABILITY

has the answer computed and has put it into action before you can consciously think about it. For instance - if you are crossing the street and a large truck suddenly appears, out of the usual nowhere, and is heading right for you, do you stop and give great logical thought about what you should do? Of course not. Your "computer" has already calculated the speed, distance and stopping ability of the oncoming behemoth. It has also predicted the terrible results if you fail to move quickly. In this situation, your ability to almost instantaneously predict the consequences has saved your life.

TRYING TO FIGURE OUT THE OTHER PERSON

Understanding the actions or motivations behind the actions of people, however, is a much more demanding task for the human computer. The difficulty of trying to understand an action taken by another person arises because you tend to automatically compute an answer as to why the other person did the thing based only on **YOUR** data. The action that the other person took was taken based on a decision the other person made based on **HIS** data. If you're going to understand why the other person took the action he did, it will be necessary for you to get **HIS** data - preferably **FROM HIM.** Getting that data requires the ability to ask the kinds of questions that will elicit the kinds of responses that will make the other person's actions understandable to you. (Excuse me; did anyone remember that this means you must LISTEN?) Until you've received enough

LIFE'S DATA STACKERS

responses to allow you to fully comprehend why the other person did what he did, you have not obtained all the necessary data. However, after having obtained all of the necessary data you may discover that you and the other person have a difference of opinion. But, since you will have obtained the data upon which that opinion is based, you will be able to understand why he holds the opinion he does. Your acquisition of his data may not cause you to agree, but at least you will be in a position to "agree to disagree" and move on. But the greatest benefit of all of having collected all that new data may be your improved ability to predict how the other person will react in the future. Professional football players watch their opponent's game films over and over again, in part, to collect enough data to be able to predict the moves their adversary will make in a given situation. Until they learned better, some quarterbacks would lick their fingers before throwing a pass - a dead giveaway to the other team. We all emit signals of this kind. The things we say, the way we touch, our body movements, and yes, even the odor we give-off can provide others with clues as to our feelings and future actions.

If you've ever taken a management training course, or read a book on how to raise your children, you're probably familiar with the admonition to "be consistent". Why be consistent? So others know what to expect from you - so others will know how you're likely to react - so that you're predictable! Your predictability makes life much easier for them, and for you.

92

PREDICTABILITY

(In some cases, of course, as with that quarterback, it definitely pays *not* to be predictable - next time lick the fingers and then call a running play).

You've probably noticed how others, especially those who are subordinate to you, attempt to learn things about you that enable them to predict your reactions. How often have you heard or asked a question like "what kind of a mood is so-and-so in" – or have been aware of others asking that question about you? Knowing that mood, they can adjust their approach to you based on what they already know about how your moods affect your reactions and decisions. If they're the type who fears rejection, they probably require a much longer period of interaction before asking you for a commitment or agreement since they want to be able to predict a yes answer and avoid the embarrassment of having to deal with a negative response. Even a stranger who meets you at a cocktail party will engage you in conversation to learn how to relate to you and to know what to expect from you.

Remember the words from that old song, "getting to know you, getting to know all about you . . . "? That's what you need to help others to do. With each exchange of information, especially with subordinates, you need to make a concerted effort to teach those who depend on you more about your life experiences and familiarize them with your intentions, attitudes, and emotional responses. This will improve their ability to

LIFE'S DATA STACKERS

foresee how you will react in various situations, or to a given philosophy.

As a rule, persons who are totally unpredictable are not well liked. Terms such as flaky, air head, unreliable or irrational come to mind. Such persons may be regarded as interesting, eccentric, or even exciting, but they are seldom valued as a close friend, employer, or employee. Perhaps some examples of both good and bad experiences will help to clarify this concept.

PREDICTABILITY IN ACTION

While working as Labor Relations Manager for a major corporation, I had a boss with a very short fuse and an incredibly extensive vocabulary of profanities. Most of his conversations, especially on the telephone, were at sufficient volume to make the windows rattle. On occasion, when he waxed particularly eloquent, the Vice President of Engineering, in the next office, would pound on the intervening wall and tell him to shut-up. Usually without success. New secretaries were fully briefed about what to expect (predict) in the way of language and noise before they went to work for him. As a result they seldom quit. In all fairness however, it should be noted that he was usually angry with some miserable situation rather than the person to whom he was speaking. Of course, until my personal computer latched on to that concept, I was rather miserable.

At the time, we operated plants in five states and were "blessed" with having to negotiate with some fifty-one union

PREDICTABILITY

locals. As the work load increased, it became apparent that we needed to add a full time labor attorney to our staff - and I was ordered to start recruiting. Finding a good experienced labor attorney would be difficult enough, but keeping one on board in the stressful atmosphere my boss had created, might prove to be impossible. How would such a person react to a boss who delivered his instructions with vulgar language and ear splitting loudness? Labor attorneys are seldom regarded as "shrinking violets" or as being willing to back down in an argument, so a disastrous conflict could reasonably be expected between the new attorney and my boss. It would be necessary to do something to prevent the office from turning into a cacophonous war zone. The obvious answer was to improve my boss's predictability in the mind of our new man. After a long search, I finally found a suitable applicant. The next move, before hiring this new attorney, was to sit down with him and describe how the Vice President acted. There was no sugar coating or hiding of faults. He was told the total truth about what to expect. The attorney felt he could handle the job and accepted the challenge of dealing with the boss.

About two years later (yes, the attorney was still employed), and after a particularly loud shouting match, the attorney came into my office. I was concerned that he might be thinking of resigning, but I was wrong. When I asked him, he just grinned and said "you know, you were absolutely right, that Vice President is everything you said he was". Since the attorney

LIFE'S DATA STACKERS

knew in advance what to expect (predict), he subsequently had no complaint. The job had turned out as predicted. He left the office with a smile - ready to once more face the day-to-day difficulties of dealing with the vociferous Vice President.

Experience can be very useful in predicting outcomes. Some years ago, while doing extensive employment interviewing, I routinely gave all applicants a widely-used intelligence test (such tests were legal at the time). After personally screening some hundreds of people, of both sexes and of all ages, I found I could predict their test results without scoring the test. After awhile it became a game of sorts - my secretary would bring me the completed application blank and I would predict the score on the yet untaken test. Usually, I could come within a few points of the actual result. How did I do it? Essentially, I evaluated the APPEARANCE of the application. It wasn't necessary to read the application or see how the questions were answered. It was simply the general look of the completed application form. The kind of handwriting or printing, neat or sloppy etc. etc. Believe me; if you're a job applicant, at any level, you always keep in mind that NEATNESS COUNTS. Now, please don't tell me about intelligent doctors with undecipherable handwriting, or persons with physical problems. Of course this method of predicting isn't perfect, but on the average, it was an accurate way of predicting intelligence test results. Why am I telling you all this? Because it demonstrates how an interviewer decides who to hire. It's based on the sum

PREDICTABILITY

total of his/her experience in dealing with people. It isn't something that you can learn in a college course, or by reading it off a list of prepared questions. Many companies make the mistake of thinking they can simply give a list of questions to almost anyone and achieve a satisfactory interview. They will even give so many "brownie" points for certain answers. That is an entirely inadequate method. The experienced questioner has learned how to handle the answers AND THE NON-ANSWERS. One carefully notes the looks, the tone of voice, the body language, and learns when to pursue some seemingly innocuous comment. All of the "fantastic five" have stacked the data from hundreds of meetings. The interviewer, without having to think too hard, can usually come up with a rather good assessment - and can sometimes predict the test score.

There are times, of course, when you just cannot predict an outcome. Like the time a machinist in the steel plant kept getting drunk on the job. How did he do it? He came through the gate stone cold sober. The security guard searched his lunch box and could not find any liquor - not even in his coffee. Numerous searches of his locker failed to turn up anything out of the ordinary. Nothing came over the fence. So how did he do it? Our problem was that, thinking conventionally, we assumed and predicted that he could be caught drinking beer, wine, or hard liquor. After all, what else could he possibly be using to get drunk while inside the plant? After shave - that's what! Once we expanded our search for answers from the conventional to the

LIFE'S DATA STACKERS

possible we discovered that he'd been drinking good old shaving lotion. It not only served to make him drunk, but it left him with very pleasant breath - which proves that it often pays to change your perspective when considering a dilemma. If you augment your data gathering by considering situations from different perspectives or viewpoints your predictions are likely to improve and you'll be able to solve more problems. A narrow, single-perspective approach to predicting outcomes can be likened to playing the old "what if" game: What if that young woman in the bar is newly divorced and looking for a good time? The "Casanova" who predicts a friendly welcome based on that "what if" could get a rude surprise. Golly gee fellows, **what if** she is simply waiting for her boyfriend - the 300-pound bouncer? You can bet that data obtained by considering multiple possibilities from a broad range of perspectives can dramatically improve the quality of your predictions (and may even help you avoid needless bloodshed).

Here's a short psychological note: Don't allow yourself to get depressed when you fail to reach goals or when things don't happen the way you predicted they would or wanted them to. Instead, consider such disappointments as learning experiences: Stop and think about what it was that you wanted to have happen and whether, perhaps, you might have set your sights too high. The goal that you predicted you would reach may have been unreachable. Leave the "impossible dreams" to Don Quixote. If,

PREDICTABILITY

instead of learning from such experiences, you continue to set overly ambitious goals and make unrealistic projections, you may well fail to reach or realize any of them and increasingly think of yourself as incompetent – just because your faulty predictions don't work out. When that happens, you feel bad about yourself. Worse, you may start to feel inferior - and that could get to be a nasty habit that benefits neither you nor your family, co-workers, employees or friends.

Even if you have limited education or are not the smartest person on the block, it does not follow that you are "inferior". I have known people with the IQ of a genius who flunked out of school and, conversely, I have known some "not so bright" people who have succeeded magnificently. Much of this is due to motivation, or the lack thereof - and there is nothing that will kill motivation any quicker than a feeling of inferiority or a chronic expectation of failure. Many a child of the inner city has an abundance of what we call "street smarts" (indicative of high, though misdirected, intelligence), but not much formal education. The only one of these people who might justifiably be considered inferior would be the genius who has chosen to totally waste his God-given talents. So start out setting more realistic goals and you will lessen your disappointments. Do a little self-analysis, and perhaps undergo a testing program to help discover your strengths and weaknesses. Select goals that are in line with your strengths while you're working on correcting any

LIFE'S DATA STACKERS

deficiencies. Remember: you, and only you, can make these decisions for yourself. But that doesn't mean you ignore knowledge acquired by others or cast aside their advice. Even highly intelligent people make a point of learning from as many other people as possible. Books, training programs, and night school classes are just three useful devices to help accomplish that end. Armed with such knowledge you can avoid the mistake of setting out to "reinvent the wheel". The man who invented the automobile did not invent the wheel, the steel, the engine, or most of the other parts of the vehicle. He simply assembled them in a unique manner. He added to the knowledge and work of others - he did not start from scratch.

After achieving a more modest and realistic goal, you can always set another one that is just a little bit more ambitious - but try to make sure it is capable of being reached. It is also important to realize that you are the only one who can decide when you've been successful. In some people's eyes I may be seen as a failure because I'm not a multimillionaire. But to me, money is not the ultimate measure of success or happiness. You must set your own goals - ones that you can reasonably expect to achieve. Get used to the feeling of being successful. It's a lot more fun than feeling like a loser.

When you have authority over others you should be realistic in setting goals for them as well. For example, parents of children who don't reach their 6th birthday until late in the year should carefully consider whether to enroll such children in the

PREDICTABILITY

First Grade at the age of five "and three quarters". Enrolling children in the First Grade at this age throws them into a situation where everyone else in the class is older and are generally more mature. In addition, educators know that boys are generally less mature than girls at this age, so boys suffer most from this early enrollment approach. Under these circumstances it is quite difficult for a younger child to ever achieve success as a social leader or to be academically superior. The child learns to accept a subordinate, submissive, inferior role - an attitude that is likely to have serious repercussions later in the child's life. Holding the child back until the next school year allows them to go through school as one of the oldest in the class, to build a more positive outlook on their own abilities to succeed in many areas. Unfortunately, too many parents, motivated by their own egos, insist on pushing their children into situations they're unprepared to succeed in. (We see a lot of this at Little League games and in ballet classes) Later, when the poor kid doesn't do well, the parents blame the failure on the child or the "incompetent" teacher. The bottom line is, we too often set-up our children to be failures when we could just as readily have set them up to be winners. Predict success and set goals that allow your children, your subordinates, *and yourself* to fulfill that prediction. At the same time, build into your mental computer the knowledge (and prediction) that an occasional failure is to be expected and should be treated as a learning experience. Expecting to fall short once in awhile helps you avoid a feeling

LIFE'S DATA STACKERS

of failure when it does happen. Keep in mind that Abraham Lincoln lost every election except one - the one that made him President of the United States.

Well, back to other examples of how important it is to know about predictability: Long, long ago, in ancient times, attorneys learned the value (and dangers) of predictability. It has almost become a mantra for the new attorney: when questioning a witness in court, "Never ask a question to which you do not already know the answer". There is nothing worse than having your star witness (or a hostile witness) come up with an unexpected and damaging response. I found this out the hard way in an arbitration case. The arbitration of a grievance filed by a union employee is handled much like any case in a court of law. Each side presents evidence by calling and cross-examining witnesses and cites and applies contract language ("law") to that evidence to support their contentions. The major difference is that an arbitrator acts in place of a judge and/or a jury.

Tom had been a particularly bad employee for several years. He was lazy, obnoxious, and frequently absent - even his fellow union employees didn't like him. There had been previous attempts to interrupt the continuity of his employment, but they had all failed. Time and again he was returned to work because of sloppy groundwork by his immediate supervisors. After each failed attempt, good old Tom became more and more arrogant and missed more and more work. After all, he had learned to

PREDICTABILITY

predict that his transgressions would go unpunished. As the new Personnel Manager, it became my job to lead the next attempt at ridding the workforce of this master of "goldbricking". Taking his supervisors aside, I made it very clear to them that we needed to build a proper case against Tom. No trumped-up charges would be tolerated - Tom violated enough rules on a regular basis to make that ploy unnecessary. I let Tom's supervisors know that I would expect them to carefully document all Tom's infractions, and that, most important of all, that they must give Tom a very clear and specific warning that any additional missteps would result in his immediate discharge. A cardinal rule in labor relations is that an employee must be warned about the penalty for an improper action to, you might say, improve the company's predictability in the mind of the employee. Tom's supervisor promised to do so. Eventually Tom was fired again for absenteeism and the case went to arbitration. All went well and things were looking good until I asked the supervisor the question to which I thought I knew the answer. "Did you warn Tom that he would be fired if he were absent one more time"? The unexpected answer - NO! That was it, we lost. I had assumed the supervisor had followed my instructions and failed to actually check before the arbitration. It was a mistake I never made again. As for Tom, he was returned to work, where he continued his insufferable ways until the day he was killed by a hit-and-run driver. Something Tom hadn't predicted.

LIFE'S DATA STACKERS

Throughout this dissertation you will read over and over again about the importance of knowing how another person has his, or her, data stacked - and conversely, about how essential it is that you make a conscious effort to know how your own thoughts and opinions have been formed. I cannot emphasize this too much. It is the basis of all good communications. It's not enough to know where the other person is "coming from". You must also know where you have been.

Doctor, lawyer, merchant, chief;
All need to know this,
Or come to grief.

Webster's New World Dictionary defines the word empathy, as follows: "the projection of one's own personality into the personality of another in order to understand the person better; ability to share in another's emotions, thoughts, or feelings". To gain empathy requires us to learn about each other's backgrounds. Those who achieve success in the "real" world have learned to not only be consistent in their thoughts and actions, but to go further and communicate in terms that others will understand.

BENEFITING FROM BEING PREDICTABLE

Let's look at how a few people have done well in their professions, sometimes in spite of what appear to be daunting human relations challenges: A plastic surgeon is one type of

PREDICTABILITY

doctor that is particularly at risk these days since their patients too often have exaggerated ideas of how wonderful they will look after the operation. The doctor is expected to be a magician. All those nasty wrinkles, puffy eyes, sagging waistlines, turkey wattle necks, crooked noses, or inadequate breasts will be corrected and they will once again be youthful and perfect. When the operations are over and the doctor has done his best, the 65 year old will still not look like a 20 year old. There's only so much that can be done with scalpel and liposuction. However, the unrealistic patient would rather blame the doctor and may even file a law suit for malpractice. All of the doctor's colleagues might applaud his skill, but if the finished product is not up to the patient's personal expectations, courthouse here we come.

One of this country's most successful plastic surgeons has developed a process for avoiding angry patients and costly legal entanglements. The first step is to have an office that oozes good taste and success. The furniture, flowers, pictures on the wall, all speak of someone who knows how to do things right. The second step is the staff. All are dressed well, speak in well modulated tones, use good grammar, and above all sound intelligent and well versed in their particular activity. In fact, they **ARE** well versed and intelligent. All sound very pleasant and friendly. (You wouldn't want to sue a friend would you?) Beyond the receptionist is a well-trained person who explains in detail what you can expect. You will learn about pictures that will be taken before and after surgery, how much each procedure will cost,

LIFE'S DATA STACKERS

how to pay for it, and what to expect in recovery time. All of this might sound sufficient, but the doctor goes the extra mile: The patient is given a booklet that describes preparation, surgery, overnight needs, postoperative visits, pain, healing time, and who to call for more information. Before surgery the doctor uses modern computer imaging to show patients what changes to expect in their appearance. He also spends considerable time answering patients' questions and outlining the entire procedure. The material in the booklet is covered again during one-on-one interviews - both before and after surgery. From start to finish, sometimes a year later, the doctor and staff do all they possibly can to fill the patient's data bank with knowledge about what to expect. At each step, the patient is able to predict what will happen and when. As you might imagine, lawsuits against this doctor are quite rare. The overweight executive who has had his "love handles" suctioned off will not be surprised when the ladies fail to conceive of him as a triathlon champion. The 65-year-old lady will be content to look maybe 10 years younger, and be aware that it won't last forever. When those who have come to expect only modest results end up looking great, they are overjoyed. If, on the other hand, the results are not outstanding, the patients are not angry. Why? Because the doctor did not lead them to expect perfection. This is a case where the doctor has **NOT** made any glaring errors in his endeavors to be predictable. His practice and reputation continue to grow.

PREDICTABILITY

Contrast the predictability of the above surgeon with that of another plastic surgeon (I'm not picking on this profession - it just happens to be an interesting contrast) who did some work on a patient's hand. The patient suffered from a condition known as Dupuytren's Contracture. Untreated, this causes the fingers to curl into a claw-like shape. His little finger had been frozen at a 45 degree angle for two years and now another finger was starting to curl. The doctor assured the patient he could take care of his problems. Shortly after the operation the doctor came to the recovery room and told the patient that he had been unable to straighten the little finger. He had led the patient to believe that he would take care of something he was not qualified to handle. In his eagerness to make a buck, he failed to refer the patient to an orthopedic surgeon. He had not even hinted that the procedure was beyond his capabilities. Naturally the poor patient had expectations of a complete cure and was extremely unhappy. The doctor not only ruined the patient's expectations, he also damaged his own reputation in the community. It is small wonder that he remains an inadequate doctor in an unfortunate small town. The patient, on the other hand, went to Mayo Clinic where a skilled orthopedic surgeon corrected the problem.

Our next little excursion will take us into the land of the blue suede shoe, to the sales field - steel sales to be more precise. That is the area in which I began my somewhat checkered career, and in the process learned a bit about the value of predictability. Sales training in this particular steel company really didn't have

LIFE'S DATA STACKERS

much to offer in the way of customer relations. (It's amazing how some corporations can be so inept in the way they handle customers and yet manage to stay in business.) As new salesmen we learned how the product was made, how it was priced, and how to process orders. But the most important aspect of our jobs - how to conduct ourselves in face to face sales presentations - was completely overlooked. I guess we were supposed to acquire that particular skill by osmosis or from other more experienced sales associates. Upon completion of the deficient sales training, the Vice President called me in and told me I was being sent to the Chicago office. It would be an inside sales job that put me between the customer and the manufacturing plant. My new boss, as the Vice President had warned me, was quite hard to get along with, and had caused more than one employee to quit. The Vice President's warning, telling me what to expect, made it much easier for me to tolerate my new self-centered and aggressive boss. It was here that I learned how someone's predictions about another person can go wrong, unless he or she really gets to know the other person's idiosyncrasies. After working for the new boss for some time, I felt I knew what he wanted when dealing with customers. I pretty well knew what to expect - I thought. Then came the day that a crisis arose with one of our best customers while the boss was out. Our customer, a large appliance firm, was in trouble and needed to change specifications, deliveries etc. etc. I worked with the customer and the steel plant to successfully solve the problems. Upon the

PREDICTABILITY

boss's return I advised him of my actions - expecting an "atta boy". Instead, he bared his beaver-like teeth and delivered a tirade on how he should have been consulted and things done differently - this in spite of the fact that the problems had all been solved and the customer was completely happy. All of this, of course, was a good example of poor management. The boss who simply cannot delegate any authority to others is a poor manager indeed. As you can well imagine, my perceptions of what he wanted done were adjusted very quickly. My obvious course in the future would be to take no action without his advice and consent. Right? No, wrong. That is what he led me to expect with his words. I should have been paying more attention to his past actions to determine his true "reality". You can almost guess what happened next. Another similar situation arose, and, following his previously screamed instructions, I took the problem to him. Imagine my surprise when he looked up and quietly said "well, if you can't handle this, perhaps we should get someone who can". So much for my ability to predict.

Actually, I could not have predicted his actions with any degree of accuracy since the boss was constantly changing his mind. Actions are what my predictions should have been based upon - not the things he said. In retrospect, I probably should have asked him more questions to find out how **HIS** data was stacked - although he really didn't like being questioned. However, if you are dealing with someone who is always going off in new directions, you usually can't win. The best you can do

LIFE'S DATA STACKERS

is get as much information as you can from that person, and hopefully make some improvement in your ability to predict.

Also, please make sure that you never act in a similarly negative, untrustworthy, or unpredictable manner. Do you say one thing then do another? Do you blame others for your failures? Do you give off negative signals to your employees or friends? It's easy to do so through your body language: a smirk on the face, or turning your back. Can those you know really trust your words? When you want to communicate properly, you must not only employ visual, oral, and written techniques, you must be sure to employ them consistently.

Sometime later, I had the opportunity to transfer to the Company's Milwaukee office and take over a position as an "outside" salesman. Calling on accounts all over the state. By this time I had learned the value of being honest with my customers and keeping them apprised of the status of their orders. (Make sure they knew what to expect) This was during war time and there was a severe shortage of steel. Customers were barely scraping by on limited supplies of material, and delivery dates were critical. I made it a point to let my accounts know the minute there was a delay in production or shipment. They didn't like the delay, but at least the knowledge made it possible for them to juggle their schedules. When they knew what to expect, they could work around it.

PREDICTABILITY

One of our other salesmen had a different approach. He seemed to have an ego problem of some kind. He simply could not bring himself to tell a customer that he did not know the answer to a question. Worse, he was too lazy to make the necessary effort to get the answer. Instead he would make up false stories and promise delivery schedules that he knew could not be kept. Inevitably the customer's expectations were shattered, tempers were lost, and production lines unnecessarily shut down. One of his customers called in one day and asked for "that alleged salesman of yours". The disgust and sarcasm in his voice were quite clear. When the war ended, so did the orders from his customers.

Of course you need to be honest with others, but also to let them know what to expect - to improve your predictability. If you do not strive to be predictable you may end up like one of the two Big Bad Bobs:

TALE OF THE BAD BOBS

Bad Bob#1 was the Human Resource Manager for a major computer manufacturer. As such, he presided over a rather large staff of well-educated men and women. There were times, of course, when someone would decide to leave the company. A policy manual (which was too thick, and was half written by Bob) dictated that department heads should conduct exit interviews to ascertain why their employees were leaving. The

LIFE'S DATA STACKERS

purpose of this was to try to uncover discontent about things such as salaries, benefits, or poor treatment. Departing employees were always welcomed into good old Bob's office on their last day of work. The employees, expecting (predicting) that Bob would actually be interested in what they had to say (since that was the stated purpose of the interview) would start telling their reasons for leaving.

Bob could not bring himself to just sit and listen for long. He had to start interrupting. Soon he would begin delivering a scolding lecture enumerating point by point where the employee was wrong. He really never understood that the employee's viewpoint (reality) was entirely different from his. It was not long before everyone knew it was hopeless to try to tell Bob anything. Rather than get a nasty lecture on their last day, the mean nasty ungrateful wretch of a quitter would simply mouth some meaningless platitude about everything being just fine. Bob never did learn anything from those exit interviews and the Company never did benefit from the good suggestions Bob might have received had he, according to the exiting employees' original expectations, actually been interested in what they had to say. In this case, by being unpredictable, Bob had discouraged people from communicating with him.

Bad Bob#2 was the Operations Manager at a well-known celebrity's music theater. A whole book on "inhuman relations" could probably be written about this throwback to the managerial dark ages. Name a poor management practice, and it was one of

112

PREDICTABILITY

his areas of expertise. The litany ran the gamut from berating subordinates in front of other employees and/or customers, to poorly thought-out personnel policies. Under these circumstances it was inevitable that there would be a high rate of turnover. Once people found out about him, they bolted from the theater like a herd of spooked deer. Obtaining good replacements was not easy - his reputation had gotten around - so he requested a week's notice from anyone who planned to leave. He predicted that this would help solve his replacement problem, but he screwed that up too. The first person to give him prior notice was immediately fired. Although there were many more quits, no one else gave prior notice. The employees could predict what was going to happen and acted accordingly. Bad Bob, however, had his expectations ruined. Like many others, he did not understand that once again "actions speak louder than words". Words do mean things, but your actions will speak even louder when people are trying to find out how to deal with you.

Many years ago, a famous leader of the United Mine Workers Union is reputed to have invented the "wink and nod" technique. When government officials ordered him to tell striking miners to return to work, he would give a great speech telling the miners to do just that. However, when he told them not to picket or use violence, he would wink and nod his head in a "yes" motion. Similarly, when he told them to go back to work, he would wink and shake his head in a "no" motion. Yes indeed, actions often speak much louder than words. In the above case, it

LIFE'S DATA STACKERS

was intentional. But our actions often result from subconscious decisions made by our internal computers. In the case of Bad Bob#2 above, he blamed his poor management practices on the subconscious influence of rotten input his personal computer had received during his earlier days in the military. These subconscious influences from sometimes forgotten sources of input are the ones we must guard against. It's important that we become aware of and control them so we can become aware of the messages we're actually communicating to others.

MORE EXAMPLES - GOOD OR BAD

Psychologists often need to explore a patient's early years to get some clue about that patient's experiences - to learn how the patient's data has been stacked. One simple example concerns a young man I know of who could not tolerate someone holding him close, not even his mother. In school gym classes he would come close to panic if grasped in a tight wrestling hold. He did not know why, he just knew he was helpless to prevent the sensation. Eventually his parents figured out the cause. When he was eight months old, the young man had a problem with a tear duct in one eye. Doctors wrapped the baby in a sheet so he couldn't move. It amounted to a simple straitjacket. The doctor then ran a probe through the baby's tear duct. This was done about eight separate times, and with light or no anesthetic. According to the doctor, there was no pain, however, the psychological damage from the baby's confinement and fear of

PREDICTABILITY

treatment was long lasting. These facts, when told to the boy as he grew up, enabled the young man to understand and deal with his claustrophobic reactions. Later, he was quite successful operating within the cramped confines of an Air Force F-16 fighter.

In this, and many other such cases, it's often necessary to enlist outside help to learn who, or what, created our current realities. Later we will look more closely at how to conduct this reexamination that can make drastic changes in your outlook. Ted Bailey, (our hero from Chapter One) for example, was able to change when he realized his teenage experiences had introduced bad data into his personal computer, but it took help.

The value of being consistent and/or predictable can be seen in social, political, family, or business affairs. The examples are endless. We only need to sharpen our powers of observation to see this phenomenon. I recall the Vice President of a large manufacturing organization who had a rather dubious reputation for being an extremely hard-nosed arbitrary boss. He was said to be somewhere to the right of Attila-the-Hun, and often walked through the plant barking orders, comments and complaints. To him everything was a Communist plot and he often spoke loudly about his dislike of minority groups. Rules of good management were violated every day. Employees were castigated in front of their peers, he never listened to any opinion that did not coincide with his own, he never delegated authority, but often delegated lots of responsibility. Does that profile sound familiar to any other of you corporate slaves? In most unionized plants, as this one was, there would be a steady stream of grievances filed against this kind of management throwback. But surprise, surprise, the plant ran smoothly and without excessive labor trouble. The secret? Despite all of his problems and faults, he was predictable. More than once I saw employees, who had been exhaustively chewed out, walk away with a smile on their faces. Their comments would be something like - "oh that's just Jake, he always talks like that". They knew what to expect and so were not surprised or bothered. This is not to say that the plant could not have been a lot more productive with better management, but it shows how much people can tolerate - even under a dictator, so long as he is consistent. If a predictable jerk is tolerable, just imagine how your friends and associates would view a nice person like you if you were more predictable! We all feel more comfortable around people who do what we expect. It is good to know how to conduct ourselves in ways that will make us predictable to our co-workers so that we can avoid needless conflict.

Sports Note: As I am writing this particular chapter there is a lot of news coverage about a player's strike in the National Hockey League. Weeks have gone by without a resolution. One thing caught my ear - the owners were presenting a "final offer" to the union. And then the next day, after it was rejected, they were working on a final offer. I'm not sure how many "final" offers they made, but what did the owner's actions really teach

PREDICTABILITY

the union? It taught them that the word "final" had no real meaning. When the owners used the word, the union had no reason to expect, or predict, that it was truly the last effort. The owners taught the union to keep coming back for more. It is a far better practice to insure that the other side knows and believes you mean what you say. You cannot be creditable if people cannot depend on you to be consistent in your actions and to rely on what you say. People prefer those of whom it can be said, "their word is their bond", or "if she says it is so, it must be so". This is more than saying the person is honest, it is also saying they are reliable, and can be counted on to act in a dependable manner. That they have INTEGRITY! (from the Latin "integer" meaning whole or seamless)

We can all benefit by observing how the military services train their men and women to consistently respond to orders. One of the first things one learns in the military is self-discipline and to respond almost automatically to direction - not just when you feel like it, but consistently. Every commanding officer needs to know that his troops will respond properly, and predictably, to directions in combat while, at the same time, being prepared to adapt to changing situations. The best planned and well-timed maneuver will turn into a disaster unless the troops execute their orders in the manner their commander prescribes and at the right moment. To improve their soldiers' predictability, commanders create realistic training scenarios that give recruits an experience as close as possible to actual combat. They use smoke,

LIFE'S DATA STACKERS

explosions, noise, bad weather, and sometimes gunfire with live ammunition. They also direct simulated enemy forces to make unexpected moves. It's essential that when soldiers (or sailors, or airmen) go into real combat, they know what to expect and how to react so that, in turn, their commanders know what to expect from them. Realistic training goes a long way in preventing panic under fire and otherwise preparing soldiers to perform in a predictably effective way.

SAVING A SALES TRAINING PROGRAM

Well now, let's take a look at how a major appliance manufacturer suffered from a lack of predictability, and then later eliminated a major problem by improving predictability through the use of data stacking.

The Company manufactured home laundry appliances and distributed the product nationwide. There was a large sales staff that sold the product to department stores, discount chains, hardware stores and other appliance outlets. In addition to domestic sales personnel there was a second group that concentrated on sales to the commercial, or coin-operated, side of the business. It was essential that each of the salespeople be well trained and extremely knowledgeable about their respective type of product. Knowledge of product has always been a significant factor in achieving success in the sales field. Also, the technical nature of this electro-mechanical product demanded more than a cursory familiarity. Retailers would continually look

PREDICTABILITY

to the sales personnel to deal with the tougher technical complaints received from the store's customers. After all, the salesmen were from the home office and were expected to have all of the answers.

Like most appliance manufacturers the appliance company also had a large service department. In this case the service department was comprised of three groups: The first, an in-house group, operated a large warehouse from which they shipped replacement parts to stores and/or distributors. The second group, also an in-house group, consisted of administrative personnel who manned order desks. A third group was made up of people known as Service Representatives. Their job was to travel all over the United States making calls on dealers to hold training schools for the dealer's repair people. In the industry these traveling teachers are usually referred to as factory representatives. If you are going to teach technicians how to fix a complicated product, you had better be very well trained yourself. In past years the Service Representatives had been selected from various parts of the Company, including the hourly work force. These people were often quite good mechanically but were generally lacking in customer relation skills. At the same time, the Company was hiring salesmen with great human relations skills, but with little mechanical know-how.

A new program was instituted using mostly recent college graduates, with good human relations skills, and putting them through the Service Representative training program. In

LIFE'S DATA STACKERS

this way they would obtain an in-depth knowledge of the Company's products before going out into the sales field. Management also hoped that with their better education the new recruits would eventually become better sales managers. The theory was good, but it soon ran afoul of reality.

The initial phases of the program immersed the trainees in all the intricate details of clothes washers and dryers. They learned to assemble and disassemble every model and product, and all the little tricks to make the job easier. They spent several weeks studying manuals and stripping down machines. It was not enough to know what the part was, they had to know its function and how it was made. Part of the "final examination" for this phase consisted of the trainee stripping down a washer and dryer to their last nut, bolt, wire, belt, motor, and piece of sheet metal. Next, all the parts from both machines were intermixed into one big pile. Now the trainee was asked to reach into that pile and correctly assemble a workable washing machine and a dryer - and don't take too long in doing it. Once in a while, when some of the trainees thought the job was impossible, the instructor would give a personal demonstration. The instructor would not only take the machine apart, but he would then reassemble it blindfolded. (Try that one someday oh weekend do-it-yourself handyman.) Upon "graduation", the trainees were sent out on the road - and this is where the program came apart. Their "territory" was the entire United States, which meant living on an airplane and out of a suitcase. To make matters worse, the customers

PREDICTABILITY

normally could only make their repair people available after normal business hours, or on the weekend. Economics and customer's schedules made it necessary for the Service Representatives to be away from home a minimum of two consecutive weeks at a time and sometimes as long as a month. Between trips they would work in the office for perhaps a week before starting out again. Bachelors did not mind it at all. They were able to live off the expense account most of the time. However, for some of the other new graduates, many of them newly married, it was an unexpected nightmare. Now remember, the greater the difference between the expected and the unexpected, the greater the unhappiness. The turnover rate went out of sight.

The solution to the problem was quite simple, and was based on the same technique used on the labor lawyer hired at the brewery: The company improved its predictability by telling job candidates what to expect. In discussions with the trainees the company had learned what should have been obvious. It wasn't the work itself that grated on the new Service Representatives, but rather the unexpected time they had to spend away from home. The cure began in the college recruiting offices. During interviews candidates were given a full and detailed description of the training program, as well as the reward to be expected upon completion. In fact, interviewers went a bit overboard in stressing the negative aspects, especially of the travel requirements. Before they were hired, candidates

LIFE'S DATA STACKERS

were asked to talk it over with their wives. Supervisors also talked to the wives of the final candidates. When the new employee came to work, they knew in detail what to expect. The travel schedule remained just as tough, but this time they were expecting it.

Then one additional step was taken to further improve circumstances for the wives of the new Service Reps. Moving into a strange and fairly small town was a new experience for most of them. Their expectations (predictions) were that they would have friends to associate with while their husbands were gone. Unfortunately, small towns can sometimes be slow to warm up to "outsiders" from other parts of the country. Too often the wives were left alone for weeks on end. Husbands (the trainees) bore the brunt of their subsequent unhappiness. To help overcome this, the Company regularly sponsored a number of social events to which the trainees and their wives were invited together with several older employees. Friendships were quickly established and the problem solved.

PLEASE COMMUNICATE

Hopefully you have already picked up on a very essential component in solving all of these predictability problems: Communication. Don't just sit there - talk to people - and listen, listen, listen. Only by exchanging information can you ever hope to know, and solve, human relations problems. The management of the washer company didn't learn about the feelings of the

PREDICTABILITY

trainees by going to some back alley fortune teller, they talked to the trainees!

When people know that your interest in them is sincere and you're not just being nosey, they'll open up to you. Often the best way to demonstrate your sincerity is to begin by sharing something about yourself or one of your own problems. Another method is to first ask the other person if you may ask them a question. Once they give you permission, you can ask the question without it seeming to be an invasion of their privacy. I've pointed out the dangers of asking a question to which you do not know the answer, but that rule doesn't necessarily apply in social situations. You're not putting your friend, new acquaintance, or employee on trial. Among social and professional acquaintances and associates, welcome the unexpected answer - it may be of critical importance to gaining an understanding of how their data's stacked.

Also, when listening, take note of little remarks or facial expressions that indicate a depth of feeling beyond the content of the words. A departing female employee was asked how she got along with her boss. "Oh fine", she said, "I kind of questioned his scheduling, but we got along OK". "I've decided to stay home and take care of the kids". It would be a mistake to assume in this case that the relationship between the departing employee and her boss was, in reality, alright. The throw-off reference to scheduling needed looking into. More in-depth questioning revealed that the boss was being terribly unfair in his scheduling

LIFE'S DATA STACKERS

and treatment of the employee - and that was her real reason for quitting. How it is said, is just as important as what is said. It would seem that the employee's internal computer had long ago calculated that to tell the real truth might get her in trouble. Once this piece of data was unstacked, she could feel comfortable telling the whole story.

There's another potential pitfall for the conversational neophyte: failing to listen to the answers to your questions. **Do not ask a question unless you are willing to LISTEN to the answer** - the *whole* answer - not just an opening sentence. Too often a person will hear the first few words, make an unwarranted assumption as to what comes next, and jump in with an incorrect, inappropriate, or insensitive response. First off, this is terribly rude. Secondly, it's terribly stupid. Never assume from your own data how the other person is going to complete their sentence or thought. Some people just can't shut up long enough to allow another person to say anything. This is really a form of conceit. Ask yourself - why is what I have to say more important than what my friend has to say? Stop predicting what they are going to say and stop finishing their statements. The one most important thing you can do is learn to listen, listen, listen, and listen! It is amazing what can happen when you let a new thought fight its way past your open mouth and into your brain. Hot air from open mouths have blown away more good ideas than trees by hurricanes.

PREDICTABILITY

When, instead, you open your ears to another's ideas, the other feels flattered by your interest and will be much more willing to continue sharing his feelings with you. Awareness of those feelings will make it easier for you to know how that person will react to your future actions. Knowing why they think and feel the way they do enables you to communicate much more effectively with people.

I've said a lot up to this point about trying to improve your ability to predict the actions of others, and have also written at length about improving your own predictability by telling others what to expect of *you*. However, before leaving the subject of predictability, we need to think about how you can help people learn more about you. Certainly, as stated earlier, it helps a lot to be consistent with your words and actions. To help accomplish this, you must know something about yourself. There is a fine old expression that applies here: "to thine own self be true". Follow it! Let your words and actions reflect how you really feel and what you believe. If some of your beliefs are not popular with your associates or society in general, then you need to examine them carefully. By yourself, or with the help of a friend or counselor, ask yourself the same questions you would put to someone else. Find out how you came to believe what you do, and make sure the foundations of your philosophies are still valid.

LIFE'S DATA STACKERS

Remember, the old computer in your noggin never makes a mistake, but did you throw in a load of garbage during your childhood? At this point in your life, or after having acquired a few more years of experience, you may well decide that your previous input was either wrong or insufficient. Ted Bailey's idea of being perfect came from observation and listening to his father. Later in life he realized, in response to being questioned and acquiring new information, that he had been wrong. You may select as your interrogator a psychologist, a clergyman, a counselor, or simply a good caring friend. It's usually easier to have someone else question you rather than relying on self-examination. On your own you might avoid asking yourself those questions to which you don't want to know the answer.

Once you've learned about yourself by evaluating your previous input, remember to be predictable: do not speak falsely. When you say one thing, but believe another, the insincerity shows through. It becomes difficult, if not impossible, for others to know whether you are expressing your true feelings or simply lying. No one will be able to trust anything you say. Not being able to know, or predict, how you truly feel, they will be left with no alternative but to discount what you say and mistrust the motives behind your actions. The least offensive term that might then be applied to you will be, "unpredictable". Use tact and diplomacy, not lies, when you disagree with others. Once again, listen, and communicate. Exchange ideas and information rather than accusations.

PREDICTABILITY

CHAPTER FIVE

THE
FAMILY:
FOR
BETTER
OR
WORSE

I have long been a believer in the value of using appropriate examples to illustrate ideas and principles. For that reason, and because people tend to remember stories better than a listing of facts or procedural steps, I'm devoting the balance of this book largely to providing additional "real life" cases showing how the principles I've outlined can or have been applied in a variety of different situations. Since people's backgrounds and situations are unique, I'll relate a wide variety of situations in the hope that at least some of them will relate to your own experience.

THE FAMILY: FOR BETTER OR WORSE

We'll deal with issues you may face with your family, your neighbors, and at work. Interspersed will be a few friendly suggestions and/or "rules" to follow. I'll illustrate how people use their fantastic five senses to first "load", or stack, their personal internal never, never wrong computers. This, I hope, will help you come to see how each person develops their own unique "realities" and, ultimately, how they come to make predictable decisions. It's the total of all these "realities" that combine to become our individual personalities. Hopefully, you'll also begin to see how your own predictions, or expectations, have influenced you in your assumptions about others. Even more hopefully, you may find some of the "rules" to be beneficial in dealing successfully with others. Intertwined with all of this is the ever critical and mandatory need, and desire, to communicate with others. The televised speech, conversation around the dinner table, a baby's cry, orders on the assembly line or a lover's whispers - all are used to transfer information about ourselves to one another.

For better or worse, we **all** are the sum of many parts. With a bit of introspective thinking, we can become as predictable to ourselves as we already are to others. When we become more predictable to others, it is easier for them to live with us. Oh, you don't think you are predictable? Go talk to your parents, your spouse, or co-workers - they may surprise you with their answers. There is nothing wrong with being consistent in your behavior, and I'm sure you would like to see more of it in

LIFE'S DATA STACKERS

others. It is essential that we learn why we make the decisions that affect every facet of our lives. Our "computers" have been stacked with data from an unlimited number of sources I like to call DATA STACKERS. The five senses are the conduits for feeding the information from these STACKERS into our brains. DATA STACKERS are all around us. People, places, things. The family is one of the earliest and most potent DATA STACKERS we ever encounter. The things we see and learn in the home provide some of the strongest impressions our memory banks will ever receive. That is where so many things begin and so will I.

HUSBANDS, WIVES AND LOVERS

Can you guess where one of the biggest breakdowns in predictability among women today occurs? It occurs at all income levels. Education seems to have no appreciable effect. The color of skin makes little or no difference, and it has continued for centuries. Give up? It is that timeless ephemeral dream that a woman will change a man once she's married him, or once she's established a "lasting" relationship with him. Give it up ladies - it ain't gonna happen. Don't take my word for it; look at what has happened in your own life. Is it at all possible for any woman to change a man? Yes, but unless she is a well trained and experienced counselor, and he is truly willing to do what's required, it is very, very unlikely any real change will occur. This is not really a gender specific phenomenon, since

THE FAMILY: FOR BETTER OR WORSE

men are no-better at changing women. The ladies just seem to have a greater need to alter the ways of their partners. "If you really loved me, you would do it". Look folks, you're overlooking something very important: You're asking your partner to forget everything the "fantastic five" have been stacking into that person's internal computer for many, many years - years of strong influence that happened before you were ever in the picture. All that good(?) information has created an individual reality that does not include you. Your assignment, should you choose to accept it, is to learn about that reality BEFORE you get into a serious relationship. Perhaps we should establish a kind of mantra that says "learn the reality and predict your future". Learn the reality and predict your future, learn the reality and predict your future!!!

One wise woman made this comment, "Too many women have a kind of conceit. They think they are so unique and extra special that their male friend will do anything for them". Maybe it has something to do with the idea that men are the sexual aggressors, and therefore all she has to do is flaunt her charms and he will do cartwheels to possess her. To what extent this may be true, I do not know, but those ladies should beware. That attitude will only work until they run into the fellows who remind them that women are like street cars - there will be another one along in a few minutes.

In college there were always a certain number of male students who seemed to feel that getting drunk on a regular basis

LIFE'S DATA STACKERS

was the mark of a man, a good fraternity member, a sociable fellow - or so, at least, their data was stacked. Along comes some unsuspecting coed who likes everything about her hero except for his drinking. "Oh well, I can change that after we are married". And so it is that one more couple embarks on a journey doomed to failure. Unless someone, or some organization such as Alcoholics Anonymous, can reach into the young man's computer and change around some of his previously acquired data - "it ain't going to fly Orville". In another instance I know of, a young man married a woman who had been somewhat loose in her morals before marriage. He too, like the college coed, felt a change would occur after the ceremony and she would be faithful only unto him. After a year or two she drifted back into her previous ways, and eventually became a "housewife prostitute". When he went to work, she went hunting. Once again, change is not impossible; it is just improbable without expert professional help, a strong desire on the part of the individual to change, and a close examination of what's stacked inside that person's human computer.

These are only two among the millions of scenarios that are played out every day all over the world. The cast of characters and locales are different, but the basic situations are the same. I am sure that each of you can very readily provide many, many more illustrations from your own life. Then there are TV talk shows that are awash with miserable examples. Always there is the hope that the other person, through an

THE FAMILY: FOR BETTER OR WORSE

application of love, kindness and persuasion, will change. Lots of luck! If you succeed, you will be one of the very few.

Those of you who have read through the first four chapters may have an inkling as to what course you should follow if you're to have any hope of affecting change in a "significant other". What you may not realize is that it requires that you get over that romantic idea of love at first sight - or at least that such love is enduring. Sure, you may be strongly attracted to the other person, and sure you find that person to be a really fun date, but what do you really know about him or her? Try to be aware that being "great in bed" is often the first casualty in a relationship. Oh it is exciting and perhaps immoral before marriage, but after the ceremony you had better be able to rely on something more than flaming passion. All of you who would begin the process attempting to change your present or future mate by asking questions are correct, and get an "A" for the course. Now recite - LEARN THE REALITY AND PREDICT YOUR FUTURE. Also, the advice to look at your intended spouse's parents if you want to see the future, has good foundation. Be assured that it is in the home where the human computer gets a majority of its initial information. There are many sayings that mean the same thing. "As the twig is bent, the tree will grow". "The apple doesn't fall too far from the tree". "Like father, like son". Perhaps we should create a new saying: "as the data is stacked, the computer will act". Go and have dinner, or attend some other social event with your true love's

LIFE'S DATA STACKERS

parents- an informal one is best. Watch the relationship between the parents. Is the wife one who expects to be a queen on a throne with the husband scraping and bowing? Does the husband treat his spouse like a slave and with little or no affection? No matter how much you may want to deny it, daughters who emulate mothers, and sons who mimic their fathers, are more the norm than the exception. Study the parents, take considerable time to do so (not just one quick visit) and learn all you can about their relationship. This thought may make some teenagers want to vomit, but eventually, as they get older, the family traits become more and more obvious. Numerous studies link the actions of alcoholics, child abusers, wife beaters, long term welfare recipients, braggarts, criminals, etc. to experiences during childhood years. It can go one of two ways. Often the child will think the parent is a proper (perhaps only) example, and will learn the same negative traits. Or, having seen the damage inflicted by an alcoholic husband on his wife, the child may vow never to touch liquor. Also, on the positive side, those same years, in a good family situation, can teach kindness, love, consideration, faithfulness and other good characteristics. For example, history records that families that dedicate themselves to public service tend to do so over several generations. Despite what we too often see in Congress, not all of our representatives sought political office for personal financial gain. It all depends on what reality the fantastic five have provided each of them.

THE FAMILY: FOR BETTER OR WORSE

Your job is to ask question after question, and listen, listen, listen. You should especially learn all you can about that individual with whom you want to spend the rest of your life. Quite often your questions (now please, do not make it a "third degree" - spread it out - a question a day may keep the "hell" away) will cause the other person to reevaluate the basis for their actions and/or philosophies, and they will change. While you're at it, don't forget to keep your eyes open for the actions that speak louder than you know what. Use all your five senses to the extent you can. You need all the help you can get. Learn how the data is stacked in your prospective companion's mind - learn what their reality is. Then you may be able to predict at least some of what you can expect in the future. At worst, you will have a much more solid foundation on which to build your relationship.

However, due to a lack of complete information, not all predictions are 100% correct. I hearken back to the early days of my courtship of a lovely blond, pure Norwegian young lady from Minnesota. We had been introduced by mutual friends and had dated for several weeks, when she invited me to meet her parents in Minnesota. It was the Christmas season, and in Minnesota-land, that means it's lutefisk and lefse time among the Scandinavians. For the uninitiated, lefse looks like a Mexican flour tortilla but is made from potatoes. Lutefisk is cod fish that has been soaked in lye to preserve the flesh and dissolve the bones. Lutefisk is often stored in a dried state and has to be first

LIFE'S DATA STACKERS

soaked in water (this also helps to remove some of the lye) before boiling. The cooked fish is rolled up in the lefsa along with mashed potatoes and melted butter. My darling had told me about this holiday custom, but I feared not. In my family's home I had often enjoyed eating cod fish, and so predicted that I would like lutefisk. Then came the fateful day. It may have been the smell, or perhaps the consistency, but whatever it was, I nearly choked. It was said, by nearby observers, that I turned a rather interesting shade of green. The family was greatly distressed. Especially, when in desperation, I rolled the lefse around a hot dog. To make a bad situation even worse, I did not like to drink coffee. This, in a household where a pot of "egg" coffee was constantly on the stove. Well, both sides had their expectations and predictabilities changed in that one evening. I'm sure the young lady's parents had hoped their daughter would bring home someone with a "proper" appreciation for Scandinavian cuisine. Instead they got this outlander who salivated over Pennsylvania Dutch scrapple made with left over pig parts. Well it was a good learning situation for both of us - and after many, many more exchanges of information, we have managed to stay happily married for over forty years. But I still won't eat lutefisk.

For many women another major breakdown in predictability occurs when they begin working outside the home. This is especially true for those who have children. Women's magazines and organizations tell them they can "have it all". A good full time job, darling well brought up children, and a

THE FAMILY: FOR BETTER OR WORSE

faithful, attentive, and housework-sharing husband. Many women dive into the "working world" without asking enough of the right questions - and thus their expectations often crumble in the face of increased clothing and transportation costs, higher taxes, unsuitable child care, an uncooperative husband, and considerable stress. Once home from work, husband and wife must cram all of the household chores in and around an effort to provide "quality time" for each other and for their children. The rosy predictions are crushed on the hard rocks of reality. The great disparity between what was expected and what really happens, frequently causes tremendous unhappiness. Once again, a little more prior investigation would have revealed some of the problems. Knowing what to expect would not have made the problems go away, but the couple would have felt better and possibly removed most of their feelings of psychological stress. Some realistic investigation can usually help to solve many of the problems ahead of time, and make those that are unsolvable, easier to bear. This is similar to the way my labor attorney friend could tolerate the bombastic boss because he had been forewarned, and knew what to expect.

Money, dirty filthy lucre, has always been another area of contention between husbands and wives. Keep in mind what you have already learned about people getting their data stacked at an early age. Imagine for a moment what happens in the following situation: The wife is raised in a family where her father came home and turned his paycheck over to her mother. The mother

137

LIFE'S DATA STACKERS

controlled the checkbook and paid all the bills. The young wife's new husband, however, was reared by a father who handled all of the finances and the mother had to "beg" for spending money. Will there be a conflict after the young couple gets married? Almost certainly. Can a bitter battle be avoided? Probably, provided the couple sits down ahead of time to discuss the differences in their upbringing. Examining the philosophies observed in childhood, in contrast with what they know as adults, will most likely give them new viewpoints. They should be able to see the faults of both parental approaches and work out their own satisfactory method.

Sex: another opportunity for marital problems. Physical and religious reasons aside, there are still plenty of other pitfalls. The "puritan" marries a "flower child". What is "normal" for one person may be "bizarre" for another. People reared in different neighborhoods with different customs and/or mores may soon clash. All can lead to serious conflict. Failure to share "realities" prior to marriage may lead to some unpleasant surprises on the wedding night, and possibly for many years thereafter. The advice to discuss these things before the ceremony is not new, but it is too often ignored or given short shrift. Some will claim that living together before marriage will solve this problem. (An opinion voiced by people who cannot or will not accept responsibility) However, misinformation about your partner will doom that type of relationship just as surely, and probably more quickly, than a conventional marriage. After all, the "glue" of the

THE FAMILY: FOR BETTER OR WORSE

wedding ceremony (and perhaps the cost of divorce) is missing. If it were present it would usually force the couples to at least undertake <u>some</u> discussion of their problems before parting company. For the unmarried - why talk about it? Just split! My intent is to once again point out that it is the breakdown in communication and the resultant lack of predictability and understanding that causes the subsequent unhappiness. The unexpected is unwanted! The unexpected causes problems! The unexpected causes pain!

However, all the discussion in the world cannot overcome an inability to accept the obvious. If either your upbringing or heredity has rendered you unbelievably naïve your data stack may be immune to change. Consider, for example, the case of the man who "had so many children he didn't know what to do". After his wife had presented him with seven offspring, assuming he must have had terribly active sperm, he decided to have a vasectomy. Now the doctor either failed to explain to Al (we will assign him that plebeian nom de plume) that he should expect to become completely and permanently sterile - or - Al was just plain stupid. Long after the operation, and more than nine months after any latent sperm should have remained, Al came into my office to show me pictures of his newly born eighth child, and pass out cigars. Of course I had to marvel at this seeming "miracle" and offer congratulations to the proud "father". There was however, one other odd aspect to this family,

139

LIFE'S DATA STACKERS

which I noted when Al showed me a new family portrait. For some reason, none of the kids looked like good old Al!!!!

Addendum: Maybe part of the explanation for this apparent "miracle" was Al's response to a request from several male co-workers that he allow his wife to spend the weekend at the beach with them. They told Al they wanted someone to cook meals and sit in on their card games from time to time. Al gave his permission, but laughed as he told me about it later. "Hell", he said, "Those guys are nuts. She's a lousy card player". Look folks, I don't make these things up. It really happened just that way!

Did you hear the one about the 85-year-old man who was having his annual checkup? The doctor asks him how he's feeling. "I've never been better!" he replies. "I've got an 18 year old bride who's pregnant and having my child! What do you think about that"? The doctor considers this for a moment, and then says, "Well let me tell you a story. I know a guy who is an avid hunter. He never misses a season. But one day he's in a bit of a hurry and he accidentally grabs his umbrella instead of his gun. So he's in the woods and suddenly a grizzly bear appears in front of him! He raises up his umbrella, points it at the bear, and squeezes the handle. The bear drops dead in front of him, suffering from a bullet wound in its chest". "That's impossible" says the old man. "Someone else must have shot that bear".

THE FAMILY: FOR BETTER OR WORSE

"Exactly" said the doctor. (Don't know the author-just one more internet joke-it fits)

PARENTS AND CHILDREN

"Monkey see, (or hear) Monkey do" might well describe the predominant learning style of children in most homes. As noted earlier, a child's view of the world is largely shaped at home. The Fantastic Five are operating 24 hours a day, and the home is the major, major source of information. For better or worse, parents are really big time DATA STACKERS!!

Unfortunately, children are too often subjected to a learning environment best characterized by the expression "don't do as I do, do as I tell you". Mom and Dad use cigarettes, alcohol, drugs, etc. during their moments of relaxation, to have a good time or to celebrate a special occasion. It's small wonder that the ever observant child perceives these actions in a positive manner. Too few parents take the time to talk to their children about how these "crutches" should be used and/or controlled. As a result the childrens' computers fail to get the full story. They don't learn the dangers along with the pleasures. As they get older (but not old enough) they start emulating their parents. The teen age alcoholic has often been taught "well" by his parents. Parents can protest all they want, but their actions reveal what they really appear to value. This is not lost on the child. As the old expression mentioned earlier puts it, "as the twig is bent the tree will grow". What else can we expect? When parents return

LIFE'S DATA STACKERS

from a cocktail party laughing and exclaiming about the good time they had, it's only natural for their offspring to predict that they too can have a good time by drinking, smoking and supply your own vice.

This same basic scenario applies to other things like stealing, poor driving habits, cheating, self-centeredness, child and/or spouse abuse etc. etc. etc. The parent acts in a certain way, the impressionable child watches and learns to expect similar results from similar actions. If Dad and Mom are doing it, it must be correct and good. And so the internal computer gets loaded with dangerous information which, unless modified by other input, will lead to unacceptable actions by the child. Society - that great ill-defined group of people, along with educators, clergy, friends and co-workers, must provide the counteracting input. It's indeed unfortunate that too many good and well meaning parents fail to provide adequate guidance to their children. They're too busy working, reading the paper, golfing etc. to spend time carefully feeding those receptive and malleable young minds. Now consider how this effect is magnified with two-income parents who leave it to baby sitters, a child care "factory", nannies and the like to provide input for their children's data banks. Instead of emulating the parents, the children now largely have their data stacked by others. Or worse yet, the alleged care giver plops them down in front of a TV set full of garbage or mind-dulling cartoons. So much for learning "family" values.

THE FAMILY: FOR BETTER OR WORSE

It doesn't necessarily take a bank robbery to have a negative effect on a child's data stack. Let's look at a rather simple and common type of situation. A parent works in an office. Night after night and year after year the loved and admired authority figure brings home little items such as pencils, pens, notepads, etc. Often times there are comments about making personal long distance phone calls at the company's expense. There is no discussion of possible penalties, and the "thief" suffers no visible consequence. Now how do you suppose this petty theft is viewed by the "big-eared and big-eyed" little kiddies? Later, in a department store, the parents are horrified when their little darling steals a small item from a counter. Imagine the conflict that's created in the malleable little mind when the parents reprimand the child! How come it's OK for dad and mom to take (steal) things but it's not all right for ME to pick up something? It doesn't take a lot of brains to predict that "junior" may well grow up to be another petty thief.

An equally familiar scenario occurs on every highway in the nation. Parents who habitually exceed the speed limit, curse other drivers, fail to wear seat belts, drive while drunk, or are just plain obnoxious road hogs are stacking their children's data far more effectively than if they'd intentionally attempted to teach their children such behavior. These are a child's first driving lessons as well as instructions in social etiquette. Hopefully the offspring will get into a good driver training course in high

LIFE'S DATA STACKERS

school and have its data stack re-arranged – or will encounter some other outside influence capable of overcoming the bad data its parents provided. It's too bad there isn't a similar course to adjust the data of those who have learned to cheat and lie.

Thoughtful and caring parents can do a lot to make life easier for their children. All parents have to do is try to be aware of the fears created in new situations. A popular saying is that "experience is a great teacher". That is true, BUT why not let the young ones learn from older people's experience? It's not really necessary for everyone to reinvent the wheel. We all learn from the lives of others.

Compare two families - both about to make a permanent move to another city. The son in the first family bemoans his fate and cries over leaving his friends behind. (He may have overheard his parents complaining about the move.) In the second family the son says, "Wow, what a chance to make some new friends". Guess which set of parents did the best job of developing positive expectations? Gee, I hate to keep bringing up old (and trite) sayings, but they have so much truth in them. Both of the above sons were the proverbial "pitchers with big ears" and listened carefully to what the "old folks" had to say. And if you can't believe your parents, whom can you believe?

Go to any summer camp and it is easy to spot those who have been well prepared for the new adventure. Preparation - spelled PREDICTABILITY - can do wonders. Instead of moaning over the kid's departure and how empty the house will

THE FAMILY: FOR BETTER OR WORSE

be without him, let him know he can expect to make new friends, go swimming, camp out, learn new games and skills and be perfectly safe at all times. If Mother starts crying about feeling lonely etc, don't be surprised if the little camper becomes homesick. Increasing the child's predictability and positive outlook may not solve all the problems, but it sure can help with most of them.

Kindergarten teachers usually like to have parents bring a child to the school before enrollment. They want the child to see what to expect or predict, learn what a nice place the schoolroom is and have them look forward to having fun with other boys and girls. This type of orientation can generally be quite beneficial for both student and teacher. I say generally because children sometimes encounter an insensitive or cruel teacher in their early years and spend the next several years hating school. However, a good start allows the child to predict a favorable experience.

It would be nice if there were a way for single parents, who have no choice but to drop off infants at a day care center, to stack the data of their infants in a way that would allow them to understand what's happening to them. It's too soon for them to talk to their infants about what will happen to them and why they must be left there. These children are too young to understand what's happening to them or why it's necessary to leave home and mother - but they do learn something: The one they trust the most can and will leave them. The warmth and safety of their world has been shattered for reasons they cannot comprehend.

LIFE'S DATA STACKERS

Even at this young age, the child has come to expect the sound of a particular voice, a touch, a way of cuddling, a scent, a familiar bed. The best of day care centers cannot duplicate the home, and the greater the disparity, the greater the possibility of turmoil in the child. The little ones are well aware of mother's body language and guilt feelings. Strong feelings are hard to hide. It can reasonably be predicted that children raised by day care workers will often suffer later personality problems.

My wife, who has a degree in early childhood education, has operated a pre-kindergarten facility and taught through the high school level. She often observed these negative effects. There is increasing evidence supporting the proposition that, when possible, it "pays" to be a stay-at-home parent.

As a child grows older, it's a wise mother who sits down with that child and tells it what to expect. Mother is going to work! Little minds understand more at a young age than we sometimes think. Many parents have successfully prevented problems through these discussions. If you're a mother who must work outside the home, tell your children why it's necessary, when you will leave, when you will return, and that you still love them. If they know that every day Mother must leave, and for a good reason, the child may not like it, but he or she will accept that fact more readily. Of course this assumes that the Mother has presented it in a serious but positive manner – rather than with tears and moaning about how she hates to go to work and

THE FAMILY: FOR BETTER OR WORSE

leave her little darling. Improve your predictability in the mind of your child - it certainly can't hurt!

There are many other areas in which parents need to take special care. Shall we add even more activities to the schedules of our already over-organized and over-scheduled children? Oh I know, you claim it's all for THEIR benefit – and that, after all, the neighbors kids all do it, and yours cannot be left out. Or maybe your child is darn well going to follow in YOUR footsteps. Activities such as Little League, Pee Wee football, ballet or dance school, cheerleading, sororities and fraternities, soccer, Scouts, Indian Princess etc. etc. etc. you name it - none of them are bad. They can be a great way of encouraging or pushing unwilling and/or uninterested children into participation.

If you've filled all your kids' waking hours with programmed activities please ask yourself, as a parent, just WHAT it is that you expect from them? Do you expect them to follow in your exact footsteps, follow only YOUR preconceived notions of what they should like, to reflect well on you in the minds of your elite circle of friends? Or are you, perhaps expecting them to compensate for your own inadequacies and failures? How did all these great(?) reasons and philosophies get stacked in YOUR computer? Isn't it just another case of GIGO?

There can be a real down side for parents who have unrealistic expectations for their children or expectations that differ from the expectations that their children have for

147

LIFE'S DATA STACKERS

themselves. When the kids don't live up to your expectations, it makes you unhappy - and them miserable.

Incidentally, who's responsible for stacking everyone's data in a way that causes them to presume that it must always be the daughter who takes care of the parent(s) in the parents' old age? Why not the son? Do you expect your daughter to take care of you, or are you planning to take care of yourself? If you are an opera singer, do you expect your child to have musical talent? Are you an All American football player that expects your boy to be a star quarterback? Why? Is athletic ability just naturally passed down from father to son? I know a young man ready to graduate from one of the finest prep schools in the country. During a discussion about what colleges he was applying to, the young man commented that he was the only person in his class who was being allowed to decide for himself what career path he would follow. Too much parental "pride" and control will certainly stifle and cause great harm to those other unfortunate children.

How many times have we seen a parent build a successful business, amass a great fortune, only to have it squandered by a less talented or less motivated offspring? That motivation is one thing that really cannot be passed along through the gene pool. The founding father of the business may have grown up in circumstances that created an overwhelming desire for success. Many a person, raised in poverty, spurred by their circumstances,

THE FAMILY: FOR BETTER OR WORSE

has been motivated to rise above childhood misery and hunger. They are determined that neither they nor their families will suffer as they have. On the other hand, the comfortable, well fed, and perhaps pampered, scion of a rich man thinks there is no need to be motivated. After all, from their standpoint, it doesn't take any effort at all to live the good life. Daddy and Momsie have always given them whatever they wanted. No one has taught them to expect to have to work long and hard to make or keep a good income. So, bye bye motivation and bye bye Daddy's fortune.

When it is all said and done, each person is acting in a manner that he or she feels is best - according to how the data stackers have stuffed their individual computers. Remember, we never make a mistake? We do wrong things but think they are correct. When you find yourself in conflict with another person, adult or child, stop and try to examine what mental process you went through in reaching your position. How is your data stacked and why? Go back as far as necessary and reconsider.

It would be nice to end this chapter on a rosy, beautiful sunset note, but I feel it is necessary to mention a problem that afflicts too many of our teenagers - suicide. There are many reasons why a young person decides to end their life, and sometimes it is due to their inability to predict. I can never forget the young man in my high school class who hung himself in his senior year. Why? Why? Why? He was highly intelligent, but a "bookworm" who was not readily accepted by his fellow

LIFE'S DATA STACKERS

students. Today he might be called a "nerd" or some other degrading term. Did his parents do anything to improve his expectations when he went to school? Would it have helped if they had said something like, "Bill, you are much smarter than most of the other students. And many of them won't like it". When you go to school, do not be surprised when they ignore or tease you. They are trying to overcome their own feelings of inferiority and may strike out at you. It won't be pleasant, but remember you are in school to learn, and in the end you will come out far ahead of your tormentors. It won't be easy, but we will support you and help you all we can". This type of warning will not make the jibes of fellow students any more acceptable, but Bill could at least feel some consolation in knowing his predictions were accurate and that his parents understood his problems and would support him. I refer you back, again, to the labor attorney mentioned earlier in the book. He could stand up under the boss's attacks because the attorney expected them. Being able to predict lessens the negative impact in unpleasant situations. Again and again, when we hear of young people taking some self-destructive action, we find parents who, for one reason or another, have not communicated effectively with their children.

When your child heads off to school, it sometimes helps to point out that peer pressure to act in a certain way, or wear certain types of clothing, can be expected. Now is the time to talk

THE FAMILY: FOR BETTER OR WORSE

about NOT following the crowd and, instead, being a leader - a leader that sets the style instead of being a mindless robot.

Some years ago there was a formal dance at a Big Ten university. Six couples were sitting around a large table when the waitress asked for drink orders. The first person asked for an alcoholic drink, as did each of the others around the table - almost. One man's date followed suit – ordering an alcoholic drink - but made a sour face as she did so. Noticing the expression on his date's face the man asked her if she really wanted that particular drink. "No", she said. So he told her "Then order what you like, I'm having a coke". After these two independent thinkers (leaders) ordered cokes, others at the table began changing their orders to non-alcoholic drinks. In the end, no one drank alcohol.

People of all ages succumb to peer pressure because they want to do what is "expected of them" so that they can fit in with the group. Their internal computers have been stacked to make them believe this course of action is necessary. As we can see from the above example, those expectations are not always correct. Again, it can be most helpful if parents will encourage their children to test some of these supposed "rules" and assumptions.

This is a good time to describe what a group of parents and friends in Michigan do to prepare high school graduates for the future. They know how new graduates too often go off the deep end when they leave school or begin their first year in

LIFE'S DATA STACKERS

college. With that in mind, when a parent's child graduates from high school, the parent assembles a group of adults (of the same sex) who have been influential in the child's life, and meet for lunch or dinner. Over a meal, each adult will discuss experiences they had and temptations they dealt with after leaving high school. These are very frank and blunt discussions designed to point out to the new grad the impending "pitfalls" he's likely to face. There are discussions not only about the adults' own past experiences, but also in-depth exchanges about current practices and trends. All of this is designed to improve the new grad's ability to predict the difficult situations to come, and equally important, to give the grad advice on how to handle those situations. Without exception, rather than being embarrassed or resentful, the new grads have been quite receptive and have appreciated the input. It has made their entrance into the world of reality much easier.

Now let's go back to high school for a minute. A certain high school had an organization that teen-age boys could join for social and athletic activities. It was called the HI-Y club. HI for high school, and Y for the YMCA where they held their meetings. For some time this particular club languished and was unable to attract new members. "You don't want to join with that bunch of losers (nerds)". The members did not get into fights, drink or smoke, and so were obviously out of touch with the way hip students were expected to act. Expected by whom? Actually,

THE FAMILY: FOR BETTER OR WORSE

this view point was being promoted by a few loud mouthed "tough guys" who no one liked anyhow. This all changed when one student challenged those assumptions. He was popular, and a "scrub" member of the football team. Immediately after joining, he persuaded others from the football team to join, and in a short time it became "acceptable" to belong to the HI-Y. It wasn't too long before the club was the most influential group in the school and all the boys wanted to join up. Well, not everyone. The "tough guys" and street fighters had no use for it, but their opinions were no longer considered. So once again, it took only one person to restack the data for a larger group. One of the lessons we can learn here is that you should never take actions based solely on someone else's assumptions, expectations, and/or predictability. Ask your own questions, and, based upon your own background, reach a personal decision. Use all of your five fantastic senses. The tough guys, the overbearing manager, the person you married, your lover, your children, and your parents are all acting in accordance with how their own very personal computers have been stacked. Listen to them, watch their actions, ask questions, and then stack your own computer.

LIFE'S DATA STACKERS

CHAPTER SIX

LOVE
AND
WAR
WITH
THE
HOI
POLLOI

What in the world is a "hoi polloi" you ask? Well, my ever faithful Roget's Thesaurus lists the phrase under the general heading of "inferiority". It lists such meanings as "underling, flunky, second fiddle, follower, second stringer" etc. However, I prefer to go back to the original Greek meaning. They originated the term, and to them it was a collective term referring to "the masses". The every day, ordinary "common" man. I in no way regard the "common" man as inferior. Although the hoi polloi may lack high rank or privilege, are not billionaires

LIFE'S DATA STACKERS

or presidents or famous in any way, they are the millions and millions of laborers, managers, business owners, and professionals who make society work. In this chapter I plan to deal with the relationships between ordinary people – the hoi polloi - in everyday circumstances. These are your neighbors, "doctors, lawyers, merchants, chiefs", and now and then perhaps a thief. Those of us who engage in a normal amount of discourse with others must deal with dozens of different personalities every day. Even the most timorous recluse must, from time to time, interact with other human beings. Our success or failure in business, domestic relations or normal day to day activities, will depend on how well we deal with these wonderfully diverse members of the hoi polloi - diversity enhanced by the existence of millions and millions of different "internal computers" loaded by innumerable "data stackers".

HOW TO GET RID OF DOOR TO DOOR SALES PEOPLE

Have you ever spent a pleasant evening at home, doing your best imitation of a couch potato, only to have your reveries interrupted and your teeth put on edge by the insistent and all too demanding ringing of the doorbell? The door is opened to reveal the presence of that scourge of domestic tranquility - the FOOD CLUB SALESMAN!!!!!! Panic ensues and the stomach churns. You glance about for help, but your spouse, having made an immediate assessment of the situation, has made a departure at Olympic record-breaking speed. You're alone, and before you

LOVE AND WAR WITH THE HOIPOLLOI

stands this diabolically clever, well trained salesman who has already been taught all of the answers to all of the questions and objections you can imagine. He is also equally well trained to ask YOU leading questions designed to coerce you into buying his overpriced products. If you say you're not interested in buying anything, he'll assure you that he's not selling. His fiendish Machiavellian handlers have created a remorseless monster and, without pity, turned him loose on YOU! These Data Stackers have filled his, or her, internal computer with almost everything necessary to counter your predictable responses and to make the sale. Almost!

Freeze frame!!! Now, take a good long look at this creature before you. All of his, or her, five senses have been utilized to thoroughly stack their data to create the necessary mind set to overwhelm your every rejoinder, answer, retort, or rebuttal. Now it's time for you to take advantage of what you've learned in the previous chapters, to rid yourself of this consummate selling machine. You KNOW all your possible and very predictable responses have already been thought of and his computer is ready to spit out an irrefutable logical answer. But the training is only ALMOST perfect. The chink in the armor is communication. Certainly the salesman has been taught to communicate his sales pitch to you, the customer, but you don't have to receive it. The simple secret to driving door to door salespeople absolutely berserk is to CUT OFF

LIFE'S DATA STACKERS

COMMUNICATION! A conversation destroyer might go like this:

> Salesman: I represent the Little Whizzo icebox company.
>
> You: The sky is blue.
>
> Salesman: Oh yes, it is a pretty day isn't it.
>
> You: My Aunt Minnie has false teeth.
>
> Salesman: She does, how does she like them?
>
> You: Downhill skiing is a wonderful sport.
>
> Salesman: Yes it is. I like to ski also.
>
> You: New York is full of people.
>
> Salesman: Could I please tell you about Little Whizzos?
>
> You: I really enjoyed Tom Clancy's latest novel.

Etc. etc. etc. -- but not for long. Very quickly, the Little Whizzo salesman will go mumbling on his way.

The whole idea here is to cause a complete breakdown in communication by providing completely irrelevant and UNPREDICTABLE responses. You never never acknowledge anything the salesperson says, and always always respond with a completely unrelated topic. If they pick up on what you say, such as the skiing, you immediately change to another topic. Never provide any additional data that his computer can utilize. Such conversations don't usually last long. The salesperson may think you're weird, but what do you care? This is certainly not a good human relations approach - just keep it in mind as an example of how to use your understanding of data stacking to subvert a sales pitch.

LOVE AND WAR WITH THE HOIPOLLOI

I had a friend in Portland, Oregon who once used his understanding of how salesmen's data is stacked, to have a bit of fun with an Arthur Murray Dance Studio salesman. The Studio salesman called and advised my friend that he had been selected, out of hundreds of others, (yeah right) to win a series of free dance lessons. My friend knew that the salesman's data was stacked to use people's desire to get something for nothing as a way to lure prospects into the studio for the standard high-pressure sales pitch for additional expensive lessons. Knowing that an outright refusal would only invite further pressure from the salesman, the "winner's" response to the salesman was - "Gee, that sounds great. I'd surely like to do that, but I can't right now". Then followed several weeks during which my buddy responded to further sales contacts by reiterating his desire for lessons, but always "maybe next week". Eventually the salesman said "you don't really want these lessons do you"? Was my friend being cruel to the salesman, or just getting even? You decide.

LEARNING TO BE AN INDEPENDENT THINKER

These kinds of salespeople illustrate what can happen when your personal computer is "over programmed" – trained so aggressively, sometimes even by well-intentioned people, that you become virtually incapable of having original thoughts or taking independent action with regard to a given subject or process. You begin to act in an almost robotic fashion - spewing

LIFE'S DATA STACKERS

out the preprogrammed message from your handlers and responding mechanically to changes in circumstances. Some parents mistakenly take the same approach of trying to "program" their children in advance to handle any conceivable challenge. When a parent does this, the child can become confused and indecisive when something unexpected occurs. The child can find it difficult to make its own decisions and respond in new or unusual situations. One of the most important things a parent can do as a primary "data stacker" is to teach children to think for themselves. For instance, when listening to a political speech, don't just say the speaker is right or wrong. Instead, point out to the child how questions are evaded, "hot button" words are used, insinuations made and help them discuss the topics more fully. Let them see that there is usually more than one answer to a problem and most likely other equally valid viewpoints. They, and you, should be asking why the politician is advocating a specific philosophy, and why he or she reacts the way they do. What is their background, where do they come from, what groups do they belong to or represent? And of course, what is the politician's voting record? These are all questions that help determine the true views and integrity level of this would-be leader. How has their data been stacked? Teach your offspring to be critical observers and listeners, and finally, to reach their own conclusions.

The over-programming of people's computers, and their consequent inability to act and think independently, has caused

LOVE AND WAR WITH THE HOIPOLLOI

the downfall of more than one foreign military regime. In World War II the Germans might have kept the Allied forces off the beachheads if the on-scene commanders had been permitted to take independent action. Instead, readily available tank corps were held back until orders were received from Berlin. The officer corps had been heavily programmed to await and follow orders from above rather than making major strategic or tactical decisions on their own. The training of officers to change plans as required to fit a developing battle situation has always been a major advantage wielded by the armed services of the United States. As in the military, in business, or any other endeavor, it's wise to recognize that there are many acceptable roads to any objective and that those who would insist on stacking others' data in a way that restricts them to following only one predetermined path, without deviation, will surely suffer for it. In the business world we often talk about the differences between those who are obstacle oriented as opposed to objective oriented. The obstacle oriented person's programming causes him to falter when unexpected difficulties arise. However, objective oriented people have had their computers programmed to look at the unusual and unexpected as challenges to be overcome on the way to the objective. The latter types are demonstrably the more capable and successful.

LIFE'S DATA STACKERS

THE BAR SCENE

Many members of the "hoi polloi" are known to visit bars and other "watering holes" from time to time - from the place where "house" wine goes for fifteen or twenty dollars a glass, to Slimy Joe's where well-watered booze sells for 50 cents a shot. The little dramas played out in either place can be remarkably similar. Oh the language may be a bit different, and the clothing from different shops, but the internal passions and thought processes are the same. When, for example, the standard over-worn pick-up line like "hi there beautiful, do you come here often"? is uttered in one place, the inquisitor might be called a "jerk - while in another place he might be called a "puking plume-plucked miscreant" or perhaps an "artless tickle-brained barnacle". (If you've never read Shakespearean literature, you may need to look-up the meaning of these epithets) In any event, in whatever establishment you might choose to indulge your fantasies in approaching a member of the opposite sex, please remember that each person has already had his or her internal computer fully programmed. Oh I know I told you earlier that you never made a mistake - according to the way YOUR data was stacked, but this is one of those circumstances where the object of your attention is likely give you that ever-helpful "additional input" to help you re-stack your data. So, to stand a chance of success, you must find out not only what your intended is thinking, but WHY she's thinking it. It just might change YOUR data and thinking. How about a young man sidling up to

162

LOVE AND WAR WITH THE HOIPOLLOI

his "target" and saying, "hello, would you mind telling me how you have your data stacked"? (while trying hard to look into her eyes rather than at her other bodily endowments)? Well, at least it would be different.

Here again, the most brilliant "conversationalist" is usually the one who has learned to listen well. When accosted by a loudmouthed antagonistic drunk who seems intent on mayhem, might it not help if you made some sympathetic remark, and then listened? "Man, it sounds like you have had a rough day" or "tell me what those bums at work did to you". The longer you listen in an active and intelligent manner, the more the internal fires will cool, and the better you can deal with his anger. When a person speaks, ask yourself why he said what he did. If you don't know the answer, start asking gentle but leading questions to find the answers. Only then can you safely choose your responses.

GARAGE SALES ANYONE?

It's absolutely amazing how some people's data has been stacked to harbor unrealistic and unfair expectations in their dealings with others. An example of this phenomenon can be found in the conduct of buyers at a garage sale. Quite often a customer will see something she likes and ask the seller to take a deposit in exchange for the seller's agreement to hold the item for them. So far, so good. Later the would-be buyer returns to say she's decided not to buy, and wants her deposit back. At this point, it's quite proper and legal for the seller to refuse to return

LIFE'S DATA STACKERS

the money. "What do you mean", screams the buyer, how can you refuse to refund my deposit"? Of course, the poor seller has lost several customers while saving the object for the buyer. The buyer apparently has had their data stacked, somewhere along the line, to expect a return of her deposit – regardless of the fact that she has no legal or moral claim to it. Just in case, like the buyer in this example, you've never heard and are lacking a sense of justice, a deposit, by its very nature, is always considered non-refundable. Our lesson for everyday living? Just because the law and fairness are on your side, don't assume everyone's data is stacked the same as yours: always make it clear to would-be buyers that their deposits are entirely nonrefundable. It's gone! You lost it Mac! I could have sold that sucker a dozen times, but I held it for you.

Would you like some additional free advice on how to run a garage sale? Before marking your prices too low, consider how antique collectors' data are stacked. Once upon a time a lady was holding a garage sale. One of the items for sale was an "antique-style" pitcher and bowl set. However neither the pitcher nor the bowl was actually an antique. As the hours passed, no one seemed interested in the set - which was priced fairly low. Then a neighbor, who was well versed in retail sales, stopped by. The lady holding the garage sale mentioned to her neighbor how she'd been unable to sell the pitcher and bowl – even at a price well below the actual value of the set. The neighbor advised her to put the price much higher so that people would perceive the set as being valuable. The lady followed his advice and the next customer to show interest in the set paid the higher price and ran off hugging the pitcher as though it were made of gold. Do you see the "what's real is real" concept at work here? In the purchaser's mind, if an item is high priced it must be valuable. She was also predicting, probably from her past buying habits, that this was a valid reality. In case you weren't already aware, many retailers use this same pricing strategy.

DOGS AND SLIMY SNAKES

Then again, perhaps you have a neighbor who seems deathly afraid of your sweet little harmless Chihuahua. Certainly those fears must be entirely irrational and based on faulty data stacking. What "normal" person could possibly be that cowardly? Doesn't EVERYONE love those scrawny little devils? Well, almost everyone. Everyone except the famous Branson comedian Jim Stafford. Stafford tells how he saved the life of his own little Chihuahua (he took his foot off its head in the toilet). But, I digress! Rather than think poorly about your neighbor, you might inquire as to the cause of the fears. My wife, for one, was severely bitten by an allegedly "harmless" little dog. Never, before that time, had she ever experienced fear of any dog. But now, since being bitten, she stays a healthy distance from all bad-tempered dogs - large or small. Her data has been well stacked, and so, perhaps, has your neighbor's. Once again, a few questions

LIFE'S DATA STACKERS

and sympathetic listening may well create a better understanding and friendship.

Even what appear to be the most pathological of fears acquire their strength by some kind of conditioning by the fantastic five. What would seem to you to be an unreasonable fear of snakes is perfectly reasonable to the person saddled with that fear. Quite often the origin of such an irrational fear is something as simple as a parent showing fear around snakes. Mother may shiver and exclaim about how they seem cold and slimy. Dear old Dad may run for an axe to dispatch this dangerous creature from the "wilds" of the empty lot next door. The child is quick to see this and will quickly become susceptible to the same reactions. Kudos to the mothers and fathers who, perhaps despite their own personal revulsion, talk to the child about the snake's good points. Tell them how pretty the snake is, how useful they are, and hopefully teach the child to hold these worthwhile creatures without fear. Why not do your part to break such senseless chains of fear? Educate yourself, and your children, as to the real nature of these beneficial reptiles and other much-maligned creatures. The only warning you really need to give them is how to identify the relatively few poisonous species. Be a beneficial DATA STACKER.

SOME BENEFITS OF PREDICTABILITY

Speaking of education, it's interesting to note that some of our most successful educators, in some of the worst inner city areas, have learned how to utilize the principle of predictability. They have learned that students want and need structure during their time in school. Providing structure in the form of timetables and objectives enables students to predict what is going to happen and what is expected of them. They are happy and more secure when they see things happening in an expected and/or promised manner. As a result, where teachers and administrators provide appropriate structure, schoolrooms are orderly and children are getting far better grades. Does this sound at all familiar? If so, perhaps it's because this is the same basic approach that many parents find to be successful at home. Just as a lack of predictability causes serious problems, being predictable, providing structure, and following through on your commitments to your children can bring contentment and satisfaction.

There are many people, as mentioned above, who have found it beneficial to use the predictability principles to further their causes. In the sixties and seventies, in the midst of the push for integrated neighborhoods, some black civil rights organizations made use of this phenomenon. It was a technique known as "block busting" and it was quite effective. A home would be purchased in an all-white neighborhood through some intermediary. Then a black family would move into the home. The usual result would be a rush to sell by all the nearby white families. What they expected (predicted), was that all of their

LIFE'S DATA STACKERS

property values would go down as soon as people learned that a black family had moved in. Of course this was a self-fulfilling prophecy, since a sudden dumping of homes on a limited market would, of course, drive down prices - with or without blacks. What the black groups realized very well, was that the unreasoning fear of the whites would cause them to sell at panic prices. They could predict this reaction with a high degree of certainty, and took advantage of those fears. The white people had created their own problem. By trying to move out like a herd of frightened lemmings, they pushed down prices. Then they sat there wondering who to blame. Since we never blame ourselves for our own stupidity or prejudice, it had to be the black people. This became easily magnified into one horror story after another - all based on self-inflicted "wounds". As a result, whites quickly had their data stacked to "know" that a black person in the neighborhood would result in lower real estate prices. This made it obvious to black civil rights groups that by moving only one family into each neighborhood they would accomplish their goals. They were very easily able to predict the reaction of whites, and used that knowledge with great success. In my own experience, when black families first moved into neighborhoods where I've lived, the neighbors stayed put despite fears of lower real estate values and provided the new families the same acceptance that would have been accorded any other new people on the block. Would you be surprised to learn that there was no resulting panic, no lowering of real estate values, and no animosity or racial division in the neighborhood? I hope that fact may restack the data in some of your heads.

HOW PREDICTABLE ARE YOU?

OK students, it's time for self examination. Let's hope you can pass the test. Stop and think about the things you say and do in ordinary, everyday situations. What do you lead people to expect from you? What have you done in the way of actions and/or words that will enable others to predict what you will or will not do? Have you ever broken a promise, been late for an appointment or perhaps jaywalked? What in the heck does jaywalking have to do with this?? Something everyone does-right? Sure, but think about the guy driving that big Mack truck coming down the highway. He has every right to expect NOT to see someone crossing in the middle of the block. Therefore, having predicted that the road will be clear, he puts the pedal to the metal. All the laws and safety practices are on his side. But YOU - you think you need to cross in the middle of the block. Of course, you have done it successfully many times before, and your internal computer says "no sweat" let's go. This time, his predictions, and yours COLLIDE. Perhaps the next time you start to commit an illegal or unwise act, you should stop long enough to determine just why it is that you must undertake that action. I guess what I'm trying to persuade you to do, is to ask yourself WHY? WHY? WHY? Why do you feel the need to act in any

LIFE'S DATA STACKERS

particular manner? As someone has said - Put your mind in gear BEFORE you put your mouth in motion.

By the way, are you one of those people who is often late for a lunch date, a business appointment, or gets to the theater sometime after the first act? WHY? WHY? WHY? Of course it's terribly inconsiderate and selfish on your part, but why do you do it. A common response is to cite the press of business, last minute phone calls, problems with the baby-sitter etc. Time to check the old internal hard drive: Why does this situation occur on a more or less regular basis? Do you need to improve your time management or organizational skills? What have the Data Stackers in your life done to you? Re-examine your past experiences to determine why you think your thoughtless actions are acceptable. Then consider the new data – starting with the realization that others don't appreciate your actions and think you're a first rate undependable clod. Now if you want to go through life being considered a clod, stay the way you are. On the other hand, by providing new up-to-date data for your brain, you can become a much more popular person.

I knew one young man who was quite popular with the ladies. For some reason, no matter how forward he might be on a date, the young women seldom complained. There were no slapped faces, no screams, no anger, although there wasn't always a second date. Why did this happen? It was really quite simple. The young man made it a practice to be predictable. And, as we have learned, when you're predictable, people usually don't become angry. This fellow made it a practice to tell the young women what to expect on a date. He told them he was bad, that he liked "fast" girls and lonely back roads. On the date, he would proceed to act in the manner he had described. There were no surprises. His "victims" knew what to expect before they went out with him. They were not taken unawares. As a result, the young ladies might say "yes" or "no" but, they seldom complained.

How about another visit to our real estate friends? Sooner or later we all get involved in buying, selling, renting, or leasing real estate. Nowadays the related contracts are quite long and full of details - which are too often ignored. A good agent will be careful to go over that contract in detail and explain all the ramifications of the various clauses. You should be told what to expect at each step of the way throughout the transaction and especially about the financial factors. For example, most contracts have a paragraph that spells out the limits on the amount a seller has to pay to fix faults the inspector finds. It will be a percentage of the sales price or a fixed dollar amount. If the selling agent fails to tell you what to expect (predict) at closing, then there can be some angry words when several thousands of dollars are charged against you.

Not knowing what to expect can also have an extremely adverse effect on you physically, as well as psychologically.

LIFE'S DATA STACKERS

Earlier I told you how a plastic surgeon kept his patients happy by educating them on what to expect during and after surgery. Now I would like to cite another example. Cardiologists have long known that many of their patients will suffer bouts of deep depression following a heart attack. This depression can often have serious consequences, including a second heart attack. A study was made of this situation. It revealed that when doctors sat down with their patients and explained that depression was a normal and expected occurrence, there were fewer second attacks. In fact, among patients who had NOT been properly counseled, the study showed that there were four to five times MORE second heart attacks. By taking the time to more completely discuss the patient's condition, to more fully describe expected treatment and the expected results, all doctors could make their patients feel much better. This applies in any medical situation, whether it's a major heart attack or a bout with the flu.

This may be a good time to bring in another of those important rules to remember when dealing with people at home, in business or government. Let me state it very clearly and, as E-mail devotees would write – LOUDLY:

**ANY ABSENCE OF COMMUNICATION
<u>ALWAYS</u> RESULTS IN NEGATIVE
RUMORS AND/OR NEGATIVE
ASSUMPTIONS.**

LOVE AND WAR WITH THE HOIPOLLOI

Now that you have read it, stop and think about it. Those doctors who failed to communicate sufficiently probably, although inadvertently, caused much of their patients' depression. There is often a great fear of the unknown. Why? Lack of knowledge is one of the major reasons many people fear change, and those negative feelings come from a lack of information. Perhaps it's because when people don't know how to drive well they tend to have accidents. When they don't know how to keep track of cards in a bridge game, they tend to lose. When they don't know a stove is hot they can get burned. When they don't know what a customer wants they're likely to lose a sale. When they don't know how much they owe they can end up bankrupt. An unexpected phone call in the middle of the night almost always evokes a feeling of dread. After all, a majority of those calls usually DO convey bad news - or reveal a very inconsiderate person. Finally, how do you feel when you're unexpectedly called in to see the boss, the principal, the commanding officer, or some other authority figure? There's almost always at least a little fear of bad news. Yes, a lack of information usually has a negative effect upon all of our activities. It's small wonder that we therefore always expect the negative when we're lacking information. Having sufficient knowledge will permit us to direct our actions in such a way as to have a more favorable outcome. We will have more positive feelings, and need I say it, a more predictable and acceptable result.

LIFE'S DATA STACKERS

A lack of communication becomes especially "deadly" during a recession or when a company has financial difficulties. Under these conditions managements who are perceived by their subordinates as operating in an "incommunicado" manner, are doomed to listen and wonder as negative rumors run wild in their organizations – and to search for someone to blame for the subsequent exodus of many valuable employees. "Why sit around and wait for the Company to go under. I'm getting out now before the lay-offs begin". No matter that a huge new chunk of business is coming next month and the Company will have to hire more people. The failure to inform the employees ahead of time can only lead employees to believe the worst.

BUYING AND SELLING REAL ESTATE

There is another area in which many of these principles come to the fore. It's in the buying and selling of real estate. There are problems, lack of information, and misconceptions at every turn. The "blue suede shoe" salespeople, the heartless mortgage lenders, fly-by-night builders, gouging title companies, inept VA bureaucrats, and finally, as the real estate agent's saying goes:

Buyers are liars,

and Sellers are worse!

Wow! Which group should I pick on first?

What do you say we start by considering the disconsolate and unloved real estate salesperson? One of the ways real estate peddlers get a bad reputation is by overzealously promoting property that has a lot of hidden problems - problems the Realtor conveniently happens to forget or fail to mention. Oh sure, there are many laws providing recourse to buyers with regard to undisclosed defects, but I'm talking about those little annoying things that crop up after you buy and are generally not worth the cost of hiring an attorney to pursue.

Having let your emotions overcome your good judgment, only too late do you discover many of the problems in your dream house – problems ranging from the smell of a "cat" house (temporarily masked during showings) to inoperative electrical outlets. You expected a perfect home, but instead got the usual collection of fix-ups. What about your inspector? Do you think your salesperson would have recommended him to you if your salesperson had ever lost sales because of him? Your salesperson, the Realtor, on the other hand, turns out to have known about the defects but didn't bother mentioning them for fear of losing the sale. In so doing, the Realtor has displayed a short-sighted approach to home sales that ignore "old George's communication rule". Remember? When there's an absence of communication (information) it will always result in negative rumors and/or assumptions. Now when you, the buyer walk into your newly-purchased house and discover a crack in the ceiling (horrors!!!!!), you assume the worst: that this crack will cost you

LIFE'S DATA STACKERS

thousands of dollars to fix! Since your agent decided not to mention the crack or research the actual repair cost for you, you naturally assume the worst and begin to plan your retaliation. The smart Realtor would have checked with a contractor ahead of time, found out the true repair cost, and drawn the buyer's attention to the crack while revealing the actual repair cost - typically far less than the buyer would have assumed. By proactively disclosing the problem and the solution the smart Realtor not only avoids damaging his relationship with the buyer and his reputation in his profession, he gains the trust of the buyer – a very important factor in any sales field. In this one situation we actually see several rules at work: The importance of communication, that "perception is reality" and the consequences of a breakdown in predictability. I didn't originate this approach to real estate sales; it came to me from a long time real estate consultant. He didn't know of these rules by name, he just knew what worked in order to make a sale and maintain his reputation.

A lack of information can also make you a victim in dealing with title insurance companies. I doubt if there is any other industry that provides so little service at such a high cost. To get the coverage, which you rarely need, you pay an extremely high premium. For the number of times the insurance is needed, it would appear that the premium should be far far less. Incidentally, have you ever seen a title insurance office that WAS NOT fitted out with really first class furniture and an

LOVE AND WAR WITH THE HOIPOLLOI

impressive building? That's where your money goes. But, you argue, what happens the one time that I really need it? Good question. Did you get a warranty deed when you bought the property? Did you read it? It says that the seller warrants the property to be free of liens, encumbrances, easements etc. Furthermore, and very important, the seller agrees to defend you if any title problem arises. So I guess we buy title insurance to cover ourselves, and the bank, when the seller fails to do what he's promised to do. But neither you nor the seller need worry if you or your attorney will simply go to the courthouse and look at the public records to determine if there are, or have been, any problems with the property. I know of at least one part of the country where the use of title insurance is practically unknown. Buyers simply spend about $200 to have an attorney review those same public records that you and the title company use. Isn't it "wonderful" how people play upon our lack of information and/or know-how? They increase our fears and dazzle us with fancy offices so we will believe they are experts, successful and above all, necessary.

"Liar liar pants on fire" is an old expression that often applies to real estate buyers. To varying degrees, when looking for a new home even the most honest of us seem to fall into this mindset - almost like a subconscious death wish: we lie to ourselves, to the mortgage loan officer and to the Realtor! "This time we're going to make a list of features our new home <u>must</u> have, and stick to it" (Oh sure, and the moon is still made of

LIFE'S DATA STACKERS

green cheese!). Well, maybe the word "lie" is too strong a term to use for this. Ok, we will call it a "reasonable" rationalization. Let's face it, there are things buyers would like to have, and then there are things you can actually afford. Buyers tend to tell their Realtors that they're searching for their "dream" home, and mislead the Realtors and themselves, in to thinking they can afford it. There are several things that lead into this trap, and cause buyers to "lie" to the Realtor about what they can actually afford. First of course is the desire to have a good home with all the amenities – just like people at their income level are portrayed as having on TV - or that other people at their income level seem to have. Then there may be peer pressure, which in most cases is largely self-imposed. You just received a promotion and now you think you must keep up with your colleagues. How did this get in your data stack??? Stop and think about it. Did your boss tell you to shape up your housing situation, or did you make an erroneous assumption based on incomplete or incorrect data? Another potent force is the desire to live in a place as nice as that of our parents. See, your data was stacked during all those years you lived at home. You came to expect that standard of living to be right and normal. As I have said many times before, it's time you sat down and examined your conclusions. What is the basis for your opinion? If you're honest with yourself, you will admit that your parents had to work many years before they could afford the home you take for granted. It did not happen overnight. Time to get realistic and do an honest appraisal of your financial situation. Forgetting what your parents or anyone else has, what do you really need for a happy home? Bring your data up to date - get your internal computer on-line now!

Oh yes, I said "sellers are worse" didn't I? Too often sellers are real communications sinkholes. Did they tell you about the leak behind the shower wall? Not on your life! The owners used the other bathroom so no one would notice. Should they tell the Realtor about the bad shingle job and how they have to go up and nail some down after every storm? No way Jose! If the swimming pool has only a "slow" leak, don't mention it. Somewhere, someone has taught these people to cover up any faults the house may have - of course, you say, otherwise the house will not sell. Maybe not at the higher price you would like to get, but a house with faults will still sell. So, shall we just admit that the seller is greedy, if not dishonest? It has gotten so bad that, in most states, a seller is required to sign a disclosure statement regarding undisclosed defects. I'm sure that a major Data Stacker for sellers is the knowledge that many other people have been successful in selling their homes while hiding defects. But there is one piece of data that too many sellers either don't know or wish to ignore: That there are penalties that can be levied against a lying seller. Such penalties can be very very costly, but are not making it into sellers' data stacks because those who are caught don't go around bragging about their lost court cases. Again, think more than twice before you allow data to enter your head as valid when it's really false. Also, don't assume buyers are blind - they often see the defects and overestimate the cost of repair! Your deception may well be hurting rather than helping your efforts to sell! Tell your buyers the truth and what it will cost to fix it. The increased confidence in your honesty will be a big help in selling your home.

FILL THE INFORMATION GAPS

All of this talk about information deficits causes me to think about how people set themselves up to be taken advantage of in almost every phase of their day to day lives. I know of one Realtor who clinched the sale of an expensive, but overpriced, home by promising to resell the house at any time for as much or more than the buyer was paying. This was an improper promise, but he made it to customers who sorely wanted to believe. They set themselves up by allowing themselves to allow the emotional impact of a wonderful view to overcome logic. This is not an isolated instance. Older people are easily taken advantage of by unscrupulous doctors, insurance salespersons, home repair people, mechanics, and sometimes their own families. Their fears of ill health, robbery and a desire for financial security will cause them to become victims of uncaring people. Instead of getting facts and asking questions of experts, they allow emotions to dictate their actions. Senior citizens often have failing memories

LOVE AND WAR WITH THE HOIPOLLOI

and/or physical problems that make it harder for them to get accurate information. What's your excuse?

Do you ever go beyond reading the sports or society pages? When buying an appliance do you go to the trouble of doing research on the product? Perhaps you simply listen to a salesperson or rely on the inexpert opinion of an acquaintance. Have you ever heard of a library? Did you look in Consumer Reports or Consumer's Digest? Have you studied the readily available annual reports on the good and bad points of new and used cars? If you're a computer nut, there is an increasing amount of information available on the internet.

The point is, there are many, many sources of information from which you can obtain more reliable data for your personal internal computer. Learn to ask probing questions about what you hear and try to detect if information givers have a personal interest in pushing a particular viewpoint. Politicians are a great example of people who give us lots of "facts" that are tainted with their own personal ambitions. Distortion and outright lies are, unfortunately, part of their game. Question, question, question. Do this, and you'll be much less likely to set yourself up as an easy mark. You will have gotten your data stacked in the proper manner.

Now, after doing all of the proper things you WILL be more than just a "common" man. Now you'll be one of the more intelligent members of the "hoi Polloi".

LIFE'S DATA STACKERS

CHAPTER SEVEN

TIME
TO
GO
TO
WORK

Putting first things first-you have to get hired!!

I trust that you are not like that inner-city youth from New York who was complaining on a major network TV program about there not being any "suitable" jobs, with high pay, available to him. This lack of what he considered acceptable employment was his excuse for dealing drugs and robbing others in his own neighborhood. He had dropped out of school, was dressed like a slob, (although much like his buddies, or should we say his "peer group") used "street talk" with very poor grammar, and had never held a real job of any kind. So, naturally, since he had no skills, no education and a lousy appearance, (not to mention attitude) he had, in his view, a right to expect a good position with a generous income. (That was his

LIFE'S DATA STACKERS

questionable reality.) After all, it would not be reasonable to expect him to start at the bottom, learn the business, and THEN move up the ladder. That would be too slow for his wonderful self! Or perhaps this "victim" of society had figured out that he should receive special treatment as just one more of his "rights"- a "right" that like so many other entitlements, didn't require him to make any special effort or accept any real degree of personal responsibility. Since none of the short-sighted employers in the area could quite see it HIS way, he lived off his welfare check, drug money, and other ill-gotten gains. It could also be argued that government "great society" programs had stacked his data with garbage. The giveaway programs had taught him that he had some kind of "right" to expect the best without having to put out any effort. A true case of "garbage in, garbage out". In many respects, the same degree of sarcasm might well be applied to another group that consists of would-be executives such as recent business school graduates. Of course, not all of them, just some of them from certain schools.

While setting up a management training program for a nationally known company, I interviewed a good number of these aspiring candidates from several very prestigious eastern business schools. It was enough to make you vomit! Too often these new grads would step off the airplane, at our somewhat semi-rural airport, (but hey, at least the airplanes all had engines instead of rubber bands) just oozing excessive confidence. More often than not they would state their expectation to immediately

TIME TO GO TO WORK

be made Vice President or, at the very least, to be promoted to such a position within five years. Well they certainly were intelligent and had the education and the nice clothes, but they seemed somewhat short on humility. The expectation that they should receive preference over current long service employees (who were also college graduates), came from their professors. Those arrogant ivory tower academics had stacked their students' internal computers with less than helpful data. They led them to expect a quick road to the top, to be carried in a golden sedan chair on the shoulders of the more common work-a-day peasants. (That means on the shoulders of those poor souls who DID NOT have an advanced degree from the same or similar prestigious institution.) What the prestigious business school graduate had in common with the inner-city youth I mentioned earlier, is that each already considered himself to be entitled to advancement and a high place in society – without having to do anything further to EARN it. Golly gee, imagine having to EARN rewards! That sure sounds old fashioned – which it is - but it's still true!

INTERNAL AND EXTERNAL RESEARCH

Hopefully we can assume that you're not one of the above types, and that you're genuinely interested in getting honest work by honest effort. So what to do? What in this book will help you achieve your goals? What can I say to help stack your data in a helpful way? Now is the time for you to do two

LIFE'S DATA STACKERS

very important things: First, examine your own thinking and analyze all that deep down data that you've accumulated over the years. What kind of person are you? What do you like or dislike? Do you hold strong religious, political, or other philosophical views and, if so, why do you feel that way? How do you want to relate to others? From the position of a prison guard or a preacher? Do you really listen to the opinions of others, or are you more concerned with "always being right"? Consider your goals and ambitions. What skills do you have to offer? What's your intelligence level? Do you prefer working with your hands, with people, with numbers, in dangerous situations, indoors or outdoors? Etc. Again, what kind of a person are you? This should be an honest evaluation. You are not doing this to impress someone else - it's for you! Only after you have completed this task, can you realistically prepare to go after a satisfactory job. Second, to the greatest extent possible, you need to study why and how employers hire people. How does the Company have its data stacked? (And stacked it is!) You have to consider the company's general philosophy plus the foibles of the manager who's looking for help. And last, but not least, you must consider the peculiarities of the employment interviewer. That may seem like quite a gauntlet. It is!

There are several ways you can obtain information about a company's philosophy: Go to the library and have a librarian show you where to find articles on the company in business publications. Check for information on the company in papers

186

TIME TO GO TO WORK

such as the Wall Street Journal, Barons, or Investors Daily. Ask a stock broker for research information on the company. Try reading business magazines like Fortune, Forbes, Business Week etc. for stories on the company's industry and competitors. Write to the company and ask them to send you a copy of their Annual Report. The annual report will probably contains some sort of statement of the company's philosophy – though it's written to make the Company look good and politically correct, of course, so don't rely on it too much. And don't forget the internet as a research tool.

Whether you're looking for a management or blue collar job, if the business is located in your area, seek out current and past employees and ask them questions. Try the local "watering hole" near the plant where employees stop after work. With current employees you will get better information if you ask them what OTHERS in the company think. They'll feel freer to mention things of a negative nature if they're only quoting what others think. It's always much easier, and safer, for a current employee to say "this is what the others think - but, of course, I am a loyal employee who feels that the Company is just peachy keen". Usually the person is telling their personal view while ascribing it to the opinions of others.

An additional source of information is the company's competition. Check with your target company's chief rivals to see what they have to say about your target company - both good and bad.

187

LIFE'S DATA STACKERS

Learning about a company's employment practices and preconceived ideas about issues that are important to you as a prospective employee is sometimes not an easy task, and those ideas may not become apparent until you're interviewed by the company, or sometimes not until long after you have been hired – especially if the company doesn't want you to know about them. For instance, you may never discover that you've been rejected for being over-qualified. For example, companies that operate factories have learned that it's counterproductive to put a highly intelligent person on a routine assembly line. That individual will learn the job quickly and then become bored. Boredom leads to trying to find something else to occupy the mind. This often leads to injuries caused by inattentiveness, or using idle time to get into trouble or file grievances. This situation is much like the bright youngster in school who gets into trouble when the teacher cannot provide suitable projects. Another example is that of companies who want to hire only children of managers for management training programs. This practice is frowned upon under current equal opportunity laws, but it's not without logical support. Experience had taught the companies (stacked their data) to realize that children of managers tended to have higher goals than others. Remember the last chapter? We think we should live as well right now as our parents did after many years of work. Manager's children think of the parent's job as a starting place. On the other hand, the child

TIME TO GO TO WORK

of a less fortunate parent might consider even a lower level manager's job as the pinnacle of success.

One fellow you would not want to run into on a job interview is the appliance company Controller I mentioned earlier. He's the one who set up several litmus tests for would-be employees (and also set low, unrealistic salary levels). However, if a candidate had an extremely high intelligence test score, all other criteria would be forgotten. He would literally have hired convicted felons and embezzlers if they did well on the test. (He tried to, but he eventually was re-educated.) On the other hand, this Controller would never hire anyone having a large family. After all, he couldn't have them running up big bills on the company's medical insurance! One other problem, among many, in this Controller's mind would be if the candidate lived more than ten miles from the plant. The Controller expected a fair amount of overtime and did not want to spend money for someone's dinner. They should live close enough to be able to go home for supper and then return to work! Behind his back he was called C.O.D. – "Clutch On the Downhill" (so cheap that he bought stick shift cars that he would put into neutral to coast downhill to save on gas). This kind of information can be very hard to learn ahead of time, but do try. As you can see from the above examples, the Controller really had some bad data stacked into his computer. It took a lot of work and time to get rid of some of those ideas, and job candidates were wise to learn about them before interviewing with him.

LIFE'S DATA STACKERS

Now we should take a hard look at YOUR expectations. Have you programmed yourself for success or failure in seeking employment? That self examination, mentioned above, is to find out why you think the way you do so that you can select suitable opportunities and so that you can better prepare to sell yourself to compete for those opportunities. Take a hard and candid look at the things you enjoy in life, the way you would like to live, and your skills. Did your parents or some teacher call you a dummy? Did one of your "good friends" kindly advise you that you would never make it? Did, or do, you believe them? Sometimes those who would "put you down" are simply trying to cover up their own inadequacies and want to drag you down to their level. Be very careful who you listen to and try to learn their motivation when they tell you what to do or what they think of you. Good old Dad says he wants you to be a Doctor, but you prefer engineering. Mother thinks nursing is a nice career for her little girl, but daughter wants to be a construction worker. Are the parent's ideas for their own vicarious glory, or for your benefit? Who the heck is it who's actually going to have to live this life? And will it be full of happiness or thoughts of what might have been? In addition to all this self examination you can usually get free aptitude and/or skill tests at a State employment office. Use this information as a supplement to what you already know, and get ready to become a genuine high rolling brass ring grabber.

TIME TO GO TO WORK

GO ON THE OFFENSE

Your next job, should you choose to accept it, is to become a DATA STACKER!!! It's time to take the offensive! You must prepare yourself to stack the data of the personnel at your target company. Having gathered all your thoughts and information, sit down and draw up a list of your most wonderful and valuable attributes. Make it as long as you wish, but then put them in order of importance. These should be the character qualities, the skills, and the knowledge that you are going to sell to a company. Drag them all out, this is no time to be modest - just be honest. This is your sales list. You must have this before you can write a resume or participate in a worthwhile interview. Know where you have been, where you want to go and how you plan to get there.

A good resume is really a piece of promotional sales literature. It must be designed to get your fanny in the door and seated before the interviewer. If you have been fortunate enough to get good information about your would be employer, you can tailor your resume to suit the company's reality - the world in which they want to live and operate. Along the way, and of prime importance, you must raise their expectations as to your personal abilities and your value to their organization. Later on, we will talk about handling the interview, but right now we need to discuss the content and physical appearance of your resume.

Over the years I have seen thousands of resumes and almost all of them could use a lot of improvement. The weird

191

LIFE'S DATA STACKERS

offbeat efforts, such as in the form of a butterfly that pops out of the envelope, might be just swell if you are applying to an ad agency. That is, if you are trying to prove your creativity or convince them you are nuts. In the vast majority of cases that approach would be totally unacceptable. There are innumerable styles and methods in use today - some better than others. Too many hopefuls simply run down to a local stenographic service, give them some basic data, and then expect a good resume. Most often all they get is that particular secretary's canned version - often "borrowed" from another person's resume or from a book. The problem is, each resume must be unique and written specifically for the applicant. It must be written in a way that will properly present his or her strengths and accomplishments while avoiding signs of weakness.

Most of you have seen the standard resume wherein the jobs are neatly listed in chronological order. That is all very well, unless you have held ten jobs in the last ten years. In this case it's much better to write up a resume that talks about your skills, and save the job list to a short simple listing at the end. Persons over 50 might consider the same approach. Minimize the dates and short term employment while touting things like managerial experience, dealing with people, supervision, honest, hard working, quick learner, problem solver etc. etc. These are all presented in a style that emphasizes your specific accomplishments that were of benefit to your previous employers.

192

TIME TO GO TO WORK

There is considerably more to writing a good resume, but that is for another publication and time. Go to the bookstore or library and see what you can learn. Just keep in mind, IT'S A SALES DOCUMENT! Get in there and stack the company's data with your very best, grammatically perfect, and properly spelled effort. Let me say that again - PROPERLY SPELLED effort! Try reading your resume backwards and the misspelled words will jump out at you. A resume with misspelled words will come close to an automatic rejection. Some of your "socially correct" teachers may have told you that it's "the thought that counts", but employers don't necessarily agree with that philosophy. When an employee writes a letter, as a representative of the Company, it can, if poorly done, give the organization an embarrassing black eye. Now, best foot forward, chin up, and all that stuff.

Do not do what many careless applicants have done: Some of their mistakes are quite ridiculous. The shortest and one of the worst "resumes" I have ever received consisted of a business card. That's right, a simple business card. On the back the gentleman had written a message. "If you have a real good job with high pay, give me a call. Otherwise, don't waste my time". Well by golly Miss Molly, will you be surprised to learn that he didn't get a job in our company? At the other extreme was the resume of the former dean of a law school. It was beautifully typed on excellent high quality paper. His credentials were impeccable - all fifteen pages of them. This fellow had more honors than a saint and had joined more organizations than

LIFE'S DATA STACKERS

a political candidate. He had combined the lawyer's love of detail with the academic's pride in his publications. Every little marching and chowder society could be found on those pages. (Maybe it was because he was a Texan - they always like to do things in a big way.) It seems that those in the academic community love to list their many quality(?) publications and association memberships. Publications may demonstrate your writing ability, but they do nothing to prove you are a good administrator or attorney in the real world. Now, put yourself in a nonacademic job interviewer's shoes. Would you read all that crap? I call it by that somewhat indelicate term since most of it was entirely unnecessary to his "sales brochure". All that paper was filled up with lists of his various society memberships, etc. but included very little concerning his actual accomplishments. There was much he could have bragged about, but he did not. He had had absolutely no success with his job hunt when he came to my consultant's office. The very first objective, of course, was to pare that fifteen page grandiloquent monstrosity down to a manageable size. The next major move was to highlight his talents and achievements. After this was done, along with some training in how to interview, the Dean was able to obtain a satisfactory new job. I don't think I'll bore you with all the details of the resume from the fellow who had held forty-one jobs in four years. Despite all of his logical explanations, he did NOT get job number forty-two in our plant.

TIME TO GO TO WORK

One of your more difficult tasks, as mentioned earlier, is to try to determine the employment interviewer's likes and dislikes. That person is your first and often most difficult hurdle. This cat has clawed up many other victims before you arrived on the scene. Some are friendly and others are nasty, but whatever their mood, you must adjust your approach to suit him. Glance around the room as you come in to see if there are any clues to the interviewer's hobbies and activities. Look for items such as pictures of sailboats, books on music, UFOs, or photographs, which reveal his interests. There often are plaques indicating membership in fraternal or business groups. Such clues can help you to find some common ground with your interviewer. By discussing those common interests you will often achieve a more favorable evaluation and a lasting impression of your presentation. After all, there is no one more intelligent and wonderful than the person who agrees with me. Sometimes a few careful questions will bring out clues as to the interviewer's criteria for what constitutes a "good" employee. Yes, just in case you didn't know it, you, the applicant, are allowed to ask questions! In fact, if you've done your homework, you've prepared several intelligent sounding questions about the company and the job. Such questions will show your interest in the organization and your preparation, not to mention drawing out some clues about their "stacked data".

LIFE'S DATA STACKERS

MAKE A GOOD IMPRESSION

Well now Mr. or Ms. Data Stacker, what are you going to do to create that really cool first impression? You started with a good resume, but now you have to stack that data ever higher and higher.

That first impression is going to influence how the interviewer will evaluate every other statement you make. You have probably seen the conventional wisdom on interview preparation: dress right, look alert, firm handshake, sit up straight in the chair or lean forward slightly, etc etc. I hope there is no need to repeat all that good stuff. Instead, what do you say we pick on a few real-life examples of dumb things *not* to do in an interview - all of which I've personally seen job applicants do? First there was the young man (mid-thirties) who came in wearing a very nice suit, had a good haircut, his shoes were shined and he spoke well (so far, good data going into my internal computer). Unfortunately, although he continued to build on his initial good impression, he did so only up to the point where he fell sound asleep in his chair! OK OK, maybe I was getting a bit boring, but perhaps the greater portion of his sleepiness could be attributed to the fact that, as he later admitted, he had traveled too far and too long the day before and then had partied late. He was dead tired. He awoke when his head fell forward. After profuse apologies, we continued our discussion until he once more fell asleep. What kind of data did THAT put into my personal computer? Among other things, he

TIME TO GO TO WORK

left the impression of either being a poor time planner or someone who didn't think enough of the job to make a really good effort at interviewing well. Party time the night before his interview was apparently more important to him than his being well rested. From that point on, in my mind, everything he said was colored by that knowledge.

Then there was the young lady (also mid-thirties) who must have attended one too many seminars on interpersonal relations. Overall she presented herself very well and seemed intelligent and alert. If only she would have stopped saying the same thing over and over and over again! "Thank you for sharing" she would say after almost every sentence I would utter - always with that type of sweet understanding smile you would expect from your old grandmother. Before long I wasn't sure if I was in an interview or a therapy session.

Next there was the high powered Vice President of a major airline. His credentials were really quite good but he did have a few problems, the worst being his big mouth! I've seen many people who were in love with their own melodious vocal droppings, but this fellow won the blue beanie with the gold propeller. Ask him a simple question, hoping for a simple answer, and he gave you a SPEECH. A *long* one. He rolled on like the Mississippi in full flood-and, not surprisingly, the content was often just as muddy.

The moral of this story is to learn when it's time to shut up. If you over-talk you'll be stacking the interviewer's internal

LIFE'S DATA STACKERS

computer to question whether you'll be able to avoid betraying a confidence and whether you'll end up wasting a lot of time - both your own and that of your fellow employees. Such behavior identifies you as a nonproductive person, and perhaps someone who cannot bring himself to be concise in his communications - something most companies would understandably prefer.

SOME CORPORATE MISCALCULATIONS

In addition to "first impressions" there are certain preconceptions (another word for data stacks) with which you must be prepared to deal. As I mentioned a few sentences ago, you need to learn as much as possible about a company's philosophy or preconceptions about what constitutes a "good" employee - regardless of whether those preconceptions happen to be legitimate or completely misguided and wrong.

If you are over 50 years of age, and in many, many cases, over just 40 years, you already know how tough it is to find a new job. Frustrating isn't it? Yes - as well as totally unfair, illogical, uneconomic, and to say the least, illegal. Some of the commonly known "truths" about hiring "older" people have persisted for decades. It sometimes seems that the "corporate mind" (if it has one) moves with the speed and coldness of a glacier. Sure, older people were known to suffer more illnesses than younger ones - sixty or seventy years ago. But since then there have been major medical advances and improvements in living conditions that allow individuals to live healthy and

TIME TO GO TO WORK

productive lives well past retirement age. After administering corporate insurance programs for many years, I know that older employees no longer place an extra burden on a Company's medical program (older female employees might get the "vapors" on rare occasion, but they seldom need maternity leave). However, the "froze brains" of too many CEOs have not figured that out yet. They can't seem to thaw out their data stacks. The idea of increased absenteeism also springs from this poisoned well. A little logic might help here: Who is absent more, the young woman with monthly "problems", the mother with young children who get sick etc., or the over 40 woman whose kids are grown and needs to return to the work force to help pay for her kids' college expenses? All right, how about a choice between some young guy who likes to party late, drinks too much, or smokes dope, versus a man over 40 who has gotten all that immature garbage out of his system? Believe me. The older ones will be far more reliable. In one company we slashed the turnover rate among clerical employees by hiring persons over forty years of age. That may all be so, says Mr. Executive, but I want someone who will be with the company for many years. These older people only have ten or fifteen years before they will want to retire. Oh really?? How many years will the younger employees be with you? TV pundits frequently remind us about how young people should be expected to change jobs and/or careers seven or eight times during their working years. Younger employees are also intent on following "career paths" that are

LIFE'S DATA STACKERS

unlikely to end with your company - or are getting bored and unproductive when their work proves to be less than exciting. An employer should consider himself lucky to have kept a younger employee for more than five years. Also, older employees have at least one major incentive to stay that younger ones do not: they know that no one else is likely to hire them once they hit fifty!

Companies' reliance on 401K plans (rather than pensions based on years of service) has also caused an increase in job hopping among the young. It's alleged to be less costly for the employers, but I wonder how many of the corporate bean counters have gone to the trouble to take into account an estimate of the cost of the extra turnover?

Every company needs a good mix of ages. The long experience of the older employee blended with the new ideas and energy of the younger newcomers will result in a well balanced and thriving organization. Well, at least that's the way MY data is stacked - after many years of experience in many industries.

If you fall into this "over 40" group, you'll need to counter-act this preconception by establishing your credentials as a physically fit, energetic, and creative individual. Your resume and employment applications should reflect your participation in active sports, should include evidence of your good attendance record in your current position, and should show a continued interest in learning new things. You may include a list of recently attended seminars, evidence of active involvement in community

TIME TO GO TO WORK

affairs, evidence of having participated in or directed successful implementation of new company programs, and hopefully your earning of bonus awards for such activities - anything that will help to dispel some of the concerns that arise from those outmoded ideas about this much maligned group.

Another idiot preconception held by many companies is the idea that "if you haven't worked in MY industry, you should not be hired". You see the ads every day in the paper: "must have experience in XYZ business". It doesn't matter if it's in the oil field or making whoopee cushions, you MUST KNOW MY INDUSTRY. Hogwash - or even offal droppings from four legged animate objects! Sure, there is a very short period of adjustment while you learn new buzz words, but the essentials of accounting, selling, human relations, and manufacturing are much the same from one organization to another. But you have to convince the interviewer of that fact! Just as an aside, have you ever noticed how this parochial attitude often seems to disappear at the top levels of management? The chief honcho of a computer company might well be hired to run a soft drink manufacturer. It happens almost every day in our rapidly changing business world.

One final note concerning what to watch out for when you go job hunting: Don't let the advertisements in the paper fool you! The common wisdom is that you should take seriously the requirements listed in employment ads. See, your data has been stacked to think that unless you meet 100% of the stated

LIFE'S DATA STACKERS

requirements, you will not be considered. Wrongo chongo oh beleaguered one! Most companies of any size have a job evaluation system that lays out specific desired criteria for each job. When an opening occurs, the recruiter, being a bit lazy perhaps, simply copies off that list and puts it in the paper. What you see published is the *optimum*, not necessarily the *minimum* what the company will accept. More often than not, *none* of the applicants will meet *all* of the specifications. For instance, the hiring manager will usually trade some years of education for good hands-on experience. If you think you can handle the job, fire off a resume. You have nothing to lose!

GETTING TO KNOW THE BOSS AND HIS GANG

Your first introduction to the chief "ogre" will be the employment interview. Quite commonly, executives are poor interviewers, since they've usually never had the least bit of training in the art of screening people. Someone may have given them a list of questions to ask, but no one told them what to do with the answers. Being nervous, and not knowing what to ask, they will often launch into a long sales pitch. Everything you ever wanted to know, and more, about the company, their own career and what a wonderful job opportunity you may be offered. Many individuals have come away from such interviews(?) feeling positive about their chances. They didn't have to deal with any tough questions and everyone was all smiles. The question is, what did the future boss learn about YOU AND

TIME TO GO TO WORK

YOUR TALENTS? If he did all the talking, he probably learned nothing - and most important, didn't learn any real reason to hire you. Interrupt if you must, (and there are special techniques for that) but it's critical that you give your sales pitch and stack his internal computer with good data. Just one of those techniques is to key off something the interviewer has said. When the interviewer tells about one of his personal accomplishments, you can interrupt by saying how that reminds you of what you did in a similar situation. In a way you are still relating to the interviewer's accomplishments as you tell him about yours. Should you get hired, the way you handle the interview and the information you give during the interview, will remain within the boss's personal computer and will, in his mind, color every decision you make from that day forward.

There's nothing quite like being the "new kid on the block" - or the innocent among the knowing old timers. As in a marriage, you don't really learn what you need to know until you're already on the job – unless you make an effort to do so. For example, a few years ago you could have found out that if you went to work for IBM you'd be expected to wear a dark suit, a conservative tie, and a white shirt – and if you were a woman, that you probably wouldn't be hired. You could have learned all this from simply reading the newspapers or talking to an IBM representative. You could get your data stacked and predict what to expect. With that knowledge, you could decide whether you wanted to work under those conditions, whether you stood any

LIFE'S DATA STACKERS

reasonable chance of being hired, and could then make an informed decision about whether to even apply for a job. More recently, you could have found out what to expect from Electronic Data Systems from having read about the strict behavioral and dress guidelines laid down by the indefatigable Ross Perot. Both IBM and EDS were criticized for their strict rules, but those rules were well publicized and new hires knew what to expect (predict) by the time they'd decided to accept employment. Consequently, employees of those companies generally considered themselves to be well-treated, and both companies had reputations for being very well run. The "rules" had a reasonable business basis, were well communicated, and I believe, added considerably to the resounding success of the companies.

NOT ALL CO-WORKERS ARE GOOD

I wonder if the folks at IBM or EDS would ever have made the mistake of hiring the secretary who worked on the 21st floor of our office building. She would "piddle" in the elevator on her way up, and then step off as though nothing had happened. Yes, she unfortunately had both physical and psychological problems, but how did the chinks in her armor go unnoticed? Another one, who didn't have the same excuses, came to work with bare scabby legs, stringy unwashed hair, and full of stories about how she had fallen into a wash tub full of dog doo. Now don't those ladies fulfill all of your expectations

204

TIME TO GO TO WORK

for the behavior and appearance of a good secretary? Incidentally, don't look at me, I didn't hire them! However, there are organizations today where you can get away with sloppy appearance at work - organizations like those high-tech firms that see no connection between how an employee dresses and that employee's ability to produce good work. Some of those nerd birds can really dress down! At a computer firm where I worked, it was shirt tails out, dirty ill-fitting shorts, sandals on the unsoxed feet, and hair flying in all directions. More recently, many have made the additional mistake of falling to an even lower level of using foul language in the workplace. Perhaps it's the miserable Hollywood influence that's caused people to believe that such language is normal and harmless. Nothing could be further from the truth! I have news for those sloppy foul mouthed believers in the reality of the filthy fables now produced by a tarnished "tinsel town" - you will probably never get into a management position that way. There are few who will truly respect or put their trust in that type of person. Despite all the attempts to ruin the morals of the American people, the vast majority still have their data stacked against such antisocial behavior. The Bible says "as you sow, so shall you reap", and truer words were never spoken. If you dress and act like a bum, you can expect to be treated like one. Decide now how you want your fellow employees, supervisors, or business partners to think of you. Stack their data any way you like! As the "new kid on the block", you'd better get off on the right foot from day one.

LIFE'S DATA STACKERS

Whether a boss or a co-worker, each person has his or her own preconceived ideas about how people should behave on the job. For example, there are those who insist on things being done only their way, and in an exact manner. Such people have strong opinions about how systems should work and how people should be rewarded. So, while singing several choruses of "bless them all, bless them all, the long the short and the tall", let's take a look at a few of these creatures:

First let me refer you back to the brewing company Vice President who constantly swore and berated others. Do you remember the labor attorney we hired to put up with him? I know not how that Vice President got his data stacked, but I do know that his style of management, to him, seemed the best and most productive way to operate. However, none of his subordinates or fellow executives shared that opinion, and in fact regarded him as obnoxious and a person to avoid. If you were considering applying for a position under this Vice President, a few well chosen questions to almost any other employee of the company would have revealed this Vice President's management style to you. (Lest you think this Vice President's management style is one to emulate, note that the Vice President, in the same function, at a nearby competitor, earned about twice the paycheck.)

One of the largest "creatures" around is General Motors. Consider what happened when General Motors and Peter Drucker teamed up to develop the "management by objectives"

TIME TO GO TO WORK

technique. Seeing what this huge organization was doing (and if GM does it, then it must be good), the managements of thousands of companies subscribed to the sometimes dubious charms of this technique. At first glance it seemed to be a great tool to both increase productivity and assist in deciding merit pay increases. There is nothing wrong with the basic premise of getting everyone to set goals that will support and help achieve the company's general objectives. You can't argue with that. However, many companies that are quite proud of the success of this system need to get new prescriptions for their rose colored glasses. The managements of these companies have had their data stacked to believe that if they run extensive training programs, all their lower level managers will do a good job carrying out the program, and all their employees will strive hard to reach the agreed upon goals. On the other hand, their employees' data has been stacked in such a way as to make the employees wary of such programs and to motivate the employees to think, "How can I get around this sucker without having to do any extra paper work and still get a raise"? The lower level manager's internal computer tells him, or her, "here is another time-consuming program that makes my job harder, and I have to find a way to fool the people on top into thinking I've bought-in". So what happens next? The poor soul on the bottom knows better than to set goals that will be hard to achieve since failure to meet the goal means no pay raise. The supervisor, who has to approve those goals, knows they should be higher, but failure on

LIFE'S DATA STACKERS

the part of his subordinates will reflect badly on his own record. A supervisor therefore sets his own goals "not overly high" so that he may achieve them more easily. And so it goes up through the many levels of management along with all the "oh, so logical" explanations about why this is the best that can be expected. Each level of supervision also has another logical (according to the internal computers) rationale for using this approach: Supervisors don't like turnover! Every time an employee quits it means a lot of time wasted interviewing, training, and explaining to higher management why he can't hold on to his people. So, pay raises must be given, whether deserved or not. And unachieved goals mean no pay increases!

Let me cite one example: A PhD in Research and Development was undergoing his annual salary review. He and the Vice President had previously set goals for the PhD to reach that year. The VP felt that the PhD had successfully met all the goals and recommended an above average salary increase. The Salary Administration Department questioned the VP's decision when, during the subsequent discussion, it became quite clear that the PhD had taken his normal everyday duties from his job description and set them down as goals. He had simply done what he was supposed to do on a day to day basis. Having done so, the Vice President rated him as above average (gee, I wonder what "average" was supposed to be?). Yes, you can try to argue that the Vice President had not been properly trained in the system, but he *was*. It still comes down to the problem of

TIME TO GO TO WORK

supervisors not wanting to be critical of their subordinates and not wanting to lose employees – and taking too much pride in their departments. This isn't to say that this is the way it always works in all "management by objectives" companies, but believe me, it appears to happen in the majority of such companies. The moral of this story is not to go into this type of program with any preconceived ideas about its being the greatest thing since the invention of the inflatable doll. Install the program, but with the knowledge that it will constantly require very close monitoring. I do hope that I've now properly stacked your data on this topic.

One last, and short, example of someone wanting it done HIS WAY concerns a Vice President of Industrial Relations who belabored his Labor Relations Manager for not swearing enough when requesting assistance from other departments. His pea-pickin' brain seemed to think that his profuse use of profanity was responsible for whatever success he'd had in getting information in the past. He just *knew* it was necessary to brow beat people in order to get things done. I don't know who stacked his data that way, but to me it's wrong. Fortunately the Labor Relations Manager had his data stacked to treat people decently, and acquired the necessary help from the other departments in half the time it had taken the Vice President on a similar matter.

DON'T PREJUDGE OTHERS

In any work environment you have to work with a wide variety of people having an equally wide variety of backgrounds.

LIFE'S DATA STACKERS

As we've already noted many times, each of them has had experiences that are unique to that person. So beware of how your data is, or will be stacked. For example:

1. A loose dress does not necessarily mean a loose woman.

2. Long hair, glasses, and an intense look do not make a computer nerd.

3. Sophisticated speech and clothing do not equal intelligence.

4. An open smiling face may be the mask of an embezzler.

5. The boss's secretary is usually the feared Queen Bee. (This is one place where perception almost certainly is reality)

6. Neither the Constitution nor federal or state law gives you any RIGHT to dress sloppily, smoke on the job, refuse to get coffee, look weird, decide what work you will do, or be uncivil to others.

7. The biggest mouth is often the least informed.

The lessons I've related in this chapter may cause you to wonder whether you should ever trust anyone. That is not my intent. What I want you to do is be aware of the need to listen and observe before you allow your internal computer to be stacked. Others have wisely said; "you can't judge a book by its cover". This applies to people as well.

210

TIME TO GO TO WORK

Next important rule:

BEWARE THE ARROGANCE OF THE
IGNORANT AND/OR INCOMPETENT

It's often quite difficult to avoid stepping on at least some of the personality "mines" found in every workplace. One of the more explosive personality mines I've encountered was a manager whose fellow managers used to call "Freddie Fudpucker". In some respects, Freddie was like our old friend Ted Bailey. Both Ted and Freddie felt it was quite important that they not appear to fail. But while Ted simply blamed his mistakes on others, Freddie felt that lying was the better route to the top. During his career Freddie had learned the importance of acting confident and self assured, and having good production figures. He was well aware of the usual short-sighted American management practice of demanding "good" production figures each quarter and year, rather than projecting and planning five to ten years into the future. The short term was critical. Keep the old production curve going up and you would go right along with it. Well, Freddie loved impressive looking charts and columns of figures reporting on critical activities in his department. His style of arrogant coercive management proved to be quite counterproductive in Freddie's attempts to obtain more efficiency from the work force – so Freddie lied. When the totals didn't look good, he would simply revamp the criteria slightly to make things look better. The "usual stuff" finally hit the fan

LIFE'S DATA STACKERS

when the company was purchased by a larger corporation. At the request of the new owners the staff went back and recalculated the production numbers using Freddie's original criteria. Instead of the constant upward curve, the production numbers showed a steady decline over the three years of his tenure. He was the only person fired after the merger. Why do I spend so much time on this sort of thing? Because YOU must be constantly on guard and aware of how YOUR data is being stacked. No matter what kind of a job you are in, you must learn to question why things are done the way they are. Join professional groups, read books on your field, but for your own sanity and future, please remember to learn from more than one source! Freddie learned the wrong way and he finally got his reward. If you want to advance, it will be far better for you if you're known as a person who is well informed and not afraid of new ideas, rather than as a lump of clay waiting to be molded by others.

TRY TO BE AN ENLIGHTENED EMPLOYEE

One of the more important things you can do when you "join up" with a new company is to determine the philosophy of your immediate superior and those even higher up the ladder. Do they want innovation or slavish obedience? Do they want "yes men" or objective thinking? It's amazing how many people have had their data stacked to the point where they automatically assume they should never disagree with the boss. I guess too many have gotten fired for expressing an independent opinion,

TIME TO GO TO WORK

and that stacks their data really fast. After all, no one likes to have the continuity of their employment interrupted - especially with a family to feed, clothe, and educate. Through learning you make yourself more valuable and much less susceptible to being let go. However, if you're happy being a drone, fine. Stick-around and march in step to the tyrant's tune. The rest of you don't need to be afraid to quit and get out. By the way, if you'd asked enough questions before you were hired, you might have learned some very important answers.

The mindless slave-like approach is all too common not only at lower levels but also in the boardroom. Many a director acts like a mindless toady instead of stating his or her true opinion. Fear of ridicule or loss of perks and prestige all lend themselves to keeping one's mouth shut. I observed an example of this type of situation while serving as a director for a large vocational school system. The school administrators treated the directors as uninformed people who were expected to simply rubber stamp their expenditures. It had always been thus. What a rude surprise they received when one of the Directors led a revolt and started asking them to justify their positions and questioned their thinking. Sometimes it wasn't very pretty, but they did save the taxpayers an awful lot of money. I recommend this practice to school boards across the country - most of whom are paying far too much for administrators and not enough for teachers and materials.

LIFE'S DATA STACKERS

Also, once you have been hired, and have become a supervisor, *please* try to be a good boss. A GOOD boss will seek out and reward creative well informed persons and listen to ideas contrary to his, or her, own. That boss will learn more, have a more efficient and productive department, and will promote good employee relations. No matter what your field, it's far better to be a respected builder of people rather than a destroyer of personalities. So often the loud mouth is hiding a lack of knowledge. You see, sometimes they are so ignorant or uninformed that they don't know they're idiots. So, secure in the knowledge of their own "superiority" they ride roughshod over subordinates. Also you might want to remember there's always someone who just might be a bit smarter than you are. So don't set yourself up for embarrassment by becoming arrogant. Instead, try to be a person who can see through a facade of arrogance and observe the incompetence behind it.

TIME TO GO TO WORK

CHAPTER EIGHT

A

FEW

IDEAS

FOR

MANAGERS

Have you risen to the level of **your** incompetence? Are you a manager, a supervisor, a foreman, an executive, a President, a coach, a club president, a theatrical agent, or perhaps that often overlooked and under-valued homemaker? These are only a few of the titles that might be applied to people who have responsibility for managing other people or functions. And all of these "managers" are in danger of burning out too soon and at too low a level. Are you at risk? Then your personal management style is most likely the root of your problems. Poor management results in poor performance by subordinates. That in turn can put you on the slippery slope to unemployment or political oblivion. For example, the coercive manager, seeing a decrease in production, applies even more stringent controls. This simply

A FEW IDEAS FOR MANAGERS

magnifies and accelerates his free-fall to failure. Use of the human relations "rules" we've discussed in this book just might get you off the ant-acid treadmill and make you President of your bowling league.

During the exodus from Egypt, Moses' father-in-law suggested to Moses that he limit the span of each leader's control to just ten persons. Moses controlled only ten and each of those in turn directed ten others, who in turn were each in charge of ten others. In this way they avoided overloading any one supervisor, and were able to maintain good communications. Business leaders could take a lesson from Moses' father-in-law. He had the right idea. In addition, the Hebrews had another very important thing going for them: for one thing, they knew where they were going: they were getting the heck out of Egypt. If only more of today's managers knew as much! As that famous baseball star Yogi Berra is reputed to have said, "if you don't know where you are going, you will probably end up someplace else". Golfer Jack Nicklaus is said to have once commented "if you don't understand what you're doing, there is no chance you will get it right". How true those statements are, and sure enough, too many managers today have no idea where they are going or how to "do it right". So often their management style depends on whom they have worked for, and how those employers stacked their data. Like the young child who thinks the parent is always a good role model, the employee is correct in thinking the boss always

LIFE'S DATA STACKERS

knows how to do it right. Wrong! You should always challenge this assumption and open your mind to additional information: ideas gleaned from books, seminars, and the discerning observations of other managers; and your own powers of reasoning and common sense. Never base your management style on your observation of a single person - no matter how successful that person may appear (or claim) to be. His alleged success may be due to a Grandfather who started the company and still owns a controlling interest. Or, your role model may be about to get fired for ineptitude – having been promoted until his incompetence finally became obvious to everyone. It's my hope that by getting you to examine the quality of your past input, I can at least help you to do a little better than perhaps you have been as a leader and manager.

We have all met people who put on a good show and talk like "experts" - often in loud voices. In the previous chapter I advised you to beware the arrogance of the incompetent. The bigger the mouth the greater the probability the individual is hiding or attempting to compensate for a lack of ability and/or confidence. In any event, who would want to work for such an obnoxious ear banger? I cannot recall any truly good manager who ran around shooting his mouth off about how good he was and how much he knew. The GOOD manager will normally exhibit quiet confidence and will feel no need to browbeat subordinates or bray unceasingly about his personal accomplishments. I remember trying to entice the Vice President

A FEW IDEAS FOR MANAGERS

of a manufacturing company into a badly needed (for him) management training program. He cocked his head to one side, squinted at me, and assumed his very finest dominant attitude. "George", he said, shaking his finger at me, "if I needed that program, I wouldn't be where I am today". Well maybe. At company functions he was too frightened to stand up and speak to his own people. He even threatened to try and have me fired if I ever called upon him to speak. (Luckily for me, I reported directly to a really first-class President.) Meanwhile, in the plant, the Vice President earned the hatred of all his foremen, and production began to fall. As this Vice President applied increasingly more unreasonable coercion, things got worse. He also engaged in illegal anti-union practices and drank too much. In the end, he was fired. Much like Ted Bailey's father, he had been taught that to be a successful manager you had to shout, curse, drink, cheat, smoke big cigars and always make sure the other guy knows you are the BOSS - a much too common example of putting garbage in the data stack.

It is especially disappointing when a person with real talent seems to feel the constant need to be right or appear successful. There was, once upon a time, an Industrial Relations VP who would take a minor union problem and blow it up so it would look to the President like a major confrontation. The VP would proceed to easily solve this "major" problem, and then run to report his success to the President and receive kudos for his great skill. Actually, the VP's greatest skill as a manager was his

LIFE'S DATA STACKERS

ability to accurately assess the needs of HIS boss. Because the VP knew how the President had HIS data stacked, the VP knew what the President liked to hear. This tactic was necessary for the VP to keep his job. I will say it once again: learn the reality (how the data is stacked) and you will be able to predict the (your) future. The VP had learned through trial and error that the President demanded a constant record of "defeating" the union, so that is what he created. As the old axiom goes, "You get what you inspect (ask about, demand reports, set as objectives, etc.) for".

In contrast to the Industrial Relations VP's disingenuous posturing, I remember the forthright approach of the Chairman of the Board of a very large international mining company. When in conversation with subordinate managers he was always polite, spoke softly, and showed an interest in those around him. It was during a business meeting, planning the merger of two corporations, that I saw his brilliance become apparent. Without notes he quoted detailed statistics, discussed production problems, and showed an awareness of human relation concerns for a multitude of operations and products around the globe. The tremendous respect others had for him had been earned, not demanded. He was a true leader.

Sometimes it takes quite a long time to discover whether a person is a good or bad manager. A major factor in how long it takes to learn about someone's management skills is the size of the organization. Various studies have shown that it commonly

A FEW IDEAS FOR MANAGERS

takes approximately two years for a manager's style to truly impact an organization or department. The good news for new managers though, is that they will have a certain amount of "discovery" time before their colleagues decide whether they're good or just good and incompetent. Now if, when you find yourself in the position of being a new manager, you can only arrange to be promoted to a different job before that two-year period expires, people may not discover your incompetence until it is too late. You could be the CEO by that time and not have to fire yourself. The bad news is that sooner or later they WILL find out. In a large company you may have more time. A nationally known research group once undertook a study to determine how long it would take a for a new President's style to fully influence the operations of the immense Exxon Corporation. The answer was seven years. Wow! That sure gives a person plenty of time to write a new resume!

SIX FOR A FIX

No matter what your level is in an organization, whether you're a manager or a newly hired hourly employee, there are six very basic and important principles for you to consider and use. They are:

Recognition - That all persons have value.

Communication - Any absence of communication always results in negative rumors and/or assumptions.

LIFE'S DATA STACKERS

Predictability - As the computer is stacked, the person will act.

Fair Treatment - Because you want to! Not just policy.

Newton's 4th Law - For every action, there is an equal and opposite reaction.

Public Relations - That means you, Turkey - you ARE your company's PR person!

Each of these principles is critical to your success as a supervisor, and as an individual. I cannot over emphasize their importance. Observing these principles will make you much more effective, as well as more respected and liked. Therefore, we shall take a closer look at each one of them and see how they can be applied to our everyday lives.

RECOGNITION:

OK people, listen up! Here's a rule to live by: ALL PERSONS DESIRE AND DESERVE RECOGNITION!!!! Shout it out! I am! I exist! I have value!! Now shout again - They are! They exist! They have value!! There is no one who does not have some value. I may have little value as an author, but perhaps great value as a gardener. The highly paid, and valued, TV anchor person may be a lousy bricklayer. We each have our own particular skills, abilities, personalities, and relationships. Should you lack a record of exciting business accomplishments, don't worry. You may very well have great value as a parent or a

222

A FEW IDEAS FOR MANAGERS

friend. Many retirees, who have begun to feel that they no longer have value, find recognition and value as volunteers in charitable organizations. Everyone deserves to be recognized. In fact, we all expect (predict) that we will be given a reasonable degree of recognition - and when it's not given to us, we have bad feelings due to the breakdown in our predictability. Each field of endeavor has its own way of accomplishing this.

Professional baseball, football, and basketball players receive many forms of recognition. The most obvious is the size of their paychecks. As their natural talents are perfected over the years, their increased skill is rewarded by ever larger amounts of money and adulation. As if that weren't enough, there are the trading cards with the star's picture that many fans collect, and the long line to obtain an autograph (even pay for it) is certainly an indication of admiration. Performing artists also receive a hugely disproportionate share of recognition relative to the services they provide. There seems to be an unending procession of Tonys, Oscars, Emmys, and the many many exalted persons, singers, writers, directors, groups, country, jazz, heavy metal, video, soul, cameramen, ad nauseam. This is an area where people, some of whom may have considerable talent, go to great lengths to congratulate each other - sort of a "you scratch my back, I'll scratch yours" attitude. Those of us in the listening and viewing public don't have much to say about these shows. However, award shows will continue so long as sponsors are willing to pay for them and there are less-than-critical adoring

LIFE'S DATA STACKERS

fans who worship glitter over achievement. As you may surmise, I don't feel that these self-reward shows have much value. However, there are obviously millions of people with contrary opinions.

It is indeed fortunate that every person does have his or her own opinion as to what constitutes a performance worthy of recognition. At least it gives us a variety of entertainment styles from which to choose. How boring it would be if it were otherwise. In the final analysis, the money paid out for tickets, records, etc, determines the true amount of recognition. It is not however, a good way to measure the quality of the performance. There is more than one famous singer whose voice is shot, but who continues to receive great recognition and accolades. Usually this is due to nostalgia and/or the performer's showmanship, and just maybe the band plays a little louder. Yes, in show business it is easy to measure the recognition. In business, it is much more difficult.

The first question to be answered is: how important is recognition? Is this just the author's idea or do people really want to feel needed and important? To illustrate the answer I will refer back to an interesting study that was conducted in the 1950s. It is so old that I have no idea who did the work, but I attended a business seminar in 1957 where the results were discussed. However, and I cannot emphasize this too strongly: after nearly forty years in the human relations field I can assure you from my own personal experience that the findings are even more true

A FEW IDEAS FOR MANAGERS

today. Hundreds of workers were interviewed across a wide spectrum of jobs and job levels. Each person was given the survey form shown below. As shown, each form included a list of job conditions. Each person was asked to rank the job conditions in order of importance. Next, supervisors from 24 different companies were asked to do the same. I will show you the supervisor's rankings, but ask that you express your own opinion as to what the order should be. Then we will compare the supervisors' ratings with those of the workers. You can compare your rankings with those of the hourly employees and see how close you come to their opinions. Please refrain from looking ahead to see the workers' responses before you make your decision.

Factor	Your ranking	Supv. ranking
Appreciation for work done	1	8
Feeling "in" on things	2	10
Help on personal problems	3	9
Job security	4	2
Good wages	5	1
Interesting work	6	5
Promotion within the Company	7	3
Loyalty to workers	8	6
Good working conditions	9	4
Tactful discipline	10	7

LIFE'S DATA STACKERS

Each supervisor had his or her own opinion. The above is the average result for each criterion. How did your rankings compare to those averages? Did you do the ratings from the viewpoint of yourself as a worker or as a manager? The most desirable situation is one where the supervisors and the subordinates agree on the importance of the factors. Where there is considerable disagreement, it probably indicates a lack of sensitivity and/or communication. As a manager, you need to be aware of your employee's feelings and needs.

Well, how did the workers rank those ten factors? Exactly in the order in which they are listed. You heard me, from one to ten as listed above! As you can see the supervisors were not only way off base, but obviously completely out of touch with the desires of rank and file employees. I hope you did better. It's more than coincidental that the first three items are some form of recognition for the individual. The overwhelming desire to be recognized as an individual worthy of every consideration is quite clear. Equally clear is that the supervisors completely failed to understand this fact. The three most important conditions to the employees were ranked eight nine and ten by the managers. What a complete contrast! What a recipe for managerial disaster. No wonder it's said that a company "earns" its union. The level of managerial misunderstanding illustrated above shows us why that saying is as accurate as it is.

Notice the first and second place rankings the supervisors gave to "good wages" and "job security". Items the workers rated

226

A FEW IDEAS FOR MANAGERS

five and four. This mistaken perception is still quite common in industry today. Sure, you can attract people to miserable jobs with miserable bosses if you pay them extremely high wages. However, once the employees become used to those wages, they begin to search for something more. A working environment that will provide them with more dignity and self-respect. Should that fail, they will eventually leave even those highly paid positions. It is difficult to say why supervisors constantly make such a large error in judgment, but I can offer at least two possible causes: The first is the continual heavy emphasis that unions place on winning higher wages and job security. This impacts so hard and so frequently on the brains of all management personnel that it generally succeeds in stacking their data in the wrong direction. The other cause might be management's mental laziness, or fear of revealing its own incompetence. It is much easier to simply say the departing personnel quit because they wanted more money, than it is to acknowledge that you lacked the skills to manage them well. Good human relations do not come by accident. It takes constant effort, learning and consistent application of proven principles. All of that takes extra work and skill - more work than many managers want to put forth. However, if YOU are satisfied with having risen to the level of your own incompetence, then just go ahead and continue to blame low wages and job security.

Oh frustration, oh sadness, oh extreme puzzlement. Why are so many people so knot-headed? It must be due to poor data

LIFE'S DATA STACKERS

stacking. The psychological and economic benefits of good human relations have been known for decades. And yet, those practical and beneficial principles are continually ignored. Too often by those who are most concerned about being THE BOSS, rather than a leader. Is it really so hard to treat one another as worthwhile individuals? Is there some unwritten company rule that says you must degrade, ignore, and generally mistreat others in order to "battle" your way to the top? Is it really necessary that you always be demanding and in control in social situations, or at home? Are you so unsure of your own abilities that you must try to make your acquaintances, colleagues, and family feel inferior or subservient? I sincerely hope not. Give them the recognition they deserve and their data will be stacked in your favor. In fact, they just might provide you with some of the favorable recognition YOU would like to receive.

Most of you are probably well aware of many business-related outward symbols of recognition: Things such as a fancy job title, bonus checks, better office furniture, and/or equipment, extra time off and office location. Some of these can be quite important to certain people. One angry executive, at a major corporation, tried to get the Office Manager fired when he discovered that his office was 6 inches smaller than that of a fellow manager's. Sure it was terribly petty, but somewhere along the line this character had predicted that, once measured, his office would prove to be exactly as large (or better) than others of equal rank. He did not like finding that his prediction

A FEW IDEAS FOR MANAGERS

was wrong. He had a grievance! (Guess the Office Manager didn't "recognize" the importance of Mr. Nasty Executive.) But none of these factors are anywhere near as important to a person's sense of his own value to an organization as one-on-one personal recognition. The proverbial pat on the back, the display of sincere interest in the person's personal problems and/or joys, and the providing of useful information to the person about company activities.

DISCIPLINE CAN IMPROVE RELATIONS

Now, one final note on recognition. Did you know that discipline is also a powerful way to demonstrate concern and interest in an employee? Of course no one likes to be disciplined, but lack of it can readily create a negative feeling. For example, let us say a company has a rule book that provides penalties for absenteeism. John Doe (not the one in the morgue) goes AWOL for a couple of days. His internal computer, aided by the rule book, tells him to expect some form of punishment. On his return to work, nothing happens. The boss takes no action whatsoever and in fact doesn't even discuss the matter. How would you feel? At first, it might be a feeling of having put one over on the Company and the boss. But wouldn't it tweak your feelings just a little to think that you were not important enough to have been missed? I expect your internal computer was busy telling you everyone would be sorry you were gone, or no one else would be able to do the job as well as you did. You probably expected

LIFE'S DATA STACKERS

someone to chew you out and maybe hit you with some disciplinary time off. Instead you are ignored! No one seemed to care. Being ignored can be a major ego crushing experience for any one of us. Strange as it may seem, lack of "recognition" when you do something wrong, can be just as demeaning as not obtaining recognition when you do something positive. You don't believe this? Think back to how many children you have seen do "bad" things in a sometimes desperate attempt to receive attention from a parent. It happens every day at work as well as at home and school.

COMMUNICATIONS

It's difficult to provide recognition to others without using some form of communication. This would seem to go without saying, but the majority of us fail miserably in our day to day contacts with others. Communication is therefore the second of our "big five" principles of good management (and of good parenting or being a good friend.) Yes, I've mentioned many ways to recognize people for their efforts: the salary increases, the better offices etc. But more effective than these are the personal rewards deliverable through a one-on-one relationship. Direct communication between two individuals! There are of course many more reasons to communicate effectively. How about making sure that a person knows how to do their job, and just as important, what in the world is that job. Maybe you've been involved with a job evaluation program in your company. If

A FEW IDEAS FOR MANAGERS

so, you know that the first task to complete is the writing of the ever famous, and ever wrong, job description. It is amazing how disparate the employee's ideas are from the boss's. Their ideas about what the job should entail very seldom coincide. OK gang, don't you think a little communication would help to keep everyone singing from the same hymnal? The club president that makes unclear committee assignments will also cause just as much chaos and get equally poor results as the business manager. I don't care how you do it. Fathers and Mothers are often at fault in the same way. They dash off to work or play tossing inadequate garbled instructions to the kids about homework, cutting the lawn or where to meet when. The children should know what to do, right? No, wrong. Take the time both at home and on the job to communicate fully. Talk, sing, write, use signal flags, or anything else that will totally transmit ideas from one foggy brain to another. It just might make the joint more productive.

Over the years there have been innumerable seminars, books, classes, and lectures on how to communicate. There are whole college programs on the subject. Despite all this, there are always a large number of persons who DO NOT GET THE WORD. One of management's most misinformed and ignorant phrases is "everyone knows that". How anyone could think that everyone knows anything is beyond me. Most managers I've known who have uttered these words have not only failed to communicate TO their employees, they have also failed

LIFE'S DATA STACKERS

miserably in LISTENING to them. These managers hadn't the remotest idea how their own data was stacked. These same managers would typically get frustrated when people reacted in an unwanted manner. We should really say, in an uninformed or non-communicated manner.

There are some very basic means of communicating. I will touch five of them – each of which has already been the subject of many books, which I urge you to read. The first and most obvious of the five basic means is the use of sound. You know - that noise that comes out of your mouth with varying degrees of coherence? Use this method to talk to people both individually and in groups. Let others know your thoughts, the reasons for your actions, what you want them to do - and then don't forget to listen attentively to the responses. Compared to the grunts, moans and whistles of other species, the clearly spoken word is one of a human being's greatest assets. As an employee who aspires to higher position, the ability to speak in public and clearly communicate your ideas is absolutely essential. No, it's more than essential - you probably don't have a chance in hell of making it without that skill.

Visual communication is also quite useful. It's all around you. Movies, newspapers, books, pictures in an art gallery and even the graffiti on the tenement wall. All serve to communicate. However, printed words are not the only way to provide powerful visual communication. Pro-life groups use pictures of unborn and/or aborted fetuses to convey a powerful message.

A FEW IDEAS FOR MANAGERS

Environmental organizations effectively use photos of oil covered birds and slaughtered baby seals to provide the public with an instant awareness of serious problems. Pictures from the Hubble telescope show the magnificence of the skies far better than any words. In ancient Egypt, pictures represented words. Finally, in art galleries all over the world, the works of great artists have conveyed messages for hundreds of years.

One other very important, and subconscious visual stimulus, is body language. Here again, there have been many books written on the subject, but most people, failing to realize the importance of understanding body language, have not read them. Your facial expression alone can convey volumes of information - whether you like it or not. It's as though your body were saying, "Look you "homer", if you won't express yourself verbally, I'll do it my way". It may be a simple gesture, a look away, a folding of the arms across the chest, the way you cross your legs, what chair you choose to sit in, or a nervous twitch. They all convey something to other people - and you should be aware of what you are "saying" with your many body parts. First cousins to body language are some simple gestures that can, and often are, misinterpreted. This is especially true when you are dealing with people from other countries. In some Middle Eastern countries a man must be careful not to cross his legs as he would in the United States. In those Arab countries it is an insult to show the sole of your shoe to another person. In France the A-okay sign we make by joining the thumb and index finger,

LIFE'S DATA STACKERS

means zero or worthless. In the US we tap our forehead to indicate a person is smart, while in Holland it says they are crazy. Ah yes, body language and gestures can either help or destroy you.

Some of you may not think of the sense of smell as a means of communicating, but it is. Every parent knows when the baby's diaper needs changing. No words are necessary. At fairs and amusement parks, the purveyors of hamburgers learned long ago to fry onions on the grill. They don't care if the onions are sold because they know the smell will convey a fragrant, and hopefully irresistible, message that will entice hungry patrons to buy their more expensive products. And who hasn't suddenly become hungry when the smell of newly baked bread meanders along the breeze to tantalize your nose. That is serious communication. On the negative side, what is your reaction to a person with bad breath or a strong body odor? What does it communicate to you? Probably that the person has a physical or medical problem, or they simply don't care about their personal hygiene. Your data stack, not being full of medical knowledge, will most likely cause you to assume it is personal carelessness. You do not have enough information to make an accurate evaluation. Therefore, as I have stated earlier, a lack of communication will always result in negative assumptions. Most people will assume the personal hygiene to be the problem. This can be an insurmountable problem to a job hunter, a person wanting a promotion or trying to get a date.

A FEW IDEAS FOR MANAGERS

One other way to communicate is taste. Yep, the good old taste buds. One of my favorite restaurants recently tried promoting a new salad. The manager used pictures and words to convey the delectable nature of his newest offering, but he did not get the expected response. However, his sales climbed considerably after he decided to communicate with taste. A small sample salad made it possible for his customers to truly appreciate not only the appearance but also the flavors of the new menu item. Taste conveyed something that all of the other methods could not. It provided the final dimension. You can read about it, see a picture of it, smell it and touch it, but the culmination is the taste. One other example - have you ever kissed a person who has been smoking, drinking booze or just finished a cup of coffee? Did you get the taste message?

After all this good stuff is said, we have to ask an important question. Why do we communicate?? Obviously, it's so we can learn more about each other and improve our predictability to others, and their predictability to us. The more I know about how your data is stacked, the better I will understand your actions and motives, and in return, you will understand mine. There are the many forms of communication, most of which can be used alone to convey simple messages. However, it usually takes a combination of techniques to fully convey a complex "message". The exact method of conveying the data is not as important as making sure you do it in some understandable manner. Choose any of the above and get going!

LIFE'S DATA STACKERS

PREDICTABILITY

Well, now that we have said that word again, let's talk about it a little more. This is a principle that's critical to a parent, coach, club officer or any one of the many jobs that call upon you to be a "manager". Books on supervisory skills will always talk about the value of being consistent. Right! Consistency leads directly to predictability. People do not like surprises - unless it is a birthday party, and sometimes that isn't too welcome either. The intelligent manager will convey, by all means possible, his goals, his criteria for expected behavior, time schedules, and general conditions and terms of employment. These become the guidelines that employees must follow in order to do their job in an acceptable manner. A Management by Objectives program, as imperfect as it sometimes is, helps to lay out a "road map" for employees to follow to achieve the boss's desired results. It tells employees what is expected of them. Subsequent performance reviews should keep them posted on how well they are doing, so that they can do an even better job in the future. As I stated earlier, you get what you inspect for. The often used orientation program is one more example of a way to communicate with people to improve their predictability and future success. The very least you can do as a manager is to show new employees how to find the restroom. Some managers do not. It reminds me of a real estate broker who expressed her displeasure about a new agent who had not opened the office properly. The only catch

A FEW IDEAS FOR MANAGERS

was, the Broker had never told the agent how to do it. Apparently she was caught up in the old "everyone knows that" syndrome so never bothered with even a minimal bit of orientation. The Broker's attitude did not make the office run any better and, as you might expect, created a lot of hard feelings. This type of communication failure is rather simple to correct but is the type of common occurrence which is duplicated everyday in hundreds of offices across the nation. Not everyone gets the word!! Communicate before you castigate. Communicate if you want to predict. Communicate if you want to BE predictable.

Hopefully, you are beginning to see how several of these practices I have been talking about come together. Recognition, communication, and predictability are all closely related and dependent upon each other. Being predictable communicates a style of management and will gain you recognition. Providing recognition to others also communicates your personality and style. And lastly, communication (two-way) is the critical factor in recognition and being predictable to others.

FAIR AND EQUAL TREATMENT

There's one interpersonal relations error that will always cause anger and dissension in any situation: the failure to treat others fairly or equally. This is a problem that goes far beyond, and is not limited to, the treatment of minority groups. It creates trouble in any group or organization, or for that matter, whenever you are dealing with more than one person. Let me be quite clear

LIFE'S DATA STACKERS

about one thing at this point. When I speak of equal treatment, I do not mean always treating people exactly alike. None of us is exactly alike in our physical or mental attributes, and as we have learned by now, we have all had quite unique experiences during our lifetimes. Our internal computers are crammed with a wide variety of happenings, events, and conclusions. Each person is like no other. Equal treatment should always be provided in such things as benefits, working conditions, and in providing people with opportunities commensurate with their qualifications. However, the 350-pound lineman should not necessarily be given a chance to be a scrambling quarterback. To suggest that a person with no experience and/or limited mental ability should be given an "equal" opportunity at a job requiring the brains of an Einstein is not only unrealistic, but might well be grossly unfair to that person. By doing so, you are teaching such people to fail and doing great harm to their self esteem. It is not "fair" to stack their data to expect failure, and it is nothing short of cruelty to lead them to expect a chance at a job they cannot possibly do.

Companies that wish to remain free of labor union interference must be especially careful to treat people with fairness. I have had first hand opportunities to see how poor treatment has driven both factory and white collar employees to seek collective bargaining. In every case the primary cause could be traced to at least one supervisor who was being arbitrary and unfair in his treatment of his subordinates. As a manager you

A FEW IDEAS FOR MANAGERS

cannot afford to keep that type of person on your payroll. We will cover this subject in more detail in the next chapter.

When I say that we all desire and deserve recognition, I mean FAIR recognition. In one major oil company it was no great trick for a geologist to get a large annual bonus. This made perfect sense to the geologist. After all, he was directly concerned with the primary goal of the organization - the finding and extraction of oil and gas. If you were in some other department your bonus, if any, would be much smaller. The Personnel Manager found a way to save the Company a million dollars a year for all future years by lowering insurance costs. However his bonus was half the amount of a geologist who had merely done a good job on statistical analysis. An analysis that did not result in a similar amount of income for the Company. This approach is not unique. You may remember I mentioned entire corporations have their data stacked in certain directions. As an employee of a corporation, you need to learn what that direction is. If the Company is sales oriented, you can expect the big money to go to the sales department personnel - right down to the secretarial level. I recall one lazy secretary who was getting a big raise simply because she worked for an important department. That is not fair. Pay should be in relation to the skills required, job difficulty and the manner in which the employee performs - regardless of what department is involved. Ignore this principle and the union organizer may knock at your door. At the very least, it will generate an extremely expensive turnover rate.

LIFE'S DATA STACKERS

All of your people have a right to expect to be entitled to the same holidays, frequency of salary reviews, smoking/no smoking rules, absentee policies, leave of absences, pensions and other similar benefits. Most employees enter the workplace expecting fair treatment. They are predicting that you will do the "right" thing. Do not disappoint them. These principles apply to any other organization, or home, as well. Students, teachers, parents, children, taxpayers, jailbirds, and all others want and expect to be treated in a fair manner.

NEWTON'S 4TH LAW OF MOTION

Very loosely stated, Sir Isaac Newton's fourth law of motion states that for each action there is an opposite and equal reaction. This is what makes a rocket fly. The combustion gases are pushing out in all directions, but being contained in the combustion chamber of the rocket engine, they can only escape out of a hole in the back end of the chamber. If there are umpteen tons of force going out the rear, there is also an equal amount of force going in the opposite direction against the forward end of the combustion chamber and pushing it and the rest of the rocket forward. With a little literary license, I will now apply this law to human relations. Hot dog! Two major rules in one chapter! FOR EACH ACTION THERE IS AN OPPOSITE (TO YOU) AND EQUAL REACTION. Go to any schoolyard and watch the interaction within groups of boys and girls. Sooner or later some type of disagreement will most likely lead to a confrontation. I

A FEW IDEAS FOR MANAGERS

push you and you push me back. "Oh yeah"? "Yeah!" "Your mother wears army boots!" "Your mother has a mustache!" I push you harder and you push me harder. And so it goes until it escalates into fists and a general brawl. I take action toward you, and you feel it necessary to respond in an equal manner. If that "PUSH" is something other than physical, such as distrust, unfairness, lack of communication, etc. you can expect to receive a reaction of equal magnitude from the pushee. Conversely, if your "push" is of a positive nature, you can expect a positive response. Whether your face receives a slap or a caress, you will probably respond in a comparable manner. That is why smart managers use a participative style rather than a coercive approach. There are other ways of saying all this: what goes around, comes around; as ye sow, so shall ye reap; or, if you act like a turkey, you will be surrounded by turkeys. At this point we are combining the foregoing factors of recognition, communications, fair treatment, and predictability into the way to deal with other people. If you will utilize those factors, the other person will respond in like manner to you. It will be good for both of you. Shall I elucidate?

First, I'd like to present an example of an extremely bad practice. (Yes, we can learn a lot from bad examples.) Too often some out of touch member of management will hire an outside consultant to determine the feelings of his subordinates toward himself and the company. In comes Mr. Outside Consultant, the "genius" problem solver who starts to interview the subordinates.

LIFE'S DATA STACKERS

Looking you right in the eye, and with solemn voice, he promises complete anonymity if you will just trust him and spill your guts. Now what do you suppose happens when he betrays that trust? I watched this charade in two locations; one a corporate office and the other in a remote mining location. The results were the same in both places. The employees accepted the consultant's word regarding confidentiality and revealed their feelings with honesty. They thought the company was finally recognizing their value, was truly interested in their opinions, and assumed the company really wanted to make conditions better. In both cases the consultants turned around and discussed the employee's comments with their bosses. Not only did they discuss their comments, but they revealed exactly who said what. As you can well imagine, there were some very unfavorable repercussions for those who had spoken in a negative manner. Their trust was betrayed. Newton's Fourth Law went into effect at once. From the day the deceit became known, the employees gave back the same kind of trust the company had shown them. Never again was there an honest answer to an opinion poll or interview, and worse, from that day forward none of the company's upper management or communications were fully trusted. My, oh my! In the minds of the employees that really created a mighty tall stack of negative data. What a stupid way to run a company.

This same type of situation often arises in families. One child might confide in a parent about a problem at school. Should the parent betray the trust and blab to the other children or, worse

A FEW IDEAS FOR MANAGERS

yet, to the neighbors, all future trust will be destroyed. Gossip about "friends" behind their backs is a betrayal that will usually result in equal treatment for the betrayer. We all provide data about ourselves to various government agencies expecting (predicting) that such information will be kept confidential. Later we learn our ""data" has been sold to commercial businesses so that the state government can make some money Is it any wonder that so many people no longer trust their elected representatives and government agencies? As they have sowed, so have they reaped.

There are better ways to treat your employees. I'll mention one of them now, and another later when we get to the chapter dealing with labor relations.

My second, and more positive, example of management practices, I draw from a manufacturing facility I once dealt with in Columbus, Ohio. For years it had been plagued with labor unrest and wildcat strikes. For you folks unfamiliar with labor relations, a wildcat strike is a strike that takes place during the term and in violation of a labor contract. In this case, the plant was suffering all kinds of production delays and was generally inefficient. The situation had to improve or the plant would have to close, putting a lot of people out of work. Due to a dubious employee relations history, Management and labor had no trust between them and were constantly sparring over real or imagined problems. Foremen argued over turf and authority. Department heads were protecting their own little empires, and leadership

LIFE'S DATA STACKERS

from the top was in very short supply. It was a mess. Is it any wonder that delivery schedules were not being met, and that the plant's once-excellent reputation for quality was going down the tubes? A consultant was also brought in here, but with a difference. A team of corporate people trained in human relations accompanied the consultant to Columbus, where they set out to interview every single person in the organization. These were private, and truly anonymous, interviews. Those doing the interviews knew only what department the person had come from. After the survey was completed a summary of the results was shared not only with top management, but also with the employees. Both the good and the bad were laid out for inspection by everyone. As a result of the study a large number of changes were made in manufacturing procedures, supervisory assignments, management style, and communications. The changes extended all the way up the ladder. In this instance the employees' initial trust was not betrayed, and further, they were included in helping to solve the problems. There were no more strikes, and production achieved new levels of quality and quantity. Instead of remaining opponents, management and workers had become partners - partners that had finally learned to trust and appreciate one another.

There is a very important footnote that needs to be added here. The Columbus undertaking is much more than just an example of trust being regenerated between parties. I've related

A FEW IDEAS FOR MANAGERS

this case to illustrate how, in accordance with Newton's 4th Law, trust extended can bring trust in return.

However, of much greater influence in making these opponents into partners was the recognition factor. By sitting down and simply listening to each employee, the Company let them know that it recognized their importance as individuals. In a way, it's a form of flattery (in the best meaning of the word) to ask someone for his or her opinion. It's like saying not only that you recognize them as individuals, but that their opinion is valuable and worthwhile. Remember: show others that you know they exist and have value! By the way, have you ever heard of quality circles? You know, those sessions where management representatives LISTEN to ideas from their employees? They're based on the same principle.

PUBLIC RELATIONS

The single most important member of your organization's public relations staff is YOU! Oh sure, there is someone else with a more important title, and an even bigger paycheck, who may technically be in charge of this activity. But YOU, and others like you, are actually more important.

This is another one of those areas where too few organizations recognize the value of their employees. Worse, few organizations seem to understand the good their employees can do by assuring that those employees are willing and able to present a positive corporate image. Conversely, significant

LIFE'S DATA STACKERS

damage can be done to an organization when its employees can't or won't present such an image. It's certainly nice for the CEO to address a bunch of Wall Street financial types and enhance the image of his corporation by putting out a glistening list of achievements in the annual report. It's just too bad that such a financial "PR" effort can so easily be undermined when the CEO's employees proceed to destroy that carefully crafted corporate image. Employees seldom set out with that purpose in mind, but it is a predictable result of poor management and lousy communications.

I recall a metal fabricating outfit in my hometown that nearly expired because of extensive safety problems. The upper management seemed to have no concern whatsoever for the safety of the workers. Production, and a lot of it, was the only thing that management seemed to care about. Employees were poorly trained and suffered from equally poor supervision. The predictable and unfortunate result was a terrible and constant series of accidents. The employees did talk, and would communicate with friends, neighbors, customers, suppliers and anyone else who would listen. The story they told was not complimentary. In time the facility became known as "the butcher shop" and only a desperate person would go to work there. This meant the Company's ability to hire "good" employees became more and more difficult. Although none of this negative information ever appeared in the press - it was quite effectively spread by word-of-mouth by unhappy employees.

A FEW IDEAS FOR MANAGERS

Of course, this was before the invention of OSHA, so that government agency was not available to monitor the problem or take actions that might have improved the Company's practices and prevented the Company from continuing to stack its employee's internal data banks with plenty of undesirable information – information that the employees used to form negative opinions, spread negative information, and to justify the poor manner in which they performed their jobs. Theirs was truly Public Relations Department from Hell!

There may come a time when you're called upon to deal with the news media. Should you be placed in this position, the first thing to remember is that they seldom tell your story with complete accuracy, and can usually be counted on to quote you incorrectly. Uh, oh, has my own personal data been stacked? You can bet your 401K plan it has! I have *never* given a speech or taken part in a civic affair that was reported on with complete accuracy by a newspaper. I don't know why. Maybe it's an occupational hazard that journalists cannot avoid. Certainly some of the inaccuracy may result from simply not hearing or understanding what was being said - after all, no one is an expert on everything. But some almost certainly results from plain old bias. To minimize this effect it helps a lot if you provide printed press releases and/or copies of your speeches. However, you also need to do your best to get this media bunch on your side! I don't know any better way to do this than to make sure you're honest

LIFE'S DATA STACKERS

and consistent (predictable) in your communications with the ladies and gentlemen of the press.

Media reporting is an especially glaring and frustrating example of how a lack of communication will result in negative assumptions. If you don't tell them what's going on, they'll search around until they find or think-up something to write about. What they come up with on their own may not be what you want them to broadcast. Build your creditability by communicating as often as you can, and with a maximum of truthfulness. There will, of course, be difficult times when you simply cannot tell everything you know. But if you have a past history of being as forthcoming as possible, they will most likely treat you in a more sympathetic manner. More than one company has learned the importance of this when they became involved in labor relations conflicts or consumer law suits. Whether you're dealing with news media, employees, or ordinary citizens, there's a general rule that you should follow. Tell them everything - except for those very few things that you either must not or can not.

OLD CHINESE PROVERB TIME

In departing from this chapter on advice to new or would-be managers, I would like to quote an old Chinese proverb. Read it carefully and give its meaning some sober consideration. There's a lot of wisdom in this ancient oriental saying:

A FEW IDEAS FOR MANAGERS

Tell me, I'll forget.
Show me, I may remember
Involve me, I'll understand.

LIFE'S DATA STACKERS

CHAPTER NINE

IMPROVING LABOR (PEOPLE) RELATIONS

Anyone who works for a living is involved with labor relations. What do I mean by "labor relations"? It's the manner in which people deal with employees - regardless of whether those employees happen to belong to a labor union. Going just a bit further, you might well expand this definition to include anyone you supervise, whether or not they happen to be employees or can precisely be described as "laborers". Although I have, to this point, been dealing mostly with union-management relations, the scope of this chapter is broadened to consider how ordinary people deal with one another – regardless of whether they happen to be in an employment relationship. They may be members of a volunteer charity group or a citizen committee - the basic principles still apply. You're working with a group of people in an effort to accomplish some goal or direct some type of activity – which can be especially difficult if those

LIFE'S DATA STACKERS

you're directing are NOT your employees - people you can not reward, fire or effectively discipline.

Consider the interaction that takes place between you and those you supervise, and notice how data stacking enters the picture. In business, if you begin to apply proper labor relations techniques early on, you can most likely avoid a union organizing drive. Should you NOT manage your labor relations issues properly, a visit from a union business agent is quite probable. In addition, your poor management will probably increase overhead and decrease production.

Should a union already be in place in your shop or office, you can go a long way toward creating better relationships and fewer day to day problems by properly applying the techniques mentioned in Chapter 8, including the delegation of supervision authority to others. In social clubs and volunteer groups, on the other hand, if you don't, you will probably find yourself handling the organization all by your lonesome self. In either case, people don't join unions or clubs just for an opportunity to pay dues. They're looking for solutions to their problems (real or imagined), and RECOGNITION and good feelings from their supervisors. More on this later.

Let me mention one short example of how labor relations can be improved dramatically with just a little well-directed effort. A large mining company had a long and dismal history of innumerable arbitrations and constant conflict with a local union representing the company's employees. It seemed as though

252

IMPROVING LABOR (PEOPLE) RELATIONS

every grievance that was filed dragged on and on – not ending until the final stages of arbitration. The Company was spending thousands of dollars and thousands of man-hours trying to resolve these conflicts. A previous Industrial Relations Director had fought every grievance. He seemed to feel a need to defend everything, including the ill-advised actions of some incompetent supervisors. His credo seemed to be "fight everything, I must always be right, and I must always win". (No it wasn't Ted Bailey). Arbitrations were numbered in the multiple dozens each year. You can imagine how much time was wasted and how little time or money was left for more productive human relations activities. His successor, apparently in an effort to be a HERO, went completely overboard in the opposite direction. He would NEVER go to arbitration. His idea of labor peace was to give in to almost any union demand - much to the detriment of the Company's ability to manage. The President, being ill-informed by the Industrial Relations Manager, thought the new IR man was doing a great job since the arbitrations had ceased. This was a truly gross error in judgment on the part of the President, since it effectively robbed the plant supervisors of their ability to manage. The plant supervisors sensed that upper management had abandoned them and was allowing the union bosses to do as they pleased. Luckily the "give away artist" was replaced with a more "savvy" manager. Upon the arrival of the new manager at the mine, and after a reasonable period of orientation, the new manager called for a meeting with the Union Grievance

LIFE'S DATA STACKERS

Committee. He advised them that there would no longer be a seemingly "automatic" granting of grievance requests. To improve his predictability in the minds of the Grievance Committee members, the new manager stacked the Committee members' data with his intentions. He told the Committee that when a company supervisor misinterpreted and/or misapplied the labor contract, the new manager would agree with the union's request for redress. Conversely, when the new manager honestly felt the union was wrong, the new manager would fight the issue to arbitration. The union President immediately growled "Oh you want to go back to the old way with a lot of arbitrations"? Naturally the union did not like the thought of an end to the "free ride" they had been given for the previous three years. To dispel this misperception, the new manager's next step was to meet privately with the union's International Representative to explain his intentions and assure him that the new manager would be fair in his approach. His communications were firm, straightforward, and yet friendly. Subsequently, as the union saw that he would keep his word and that his actions were predictable, the grievances dropped off, the Company regained its lost ability to manage, and only had three arbitrations in the next three years. The Company won all three, and relations with the union were never better.

There are many reasons why a company is generally better off without a union. Not the least of these reasons is that the Company retains the right to manage the business without

IMPROVING LABOR (PEOPLE) RELATIONS

undue restrictions or unnecessary work rules - rules that often cause over-staffing and limit production. This quite often leads to lost jobs as the company crumbles.

In one instance, a major brewery required 1100 employees to operate a facility that annually produced some three million barrels of beer. Many years of wrangling with the unions had failed to reduce the serious over-staffing problem. The end result may not be too surprising. A new brewery was built a thousand miles away. It produced three and a half million barrels with only 350 employees. It was not long before the older inefficient plant was shut down and the eleven hundred people were without work. Sure there were improvements in machinery etc., but the real savings were in a reduced work force. Yes, the new plant also had a union, but one that was more realistic about manning requirements. I always appreciated the remark a Carpenter/Millwright Business Agent made one day. "I want you guys to make a lot of money - that way I'll have more to get out of you". He had learned from past experience that you cannot get big pay raises from a bankrupt company. Too bad more of his colleagues didn't feel the same way.

In a steel plant, where a crew of men had to handle extremely hot steel with hand tongs, the schedule called for a half hour of work followed by a half hour of rest. In these extreme conditions the "half on and half off" regime was entirely reasonable and necessary. At other times the work was much lighter and the men simply stood by and watched as automatic

LIFE'S DATA STACKERS

machines did all the work. The union insisted that the crew continue to work only half the time despite the drastic change in work requirements. Working halftime is no way to make a profit and it shouldn't have to take a major layoff to restack the union bosses' collective data bank. Bear in mind that it does not always take an inefficiency of such magnitude to cause serious problems. It can be as minor as a Maintenance crew "rushing" to a repair job in a truck going only 15 miles per hour. Or perhaps some mechanic not being able to start work until the electrician plugs in the power cord. And, we haven't even begun to consider the increased cost brought about by abuse of benefit programs.

ABUSE OF BENEFIT PROGRAMS

Most companies of any appreciable size provide their employees with a variety of benefit programs. These usually include life, health and disability insurance as well as some kind of pension or 401K program. Like the government Medicare program, Companies implement such programs with good intentions. Also, like Medicare, such programs are subject to serious abuse by both providers and recipients of the benefits. Worker's Compensation program abuse was at one time particularly flagrant in Michigan. Unions "controlled" many members of the legislature and promoted the passing of legislation mandating overly-generous benefits. To make matters worse, some union presidents would urge union members to file for benefits when they were not really entitled to them. Selected

IMPROVING LABOR (PEOPLE) RELATIONS

doctors would attest to the "serious" nature of the claimant's injuries and thousands of dollars would be spent on various awards and medical expenses. Any employee who fell and hurt himself at home would be urged by his union to report it as an accident that occurred on Company premises. We once made a calculation that showed that if we only had to pay for legitimate injuries, we could have paid three times the benefit amount. The necessity to pay for fraudulent injuries harmed both the Company and the employees. Ah yes, another union benefit. union officials at local and state levels had learned that this type larceny would help get them reelected and retain their power. The rank and file liked these "freebies" and so rewarded their benefactors. They, in fact, were the data stackers in that particular situation. It seemed that the more crooked they were, the more they got. Not a great incentive program.

As a manager, it will be to your and the Company's benefit if you can communicate the need for honesty in filing for benefits of any kind. It means you must stack the data banks of your employees with pertinent economic data to offset the "freebie" mentality. For your part, it will be mandatory that you be honest and demonstrate a consistent willingness to pay, without a lot of argument, those claims you know to be legitimate. As you build your credibility, your task will become easier.

BENEFITS THAT ARE FREE

There is one benefit you can provide your subordinates that won't cost you a cent: decent and fair treatment. This is much easier to provide without a union. Too often a union boss is more interested in feathering his own nest or doing favors for his buddies. Not all union members are treated equally by their leaders - especially if certain members disagree with some favored union policy. Time and again I have found myself defending an employee's rights against the wishes of some selfish and/or power hungry union official. Of course, I have also dealt with good, responsible union officials; and they are a breath of fresh air when you encounter them. They are typically tough negotiators who work hard for the welfare of the total union membership but at the same time realize that the company needs to be successful.

Union or non-union, you'll find that it benefits both you and your Company to apply some of the rules and principles I've discussed in preceding chapters. If you don't have a union, proper application of these rules will help you keep it that way. If you DO have a union, it will make your relations much better. One of your most important allies is good communication. Remember, "any absence of communication will always result in negative rumors and/or assumptions". For example, in a steel plant a union became quite belligerent over job security. Why? The Company failed to explain certain changes in production schedules. The workers, assuming it was due to a lack of orders,

IMPROVING LABOR (PEOPLE) RELATIONS

decided a layoff was imminent. An ounce of communication could have prevented a ton of anxiety and trouble. In office situations the same scenario has often driven some of the most capable workers to seek other jobs, resulting in a completely unnecessary staffing expense for the Company. How could people think such negative thoughts? Easily. Management didn't bother telling them anything, and their internal computers told them that this was a familiar script. Remember the old secretary's lament: "I must be a mushroom. No one tells me anything around here - they keep me in the dark and cover me with manure".

And, lest we forget, adequate communication is one of the very best means of providing the ever desired and critical factor: RECOGNITION. While you're providing this recognition, you need to be stacking the other person's data in your favor. Talk about plans for the future, economic conditions, customer relations, employee benefits, work schedules, impending legislation, and other civic affairs. Don't be shy - shout it to the sky! It is quite difficult to over communicate. Quite often company publications consist only of rings, rattles, and retirement. If you will just listen carefully, and learn how subordinates have THEIR data stacked, you'll learn the areas in which you need to focus your best efforts. Allow their "important" data to flow into your personal mental computer before you open your mouth to stack theirs. Did someone say LISTEN? In other words, you must become a "stackee" before you can become a good "stacker".

LIFE'S DATA STACKERS

FOR THE NON-UNION FOLKS

At first glance, if your place of business is non-union, you would appear to be one of the lucky ones who need not concern themselves with labor relations headaches. But not so fast Johnson! How good a job are your supervisors doing? Remember, it takes a lot more human relations effort to run a good non-union shop than it does a unionized operation. Supervisors must be constantly alert to the power of the "fantastic five" for both good and bad. Good information begets good and bad information begets evil. What data stacking has gone on in the past and what kind of data should you put forth in the future? The answers to these questions will challenge the new manager. The lack of a union quite often leads a company to assume it can throw any kind of supervision at the "troops" and not have problems. Big, big mistake oh frozen spindle brain!! This scenario will make the company extremely vulnerable to outside interference. To keep the union out, you must have extra good management. It only takes one management "idiot" to invite the union to dinner.

In one West Coast company it at first appeared that all of the salaried employees were happy and contented. They were being paid above average wages, had an excellent benefit program, noon time movies and free hot lunches. Sounds good doesn't it? So how come an office workers' union was knocking on the door? The Controller was a jerk!! He was great at creating

IMPROVING LABOR (PEOPLE) RELATIONS

"little" irritants like making it impossible for employees to plan their vacations ahead of time. And if he did allow them to schedule time off ahead of time, he would change his mind at the last minute. Overtime work was assigned in a random, capricious, last-minute manner; and he consistently followed the famous "mushroom" policy described earlier. Will you be terribly surprised to learn that the union won the election? The manager promised to reform, but his past performance caused his employees to believe otherwise. It is tough to overcome long term firmly stacked data.

Another sorry example is what happened to another company after constructing a new plant in an Arkansas town. One of the reasons for going to Arkansas was this particular town's reputation for maintaining an animosity toward unions. So what did the inept management do? They took an arrogant accountant with a superiority complex and made him plant manager. This fellow knew only numbers and spent hours impressing himself and attempting to impress others with his self-perceived ability to manage people. He wasn't about to apply Newton's "human relations" law. (For each action a similar and equal reaction.) Again, no surprise. When the employees saw that they were going to be poorly treated, they responded by challenging the neophyte plant manager - with a union organizing drive.

In one other case, a division president made it a practice to listen-in on office employees' (including higher level

LIFE'S DATA STACKERS

manager's) telephone conversations. Did someone mention that wire taps were illegal?? Heaven forbid!! This guy was a real gem of a data stacker. No one trusted him. No one would tell him anything important. Capable people found more suitable places to work etc. etc. Every good human relations precept was violated and the disastrous results were predictable. The dissension and turmoil eventually cost the Division President his job, but the damage lingered on for several years.

These miserable vignettes demonstrate some of the problems that can be caused by people who have spent years stacking their, and your, internal computers with incorrect data. Be careful or you might fall into the same category as these bad guys. Obviously, these types of situations are fertile ground for union business agents who are more than happy to plant, grow and harvest the seeds of dissention that grow there. Always be alert. Lurking behind each incompetent manager's door is a talented and well-trained union organizer. The Organizers are eager and ready to tell half-truths and/or outright lies as they entice the unwary workers with big promises of pay and control. For example, when you, as a manager, create the proverbial gap in communications, letting your employees know that they can NOT count on you for information, the union organizer finds it quite easy to fill the information void with his propaganda and big promises. (At least HE communicates.) Remember - negative information will always fill any information gap! The union's statements about YOU and/or your company will certainly be

IMPROVING LABOR (PEOPLE) RELATIONS

quite negative. You may strive mightily, with the help of attorneys etc., but the employees probably are mumbling something like "where were you the last time we needed someone to listen"? In most cases, it is now too late to repair the damage.

But enough of this pessimistic news. It's time for you to get out there and do it right. Time to turn yourself into a positive big time data stacker ready to defend your job and company from the bad guys. Who are the bad guys? They come in various forms. Some may be union organizers, some may be your co-workers, some may be the news media, some may be part of the general public, and some may be your bosses. Fortunately, in most cases, you can win out over those "bad guys" with one intelligent approach. You don't have to dream up completely different approaches to successfully deal with each different group. The principles we've discussed are, thankfully, universal.

More than anything else you must become proficient at two very important skills I have mentioned before. Because they are so critical, I will mention them again: LISTENING and COMMUNICATING!! I also suspect that you, like many, have done very little about using these tools properly. "Properly" means, among other things, that you practice both, not just one or the other. By listening, you learn what to communicate. You may know the old saying about "putting your brain in gear before you put your mouth in motion". - Very good advice, but the brain can't function correctly unless you have allowed the five senses

LIFE'S DATA STACKERS

to first input pertinent data. Certainly you have heard this message before, and maybe even read one of the hundreds of books on the subject. Did you really absorb and use the information, or just roll over and switch to another TV channel? Come on couch potato! Take an interest in improving your life. If you have been paying attention up to this point, you will know that what I am trying to get you to understand is WHY you do it. I repeat: by listening you discover how an individual has his or her data stacked. You can then communicate effectively and stack the other person's internal computer with the type of information that is beneficial to you. Actually, to be really efficacious, it's best that the communications be of benefit to BOTH parties!

The stacking of an employee's data needs to begin with the would-be employees' very first interview. While you're learning all you can about the applicant, you're also giving them information about your organization. Although you may be tempted to tell only the positive facts, don't be shy about describing some of the tough situations that may be encountered. Remember my labor attorney friend? Remember the service reps with the horrible travel schedule? Start building your credibility from day one. In most companies, the next step, after hiring, is to give the new employee some type of employee manual and, hopefully, an orientation program. Sure a major reason for these steps is to get the new hire acting in a manner pleasing to the Company. But of much greater importance is the role these steps

IMPROVING LABOR (PEOPLE) RELATIONS

play in letting the employee know what he or she can expect to happen and what the working conditions will be. The closer management's actions are to what is laid out in the policy booklet, the more likely there will be a happy and productive workforce. Do I dare mention it again? Actions consistent with written and/or oral promises lead to what, class?? Predictability!! All of you who answered that question correctly may read on. Those who did not must start all over again back at Chapter One.

Another very practical and important area, which usually is sorely lacking, is good communications about the Company's financial condition and/or viability. Is the Company profitable, just getting by, or about to go down the tubes? The more information you can give the employees the better off you will be. Some organizations do an excellent job of explaining market conditions, order status, profits or losses etc. to employees. Others try to keep any mention of these things from leaking out to the hoi polloi for fear they will (oh gracious me) learn something about the Company. Naturally such a short-sighted view, and lack of communication, results in the employees supplying their own negative viewpoints. That is easily predictable. There are some industries, such as the copper industry, (already discussed in Chapter Three) which are cyclical in nature. Some years the price of copper is high and the copper mining companies reap large profits. In other years, when prices are low, the same companies operate at a considerable loss. Old timers and WELL-INFORMED EMPLOYEES know this and do not react with panic. However, a newcomer, or someone NOT blessed with good communications from the Company, might literally run for the door and seek a new job elsewhere. Then there are suppliers, stockholders, banks, and the like to consider. More than one such company has disappeared from the American industrial scene because the financial people of a takeover company could not understand and/or grasp the conditions peculiar to their new acquisition. They are too foreign to their previous experience. Boy were some of those management people slow to get educated! Rather than learn how to operate their newly acquired facilities, they would first lay off the work force and then sell what was left - usually at a considerable loss. Did anyone notice from this example that a lack of information can be quite costly?

COMPENSATION POLICIES

Compensation is another subject about which management typically communicates poorly, resulting in a lack of understanding between management and employees. Dick and Jane sit in their little cubicles spending endless hours wondering and discussing to what extent they are underpaid. They are NEVER EVER overpaid - in their opinion. Besides, Jane knows darn well that the infamous "glass ceiling" for women is responsible for her getting paid less than Dick. Dick, on the other hand, knows with equal assurance that management is trying to impress the EEOC by giving Jane job preference and an

IMPROVING LABOR (PEOPLE) RELATIONS

extremely high salary - at least a salary higher than his. Dick and Jane have both read various magazine and news articles and watched TV shows describing and decrying these practices, so their internal computers are now stacked to expect this sort of treatment. The Company's strict policy about not revealing or talking about salaries doesn't help one little bit. Management silence simply allows the negative suspicions to multiply. Lack of information about salary ranges creates another interesting phenomenon: Most persons will OVERESTIMATE the pay of persons below them, and UNDERESTIMATE the income of those in jobs above them. Because Dick and Jane have made these inaccurate assumptions, neither Dick nor Jane wants to accept a promotion to a job with added responsibilities for such an imagined small increase in pay. Poor communications strike again!!

Just suppose that, being a good student of management skills, you have now started communicating effectively with the new hires, have run your orientation program, produced an informative policy manual, used the Company newspaper to inform people about all kinds of "stuff" and have published pay ranges. OK, that's a good start. What else can you do? How about a meeting, at least weekly, with all the members of your group to discuss their problems, production schedules, and Company problems? If you do decide to hold such meetings, bear in mind that their success or failure will depend on how you handle them. For instance, at an organization I once worked for,

LIFE'S DATA STACKERS

we had a plant manager who prided himself on having an "open door" policy. You know, that's one of those arrangements where an employee is presumably allowed to walk into the top manager's office at almost any time to discuss a problem. In theory, both parties listen to one another and exchange ideas and/or solutions. That's the theory. Our plant manager really did intend to do a proper job, but he was a technical man with very little skill in human relations. The employees were certainly welcome to come in and state their problem, but then all they would get were lectures. Once an employee had spoken long enough to raise an issue, two-way communication went out the window as the Plant Manager launched into a long-winded dissertation on how things ought to be done. He didn't really LISTEN to the employee. Oh he heard noises coming out of the employee's mouth, but the Plant Manager seldom caught the emotion and subtleties being expressed. It didn't take long for the employees to get their data stacked and stop crossing his office threshold. When your associates learn that you will truly listen, and understand, the flow of information will increase geometrically.

Related to the communications principles recommended above, are the successes many companies have had with Quality Control Circles. Quality Control Circles are sessions where upper management works closely with employee groups to help solve quality and production problems. They have been quite effective in many cases. Management, the "data stackers", take positive

IMPROVING LABOR (PEOPLE) RELATIONS

steps to assure employees of Management's interest in employees' ideas and Management's sincere intentions.

But let's stop for a minute. What do you think is the most positive factor involved in these Circles? Probably the most positively effective factor is recognition of each employee's personal value to the Company! Management comes and LISTENS, and even COMMUNICATES important production and economic information. "My little old skull is beginning to burst with the thought that someone cares, and they trust me! *Now* I don't mind showing the boss how hard I can work to help him solve his problem and help the Company achieve its goals". The more the employees can see that Management is living up to its promises, and that the internal computer input is valid, the more the workers participate and the more effective the circles become.

WHAT? YOU ALREADY HAVE A UNION? SO HOW IS YOUR CREDIBILITY?

So you already have a union shop. Well, I guess you'll just have to make the best of it. Failure to at least try, may well result in the waste of untold man-hours and huge sums of money.

One of the most critical aspects of your relationship with a labor union is the question of credibility. Without it, your contract negotiations will, at the very least, be drawn out and difficult – and, at the most, almost impossible and/or extremely costly. There is nothing more frustrating than trying to negotiate

LIFE'S DATA STACKERS

any kind of agreement between groups of people who have consistently lied to each other over the years. It takes a certain degree of trust to achieve a workable contract - trust that is hard to come by when everyone's internal computers have been filled with more kinds of garbage than a New York trash truck. A few examples might help illustrate what can happen:

There are many things that an Industrial Relations Manager can do to establish good relations and credibility with union officials. I can't tell you how many dinners, dances, installations of officers, and political affairs I attended over the years. Not as an empty and cynical gesture, but as a chance to become better acquainted with business agents and their philosophies. You don't remain enemies after sharing a back yard pool with kids, wives, and friends. Yes, over time I formed good and lasting friendships and established trust. Although sincere differences of opinion persisted, contract negotiations were much calmer and were effectively concluded because, although we were opponents, we respected one another.

The taking of "time studies" is a practice that quite often causes disputes in manufacturing organizations. For you laymen, a time study is something a company does to decide if the workers are doing a job as fast as possible. The all too common approach is to simply have an Industrial Engineer go into the shop with a stop watch and start timing each and every movement. After doing some "fancy" calculations, and perhaps changing the work layout and procedures, a new production

IMPROVING LABOR (PEOPLE) RELATIONS

standard will be set. Usually the person on the job will complain that the standard is too hard to achieve and accuses the Industrial Engineer of not giving proper consideration to all the factors involved in doing the job. This dissatisfaction creates bad feelings, lack of trust, and perhaps a costly strike. This type of situation can usually be avoided if the Engineer will take the time to communicate fully with the worker. Rather than gathering only externally-observable behavioral data, the Engineer needs to find out how the worker has his data stacked! Let the worker see that the Engineer is considering each and every factor that the worker considers important to doing the job properly. Once the worker's internal computer tells him that he has had a fair and full hearing, he will most likely be more cooperative. Also, the union will be much less apt to file a grievance on his behalf.

Ho hum, here we go again. Both parties will benefit when there has been an ample exchange of information regarding experiences and goals. In addition, there is once more consideration for that little thing called recognition. The Time Study Man has shown the employee that he considers him and his views important. Don't ever forget the importance of this factor in human relations.

We once had a plant Human Resource Manager who earned his own discharge by destroying his credibility with not only the union, but with his superiors. This fellow was quite a talker and talked a self confident and friendly game. At first he was well accepted by everyone, but after a while his lack of

LIFE'S DATA STACKERS

truthfulness got him into trouble. He would promise the union one thing and then do another. Eventually, this led to a wildcat strike that shut down the entire operation. The union officers shared the blame, to an extent, since they failed to communicate their grievance to the Plant Manager. Consequently, neither the Plant Manager nor those of us at the Corporate office were aware of the impending disaster until it struck. (You're right if you're thinking the local Plant Manager, despite the union officers' silence, should have been more aware of what was happening in his plant.) With the Human Relations Manager's credibility completely shot, and an extremely expensive wild cat strike underway, there was no alternative but to interrupt the continuity of his employment. Well, guess who had to go down and attempt to clean up the mess. Right. Yours truly.

Two things were of great help in resolving the dispute. First, during several previous visits I had become acquainted with the union president. Second, the striking union was the same International whose social functions I had attended in our headquarters city. This gave me the credibility I needed to work out an agreement that ended the strike. Nothing in writing - just a handshake and trust.

Past practice. These are words that haunt any labor relations staff. If you do it once, or have done it for one person, you must forever after continue to do the same thing. Especially if that one thing just happens to provide a benefit or a more favorable contract interpretation. Companies have long been

IMPROVING LABOR (PEOPLE) RELATIONS

saddled with this expectation. But there are ways to get around it. Contrary to popular opinion, it IS possible to overcome a past practice. It may take awhile and will certainly take some planning, but it can be done.

It may be the president of a union or even the chief Poohba of the Ladies Golfing and Debating Society who is attempting to hold you to a past practice. Whoever it is, they are not about to give up the power, control, special deal, payoff or other goodie that they have been enjoying for some time without a fight. Your particular "Mission Impossible" is to change the situation without a fight. Your basic weapon will be to use as many of the fantastic five as possible to re-stack your opponent's internal computer. All right class, shall we take a look at one small example?

During World War II there was, in this country, a shortage of both workers and the gasoline necessary to transport them to their jobs. To overcome this problem a manufacturing company started providing buses to take its employees to and from work. This free service worked well and served a good purpose. Some twenty-five years later that freebie really wasn't all that necessary. Enter, from stage right, the intrepid new Personnel Manager. One look at the bus arrangement caused most of his remaining hair to fall out. Lurking there in the shadows of this ancient "good deed" were many wasted dollars and, more important, a huge mountain of legal liability. Every time one of those old buses hit the road on one of its forty to

LIFE'S DATA STACKERS

sixty mile round trips, the Company was wide open to lawsuits arising from a bus accident. In any one accident thirty or forty people could be injured or killed. It would not take much of a lawyer to prove it all "arose in and out of the course of their employment". OK, but how do they get rid of this twenty-five-year past practice?

Well, first they began to stack the union committee's internal computers with the idea that the program was no longer necessary. After some time had passed, they advised the union that due to the low ridership, the Company was cutting the number of buses from two to one. There was no big objection since the riders would still have a bus ride home - although it would now take a little bit longer. Having unilaterally dropped a bus, and without union objection, the Company had established its own past practice. Some months later, after the number of riders had declined even further, the last bus was dropped. There was no big hoohah or problem - the data stacking was successful. It may have taken a year to accomplish the change, but that's not all bad considering it got rid of a twenty-five year old past practice.

As a last note on credibility, let me tell you about how one company ruined a troublesome union president's image within his own organization. This union official had become a constant irritant to management due to his endless and senseless agitation He repeatedly filed frivolous complaints and arbitrations. It seemed that this was how the union president

IMPROVING LABOR (PEOPLE) RELATIONS

endeavored to convince his membership that he was doing a good job for them. Remember, union presidents are political animals and are always looking for votes.

To deal with the problem the Labor Relations Manager devised a simple scheme based on his awareness of the fact that most people desire to know any kind of confidential information - especially if it's none of their business! The Company had a supervisory news letter that was supposed to be extremely confidential. It was so-labeled in big letters on the front and supervisors were instructed not to discuss the contents with anyone outside of its approved circulation.

The Industrial Relations Manager began writing very blunt and derogatory comments about the union president's inept handling of complaints and his responsibility for riling the Company. Supervisors were told they just might leave their copy of the newsletter on their desk top. When they walked out of the office, someone was sure to sneak in and read all this good "secret" stuff. It wasn't too long before the union members, having had their data stacked, began giving the president a bad time about his self-serving instigations. As a result, the union president became much less adversarial.

THERE ARE GOOD AND BAD SUPERVISORS

Those who are new to the work force, never having had to deal with a boss, enter the arena with their internal computers relatively uncorrupted, expecting to encounter at least reasonably

LIFE'S DATA STACKERS

competent supervision (unless, of course, they've watched a little too much television and have bought into some of the weird characterizations found in that and other entertainment media). With little or no training in how to recognize and deal with various management incompetencies, and with no valid previous data for comparison, they are often doomed to suffer the consequences of organizations' tendencies to ignore, tolerate, or even encourage managerial failings. Often they will even end-up emulating the dysfunctional examples of leadership they've served under.

This is just one of the prices that an organization will pay for failing to recognize, and either correct or eliminate incompetent supervisors. What? You can't imagine that any group would ever tolerate or encourage lousy management? Think again my bewildered friend! American corporations are full of incompetents that have been promoted to and allowed to remain in high levels of authority. As one management consultant put it, in describing a particularly terrible leader he'd encountered, "that plant manager is so ignorant of good management practice, that he has no idea he's doing anything wrong". Naturally, being ignorant of his own incompetence, that particular plant manager made it clear that he expected all of his subordinate supervisors to follow his example – and some of them probably did.

There are far too many misfits who are allowed to implement and promote bad practices in today's business world.

276

IMPROVING LABOR (PEOPLE) RELATIONS

In union shops this leads to grievances, slow downs, strikes, and general dissatisfaction, and in non-union operations it may encourage employees to organize. At the very least it will depress productivity and damage morale. Even more disastrous results often result in volunteer organizations where the participants are free to walk away whenever they wish.

While this chapter is not intended to be a comprehensive guide to abstaining from being or emulating bad managers, perhaps a few examples of the good, the bad and the ugly might be of interest. Note how the human relations principles come into play and bear in mind that each of the following individuals had their data stacked over many years. Also be alert to see how they, in turn, poured either good data or bad into others. This transfer of "data" did not necessarily require any intentional effort. It was accomplished simply by providing an example through words, actions, and lack of action. These "exemplary" leaders were all "data stackers" just as you are – and as your boss is - whether you like it or not. An awareness of this fact may encourage you to be more careful in what you learn from your supervisor's example and teach through your own.

An alleged manager or leader, who is reluctant to make decisions and fails to take action when necessary, can be one of the worst types of leaders to deal with. A bad manager that does take action is at least predictable and can be guarded against. With the "wimp" you never know which way he will go – if any. He is just full of surprises - most of them bad. I knew a Shipping

LIFE'S DATA STACKERS

Department Superintendent who fit that description. Through the years his incompetence led him to make a multitude of bad decisions that incurred the wrath of his various bosses. As a defense mechanism, he finally decided the best way to avoid getting into trouble was to make NO decisions. This phenomenon is more common than you may think. A poor manager who makes bad decisions will inevitably be chastised by his superiors. This in turn leads to kind of a "hide in the closet and pull a blanket over my head" syndrome. This fellow really fits the "see no evil, speak no evil, and hear no evil" personality. As you may imagine, in his area of responsibility, the inmates ran the asylum as he lets almost anyone make decisions in the leadership void he's created.

Then there's the steel mill melt shop foreman who stands as another "glowing" example of a "wimp" manager. Anyone who has gone from an hourly to a supervisory position will tell you that one of the hardest things to overcome is the changed relationship between themselves and their "buddies" on the old crew. A line is crossed, but some do not realize it. The melt shop foreman thought he was still "one of the boys" and assumed he could socialize and act as he had in the past. He never learned that a supervisor must not just be "a pal", but must also critique and discipline. (The same thing many parents fail to learn when dealing with their children.) The foreman neglected his family, piled up debts, his wages were garnisheed, and he filed for bankruptcy. As a "reward", to himself, he took frequent

IMPROVING LABOR (PEOPLE) RELATIONS

gambling trips to Las Vegas - because he "deserved a little fun". He would regale his crew with tales of his lack of responsibility while shirking his duties as a boss. This particular foreman did not remain a supervisor, however. Unfortunately, it took his replacement considerable time to unstack the crew's collective computers and regain a reasonable degree of discipline. The data stacker (supervisor, parent etc.) must set an example, not follow the crowd!

In situations such as those described above, it becomes almost mandatory that people of this type either be shaped up or shipped out. To do otherwise will cause the employees to lose all respect for higher management and will create unending problems. So, you don't believe this, or think I am being too callous? May I remind you of the "fantastic five" again? With a bad supervisor of this type, or any other mis-manager, you will see at least three of the five senses put into daily operation. People SEE body language, actions, and written communications. They HEAR verbal orders and commentary. They feel the TOUCH of a harassing hand, the boot in the rear or a threatening grasp. In some cases they may also SMELL anything from bad breath to burned toast, or in a food establishment, TASTE poorly prepared or rotten food. It is so easy to put "garbage" in, it is no wonder we get so much "garbage" out.

In contrast, the same plant that had the disastrous melt shop foreman had one of the best production supervisors I have

LIFE'S DATA STACKERS

ever met. On the job he seemed all business and was known to be quite strict. Even the way he walked around the plant emanated confidence and authority. He did not hesitate to discipline those who went astray. But guess what? This superintendent was the best liked, respected and effective boss on the property. Why? Above all else, he was PREDICTABLE AND FAIR. The men knew what to expect. His treatment, although tough, was fair, honest, and consistent. Being one of the gang was not his style, but he was ready to listen when someone had a personal problem or needed advice on how to do a job. Here was a tough no nonsense man who did the job right.

The respect that this production supervisor's subordinates had for him was well illustrated during a union grievance meeting: After long hours of argument, the supervisor was brought in to tell what had happened. When he finished telling his story the union president said - "if Sven says it's so, we believe him" - and the grievance was immediately dropped. A great testimonial.

If you are a student of management you might also want to check into and consider how Herb Kelleher ran Southwest Airlines. On the surface, his approach to management may seem far different from that of Sven, mentioned above, but was no less effective. Kelleher appears to be a gregarious fun loving individual who treats employees and customers as friends. However, unlike the melt shop foreman, Kelleher's fun and games are aimed at turning a profit and never amount to

IMPROVING LABOR (PEOPLE) RELATIONS

irresponsible goofing off. Although 84% of the Southwest Airline staff is unionized, there is good productivity and seldom any trouble. More managers should learn Kelleher's secret. "My parents instilled in me the idea that everybody should be treated with dignity and respect, and that titles, traditions, status and class didn't matter". What? Give recognition to people and treat them like decent human beings? What? Use effective communications techniques? What will they think of next? It takes so little to do it right, and yet so many do it so wrong.

All really good supervisors share certain positive attributes. First and foremost, whether "tough" or fun loving, they are consistent in their actions. Second, they are not afraid to communicate fully and often. Third, they treat ALL of their subordinates with respect and trust. Fourth, they take every opportunity to provide recognition. By consistently applying these simple principles, they bolster their associates' egos, improve their own predictability, and teach employees to respect the Company and its management. In such an atmosphere unions are not needed. If unions are present, problems are kept to a minimum.

* Los Angeles Times Magazine (June 9, 1996)

LIFE'S DATA STACKERS

CHAPTER TEN

RESOLVING PROBLEMS AND GRIEVANCES

Rapidly deteriorating weather forced the small four-place Cessna aircraft lower and lower as it flew over the barren high desert of Nevada. Snowflakes, wind, flight instruments, and terrain vied for the pilot's attention. The plane's occupants were trying to reach a gold mine, located between two 10,000 foot mountain ranges, before darkness smothered the unlighted landing strip. On this late winter afternoon, as the pilot searched for a way through the jagged peaks, the gloomy snow-laden clouds were already engulfing the mountain tops. Unable to go above the clouds, the plane flew up winding canyons and between the towering rocks. At times it seemed as if the pinion pines would become Christmas garlands on both wing tips. Finally, the tiny craft emerged from the mountain crevices and circled over the unpaved snow-covered runway in the valley. The pilot assured his passenger that the landing in the snow would be

LIFE'S DATA STACKERS

"no problem". He said that all he had to do was hold the airplane in a slightly nose high position when the wheels touched the strip. This would overcome the extra drag caused by the snow and would slow the plane considerably before the nose wheel touched down. Well, it sounded good! However, as the propeller started digging up mud and slush, and throwing it on the windshield, the passenger (me) knew the pilot had misjudged! In the process, he shattered my carefully nurtured predictability about our chances for a safe arrival. Boy did I have an immediate great big unwanted mental grievance!

Wandering among sinister escarpments may not be the easiest time for a pilot to review past data on snow landings, but it surely would have been nice if the pilot had taken the time to do so earlier that day. Then he might have realized that his assessment of the current landing situation was based on a limited number of previous snowy landing experiences. Ones that were accomplished on snow covered PAVED RUNWAYS. That's concrete, son. Hard stuff. Not soft, water soaked, clinging, don't mess with me MUD. Ah well, at least his imperfect plan, including holding the plane's nose up as long as possible, kept us from flipping over or cart wheeling down the strip. Heck, all we had to do was clean off the windshield, tow the plane over to a nearby gravel (and more solid) road, and off the pilot flew with his internal computer firmly stacked with useful new data.

A little note here about problem solving might be in order. When presented with a problem we should always try to

RESOLVING PROBLEMS AND GRIEVANCES

understand, to the greatest extent possible, the data upon which we will base the decisions we make in attempting to solve or alleviate the problem. In other words, what information, gained through education, practical experience, or the advice of others, are we relying on? Where did the data come from and is that data still valid? Did those supplying information have their own personal agendas? Were they really experts or authorities in their field? Are all the parameters exactly the same? Not likely.

In the pilot's case, he should have done a little more mental research and asked himself if this situation duplicated the conditions in his earlier snow landings. Had he recalled the obvious fact that all his previous snow landings had been on snow-covered concrete runways, and that this was a dirt strip he was about to land on, perhaps he would have felt compelled to reevaluate and use more caution – and maybe check with other pilots having more experience with snow-covered unpaved landing strips. In a similar manner, it's essential that we be aware of such discrepancies between present and past conditions and adjust our problem-solving decisions accordingly.

Now concerning grievances: what exactly are they and what causes them? According to Webster's dictionary, a grievance is "a circumstance thought to be unjust or injurious and ground for formal complaint or resentment". However, rather than using the dictionary definition, Union contracts and employee manuals tend to provide definitions that are more vague, and that limit the definition of employee grievances to

LIFE'S DATA STACKERS

cover only situations where the organization has allegedly violated some specific contract provision. So, even if an organization has brought about some catastrophe akin to the sky falling in, if it isn't covered in the contract, the employees cannot file a grievance.

Responding to such a catastrophe by sticking one's organizational head in the snow covered sandy dung pile, just because it doesn't fit the contract definition of a grievance, is no way to maintain good employee morale. The employees may not have a contractual right to file grievances in such situations, but you can be sure their memory banks will remember the fact that the company ignored their complaints. This becomes adverse data when they contemplate future organizational requests and actions.

All of us would-be human beings have grievances. If they're not about the job, they're about the kids, or the neighbors, or your spouse, or - you name it. But what is it that causes a person to feel that a thing is unjust? As it turns out, the real anatomy of a grievance is quite simple: Each person continuously makes predictions (or guesses) about what he or she hopes, expects, or thinks will happen right now or sometime in the future. The time line for fulfillment of these predictions may be as short as a minute, or as much as a week, a month, or even several years. When the time arrives that a person's prediction is supposed to come true but something different from the person's prediction happens, that person develops an individual conflict

RESOLVING PROBLEMS AND GRIEVANCES

situation, or a grievance. The feeling is roughly the same as when your check book shows you have $1000 in your bank account, but the bank statement says you are $500 overdrawn. Unless you are a de-constructionist, you will realize that these two pieces of data do not reconcile themselves. One or the other, or both, must be wrong.

When a conflict develops, it becomes necessary to determine the facts relating to that conflict. As I noted earlier, each of the predictions a person makes is based on the totality of that person's prior data. There are no mistakes in the computation. Consequently, the person feels his or her ability to make predictions is 100% correct – which would be objectively true if the person were operating on 100% correct data. Unfortunately, no one has 100% correct data about anything and, consequently, will always have some degree of incorrectness in their predictions.

Let us call the thing we predict "X" and what actually happens "Y". Using this shorthand we can say a grievance is an "X-Y" situation. The greater the difference between "X" and "Y", the more serious the grievance. Now it's time for me to stick my neck way out and state MY view on what causes grievances: ALL GRIEVANCES RESULT FROM A BREAKDOWN IN PREDICTABILITY!! Already I can hear thousands of academics and labor relations types screaming. "It can't be so, it's too narrow. It can't begin to encompass all the possible motivations behind grievances!" But it does. When a plant worker doesn't get

LIFE'S DATA STACKERS

an expected overtime assignment, a day off, or a pay increase; a parent's offspring fails to return home on time; dad is late for dinner, or when guests arrive on the wrong day - all these unexpected occurrences cause grievances.

Obviously, some problems are more serious than others, but the size of a grievance that an individual develops is roughly proportional to the extent of the difference between what the person predicted and what really happened (keep this in mind when we discuss how to resolve grievances). As for the "experts" who find my view too narrow, I have yet to have any of them describe a situation that doesn't fit within it.

Undoubtedly the most influential factor in creating breakdowns in predictability leading to grievances is poor communications. Remember? Contrary to popular corporate assumptions, not everyone gets the word! You can easily resolve many disputes and complaints by simply providing the necessary information. In an ideal world, good communication occurs before decisions are made and before trouble can start. In the real world the opposite is too often the case.

You'll find that you can solve most grievances by following three simple rules. However, before discussing these three rules it is important for you to know that, while you're in the process of following these three rules, you keep your "Mickey Mouse" ears on and listen very very carefully!!

RULE #1 - Find out what happened

RESOLVING PROBLEMS AND GRIEVANCES

Most of the time the person with the grievance will readily complain about what happened and tell you all about it. Sometimes, however, there will be other events that have occurred, perhaps years ago, which created additional problems that exacerbate the current situation. You may have to ask a lot of direct questions to uncover these other problems. There may be only one or two things or there may be ten or fifteen. Try to learn about everything that has happened to the person in the days preceding the filing of the grievance. Acknowledge each event and then ask if there are any other problems the person would like to bring up. Continue in this manner until the litany is complete. Then you must determine to resolve each issue separately, starting with the most recent and working backwards.

RULE #2 - Find out what the person *expected* to have happened

For each item you uncovered using Rule #1, find out what the individual thought, or hoped, was going to happen. Listen very carefully not only to what the person says, but to how they say it. Watch for little hesitations or minor remarks that may betray the real problem.

RULE #3 – Try to learn the reason for the difference

Once you've assessed the difference between what happened and what was expected to happen, it's time to encourage the alleged victim to try to think of the reasons why events turned out contrary to his or her expectations. Do NOT

LIFE'S DATA STACKERS

provide YOUR opinion as to why - it must all come from the person with the complaint.

Because of the way that information and experience are cross-indexed and filed in a person's memory banks, grievances are stored in a person's brain in a manner much like a chain, in that dragging up one grievance may drag up a lot more. What you're trying to do when you're resolving grievances is to get those irritations and frustrations to discharge from the person's mind. Often merely asking the person what he or she thought was going to happen will force the person to consider both sides of the problem in their mental computer. Since the conflicting data does not easily reconcile itself, the person will likely become frustrated. On occasion, before the grieved party will reach the point of irritation, you may have to go a little farther and ask him or her to explain the difference between the actual and the expected. Once the grieved individual becomes agitated, continue asking for explanations until the real answer tumbles out and the person no longer appears to be irritated or upset. One at a time, discuss the litany of problems you learned about using rule number one. Work your way down through the entire list, bearing in mind that your first question will normally only elicit less important third or fourth level grievances. People tend to be too emotional about their major problems to discuss them rationally at first.

As a final check to make sure you've bled off all the irritations, after your subject appears to have gotten past the

RESOLVING PROBLEMS AND GRIEVANCES

irritation stage, ask how he or she now feels about the situation. If there's any irritation left, you'll soon find out about it. Handle additional problems as further X-Y situations. You will be surprised, however, how often the above technique, on its own, will resolve an individual's grievances.

Obviously in a situation where a person has, in fact, been treated unjustly or unfairly, something must be done to correct the problem. The above techniques will certainly not repair an inequitable situation. Correcting such a problem may be beyond your power, but just taking the time to really listen will often make the person feel better. In cases like Ted Bailey's, past actions could not be changed, but reviewing them and understanding the reason for the conflicts, made it possible to alter the future. Some real life examples may make it easier to understand how it all works:

So there we were in a grimy steel mill lunch room. Particles of graphite (by-products of the steel making process) made a dark slippery coating on the chairs and tables - and the men. The purpose of the visit was to encourage contributions to the local United Fund campaign. The sweaty bunch before me had made it quite clear that they wanted nothing to do with the United Fund. It seems that their "leader" had a grievance. A somewhat shortened and simplified version of the dialogue between me (GDJ) and their leader (AL) went something like this:

LIFE'S DATA STACKERS

GDJ: Al, why don't you want to contribute to the United Fund campaign? Your union is one of its chief supporters.

Al: I won't contribute a penny when I know that some of my money will go to the Red Cross!

GDJ: Well Al, is there any other reason you would not contribute? (Was this his only gripe?)

Al: No, the Red Cross is the only organization I don't like. I would not want my money to go to them.

GDJ: Tell me Al, what happened to make you dislike the Red Cross? (Rule #1)

Al: During the big flood a couple of years ago my house was under water. The Red Cross gave me some money, but later they came around and wanted it back. Said they would take me to court if I didn't pay.

GDJ: I see, you thought the money was a gift, (X) but it turned out to be only a loan? (Y)

Al: Yeah, those S.O.B.s!!

GDJ: Al, can you think of any reason why they made it a loan instead of a gift? (Rule #3)

Al: Sure they just wanted to make a lot of money on the interest they charged me!

GDJ: What was the interest rate? Was it higher or lower than what you would have paid somewhere else?

Al: Well, it was pretty low - not much at all really.

GDJ: Do you really think they would make much money with that low interest rate?

RESOLVING PROBLEMS AND GRIEVANCES

Al: No, I guess not. (Now we have gotten rid of the profit motive- but wait)

GDJ: Al, was there anything else that bothered you about that loan? (Find the underlying problem)

Al: I think it should have been a gift. We were really broke at the time.

GDJ: Why do you think they did not make it a gift?

Al: I suppose what with all the disasters all over the country they couldn't very well give money away to everyone. (This response came after several less reasonable guesses.)

GDJ: Right, and if they had no money who would pay the people who came to help, or for the blankets and other supplies they did provide free of charge? (Input some new data)

Al: You know, I never thought of it that way.

GDJ: Al, do you have any other problems with the Red Cross? (Check again for other hassles)

Al: No, I can see they were just doing the job the best way they could.

GDJ: How about that United Fund contribution?

Al: Sure, me and the boys will sign up for the payroll deduction program.

The actual discussion in this case took about fifteen or twenty minutes and involved many more questions and answers. Hopefully, you see how it works in this shortened version - as they say on TV, edited for your home viewing. You'll want to

LIFE'S DATA STACKERS

use your imagination and ingenuity to figure out ways to ask those three basic questions.

What happened?

What did you expect to happen?

Can you think of any reason for the difference?

It's best, however, to avoid using these exact same phrases over and over again. If you do, they may sound like some "canned" program.

Often you'll know ahead of time what the answer to the "what happened" question. And often the "victim" will tell you without any prompting on your part. You may also get the answer to the Rule #2 question without having to ask. So much the better. In that case, go directly to Rule #3.

HOW TO LOSE (ALMOST) A MILLION DOLLARS

Unpredictability, despite its tendency to cause grievances, can, admittedly, be a desirable attribute in some situations – but rarely without tremendous risk. That gold mine I mentioned earlier was located in a desolate area. Roads, seemingly absent of any traffic, vanished into the distance. The silence was complete except for the soft whisper of the wind through the sagebrush and cactus needles. Down on the alkali flats near the mine, dust devils, those silent white tornados, swayed up the valley. Other than your own heart beat, there was little to hear. Through an

294

RESOLVING PROBLEMS AND GRIEVANCES

area like this the mining company had to ship millions of dollars worth of gold to distant Reno. In this empty landscape, a modern version of the old West's stage coach robbers was a real possibility.

To avoid that risk, management took-on another, seemingly more acceptable, form of risk: the risk of being unpredictable. Instead of shipping out the gold by truck on a regular schedule, whenever a shipment was ready, the management would secretly arrange for a small aircraft to fly in and land on the road next to the mine office. In five minutes the gold would be loaded aboard and the plane sent on its way back to Reno. This random, unscheduled approach of course required a little extra logistical planning since, for each shipment, an armored truck would also have to be separately scheduled to meet the plane, take the gold, and safely transport the gold to its ultimate destination. Instead of being on a regular schedule of pick-ups and deliveries, like the airplane, the armored truck had to be separately arranged for with each gold shipment. Only the mine Superintendent knew when the plane would arrive and, therefore, approximately when it would depart and return to Reno, and when an armored truck would need to be at the Reno airport to meet the plane. It all worked out very well - most of the time.

There was, of course, that one occasion when it almost went very wrong – when risk of being intentionally unpredictable almost caught up with management. The plane came in right on

LIFE'S DATA STACKERS

time, nearly a million dollars in gold bars were loaded aboard, and the plane returned safely to its base in Reno. That's when the pilot learned that someone had screwed up. After landing, the pilot taxied the plane over to the dark parking area near a deserted hanger where the armored truck was supposed to be waiting. The pilot's prediction - that he would make a quick exchange and head on home for dinner – turned out to be significantly different than reality and dissolved into (guess what?) a grievance. Of course the unpredictable happened – or, in this case, the predictable result of being so unpredictable: The armored truck failed to show up! The result? Frustration! Anger! Since there was no one there to take him through "the three steps" and resolve his grievance, the pilot locked the flimsy door on the aircraft and departed for home. Right! There, in one of the country's largest gambling cities, filled with people desperate for a stake, he left a million dollars in gold sitting out on a lonely remote ramp. The gold remained there, unattended, all night. Luck and closely guarded secret shipping schedules were the only deterrents to an easy theft.

The pilot may have had a legitimate grievance against management, either for failing to schedule the armored truck or for not planning for this contingency. But instead of seeking further guidance or otherwise arranging to properly secure the gold shipment, the pilot retaliated by essentially abandoning his precious cargo – a grossly negligent act to say the least. This, of course, gave management a legitimate grievance against the

RESOLVING PROBLEMS AND GRIEVANCES

pilot, and cost the pilot his job. Isn't it amazing how these things can snowball? What questions would YOU have asked the pilot if you were the mine manager and the pilot had called you from the Reno airport with his grievance? What would you have asked the mine manager in an effort to resolve his grievance against the pilot?

LATE TO WORK

Far more common than gross negligence on the job is tardiness. Picture, if you will, good old John Doe, looking somewhat wild-eyed and angry, hurtling through the office door an hour late. Between unprintable expletives he complains to his boss how this offense is not his fault. (Of course) It's that bunch of miserable traffic cops on the freeway. They're out to get innocent commuters like him instead of chasing real criminals! Shall we take a closer look at a shortened version of this little debacle?

Are the cops the real culprits? Is the traffic stop the REAL reason for John Doe's anger? Will the answer be found before John loses his job? Can we get John to reveal the underlying truth? Time for questions and answers. The first question, following rule #1, was already taken care of when John voiced his self-serving explanation to his boss. A simple little tale about his making an illegal U-turn to get out of unusually heavy traffic. Now the boss can go directly to discovering what it was that John had expected to happen:

LIFE'S DATA STACKERS

Q. John, it's too bad you got a ticket, but what did you expect to happen?

A. I've been taking that little shortcut every morning without the cops stopping me. They should have let me go the same way today.

Q. Why do you suppose this morning was different?

A. I guess it was because of the unusually heavy traffic today. (This after several other reasons)

Q. How do you feel about the cops now?

A. Oh I guess they were just doing their job - but darn it, I never expected the traffic to be so heavy. It loused up my commuting schedule. (Oh Oh, new grievance)

Q. John, I gather that you expected the traffic to be lighter. How can the extra cars be explained?

A. I don't know. It was almost twice as heavy.

Q. John, did you leave home at your usual time? (help John see other possible reasons)

A. No, I was about a half hour later than usual, but I expected the traffic to be about the same.

Q. What reason can you think of for the extra cars?

A. Apparently I hit the freeway during the worst time. When I leave earlier I don't have the problem. (John really knew the answer all along - but he had another complaint.)

Q. When you left home a half hour late, did you really expect to have no problem?

RESOLVING PROBLEMS AND GRIEVANCES

A. Not really, but damn it, I wouldn't have been late if my wife hadn't forgotten it was her turn to take the kids to day care. (Ah ha! Now we are getting closer to the *real* problem)

At this point we will exercise a little discretion and NOT delve into John's complicated domestic problems, although John obviously needs to give them some serious thought. There may be far more than a day care problem involved. The problem also might include disagreements over whether Mrs. Doe should stay at home with the rug rats. Again, it may go all the way back to something that happened before they were married. Ah yes, we can all imagine the many self-serving campaign promises made by both parties.

What I've attempted to illustrate here is how John initially talked only about a low-level complaint - one that he may have really believed was the basis of his grievance. Each complaint or issue had to be addressed before moving on to the next level. Eventually they reached the highest level - the point where it became increasingly clear that his major problems were of a domestic nature; between him and his wife - problems that were much too serious and full of emotion for him to talk about early in the discussion. In fact, he may very well have been unaware of these underlying causes of his anger. He had to be led through a whole series of excuses and less important matters before getting close to the real reasons for his unhappiness. This

LIFE'S DATA STACKERS

type of "investigation" can take considerable time, but with a valuable employee, or a loved one, it's worthwhile.

Oh dear, in all the "excitement" we seem to have forgotten someone: John Doe's boss! Would one of you good people please volunteer to resolve HIS grievance? It seems he has an employee with a very bad record for being late and/or absent.

Another example of a problem caused by poor predictability is a situation that has become much too common lately involving the use of *au pairs* ("nannies" to those of you from Rio Linda). Those of you who aren't wealthy enough to take advantage of this program may need a little up-front explanation. In families where both parents work outside the home, the parents must address the problem of child care. Heaven forbid that one parent should stay home with the little ankle biters. Just because one partner earns over $250,000 a year, that's no excuse for the other to stay home and actually spend time raising the human beings they have brought into the world. After all, the other member of the team can earn another $250,000 - and everyone(?) knows you can't possibly support a decent style of living on anything less than $500,000. Right? So, if your income is sufficiently high, you might consider engaging the services of an au pair. The term au pair has its origins in France and is defined by Webster's Dictionary as follows: "designating, of, or in an arrangement in which services are exchanged on an even basis/an au pair girl who helped with the

RESOLVING PROBLEMS AND GRIEVANCES

housework in return for room and board". That may be the definition, but too often is not how the program is "sold" to unsuspecting young women from other countries. The recruiter's pitch is more along the lines of "an opportunity to enjoy a cultural exchange, to travel in the United States, to live with an American family and actually receive pay, room, and board for only a few hours of work!" The rude awakening comes shortly after arrival. Quite often the ugly reality is that the poor girl becomes some sort of domestic "slave" for those upwardly mobile parents. Unending babysitting and the bulk if not all of the housework may be dumped into her inexperienced hands. Now, these young ladies obviously have a very legitimate reason to complain. If we were to use our X-Y technique for assessing the basis of grievances, it would not take long to reach a complete understanding of the grievance of an au pair in this situation. Too bad we cannot solve the problem for them! This is the type of situation where one can only listen with sympathy unless there's some way to intercede and improve their situation or even help get them back home. The point is, the X-Y technique can lead to resolving many grievances by getting people to reexamine their actions. However, when a person has truly been unfairly treated etc. then the problem can only be solved by addressing and resolving the actual cause of the inequity.

LIFE'S DATA STACKERS

LEROY

Now it's time to return to a really down-to-earth true life situation, or, The Case of the Contrary Steelworker:

> There once was a guy named Leroy.
> A confused fellow he was, hoo boy!
> Suspicious and sneaky in his work,
> The Company considered him a total jerk.
> He stuck his nose in where it didn't belong,
> And filed his grievances all day long.

Sure the "poetry" is miserable, but so was Leroy. Long and lanky, wearing dirty work clothes, he would wander about the plant asking questions and avoiding work. The chip on his shoulder was exceeded only by his know-it-all and suspicious attitude. He sucked up information and rumors like an indiscriminate overpowered Hoover vacuum. No cause was too small, no rumor too wild or challenge too great for this dusty knight of the scrap yard. Every time we in management turned around, there was good old Leroy with yet another complaint. In his view, someone was always picking on him, screwing up his work assignment, or cheating him on his paycheck.

Being "unselfish", whenever he was unable to dream up a personal problem, he would generously volunteer to champion someone else's complaint. His litany of problems was unending. Management personnel wasted hour after hour listening to his recitations and even more hours rehashing them in union

302

RESOLVING PROBLEMS AND GRIEVANCES

grievance meetings. When one problem was resolved, Leroy would be in with another. This went on for several years.

Finally, armed with the X-Y theory of resolving grievances, I invited Leroy into my office for a little "heart to heart" talk. The session lasted most of the afternoon, but I'll condense it down to the essentials.

This case will illustrate the manner in which many people create an anchor chain of events that cause them untold misery - an anchor chain that weighs them down without mercy as they forge one heavy link (bad situation) onto another. The victim, swinging on the end of the chain, generally has no idea where the first link is attached. As a data "unstacker", it is your job to find the first link and break it free.

At the time of our discussion, Leroy was on temporary assignment in the Melt Shop. This is the part of a steel mill where the steel melting furnaces are found. Smoke, noise, heat, and molten metal combine to make it a place of danger for the careless or unwary. For protection, the men working there wear wool or aluminized asbestos clothing topped off with broad brimmed white hard hats. Leroy's normal job was in the Shipping Department, where he wore a smaller red hard hat. However, due to layoffs, he had been bumped back into the Yard Department. This was an area from which laborers were drawn, as required, to fill vacancies in other departments. It was sort of a labor pool. At the time in question, Leroy had been sent to work in the Melt Shop. So what was Leroy's complaint this time??? As it turned

LIFE'S DATA STACKERS

out, he was incensed over the fact that when he was assigned to the Melt Shop he was told to take off his small red hard hat and put on a broad brimmed white hat. That caused Leroy to become quite upset since he wanted to continue wearing his own (security blanket) red hat. Gee, that sounds pretty terrible doesn't it? I warned you - no cause was too small for our dubious hero.

As inconsequential as the "hat issue" may seem, it was the place to start. Remember, a person will usually start with a minor complaint rather than something really serious. Their major hassle would create too much emotional turmoil, or in some cases the complaining "victim" might not even be aware of the real underlying difficulty. You have to start with the small and patiently work your way to the individual's major hang-up.

The first step was to find out what had happened. Leroy readily told me how he had reported to the Melt Shop and was immediately told to take off his small red hat and put on the broad brimmed white hat. Despite his protests and arguments, the foreman insisted he change hats. It is unfortunate that the foreman did not bother telling him the basic and perfectly sound reasons for his order. (More on that later.) Poor communication strikes again - and negative assumptions filled the gap.

The second step was to decide what Leroy had expected to happen on this assignment. He told me he had assumed he could probably wear his usual red hat - one that was comfortable

RESOLVING PROBLEMS AND GRIEVANCES

and lighter in weight. You see, Leroy had made a prediction based on previous experience. When he took assignments in any other department, he was allowed to keep his trusty, if filthy, red cap. Now, absent any communication to the contrary, he had reason to think he could do the same in the Melt Shop.

Time for step three. "Leroy", I asked, "can you think of any reason why the Melt Shop foreman insisted on you wearing the white hat"? It took some mumbling guesses and a few more questions before he could come up with the correct answer. I had asked him what happened when molten metal splashed out of a ladle. He knew, and acknowledged that the wide brims were to keep the metal from running down his neck. Then I asked him if it was hard for the crane operators, in their lofty perches, to see the men on the floor through all the smoke. He had to admit that in the dense murky atmosphere, the white hat was much more visible to the crane operators. When molten metal is being transported and poured, incandescent mercury-like splashes spray in unpredictable directions. Good visibility, and a hat that keeps hot metal off your neck, are life savers! The foreman knew the reasons and should have reminded Leroy of them. I knew the reasons as well, but it was important that I wait for Leroy to realize and voice them. Each person must be allowed to find the reasons on his own, or he will be unlikely to make the correct decision about what is right or reasonable under the circumstances. We cannot and should not try to make such decisions for others.

LIFE'S DATA STACKERS

The final step was to ask Leroy how he now felt about wearing a white hat. Reluctantly he admitted it was the best thing to do, but very quickly exclaimed that the real problem was that the Melt Shop supervisors didn't like having Shipping Department people working there. Oh, oh, here we go again - down to the next level.

Again, step one. " Leroy, what happened"? "Why do you feel that way"? Well, there were a multitude of reasons. The foremen seemed belligerent and the newcomers got all the low level grunt work. Leroy felt the newcomers were being assigned to all the dirty hot jobs. They had to wear long heavy and hot wool coats. What had he expected? He had hoped for some of the easier jobs, ones with some relief time. He wanted to do without the wool coats. In searching for a reason for this seemingly unfair situation, Leroy came up with only one simple answer (the wrong one). He felt the Shipping Department men were hated because they had displaced some regular Melt Shop employees.

As you may well imagine, once this mental attitude took hold, almost anything the Melt Shop people did or said would be taken the wrong way. Leroy predicted antagonism, so his little pea-picking brain found it everywhere. In his mind, this animosity was the cause for his receiving undesirable job assignments.

Since our "hero" couldn't get it right on his own, it was necessary to ask a couple of simple questions: "Leroy, do you expect the foremen to follow the provisions of the union

306

RESOLVING PROBLEMS AND GRIEVANCES

contract"? Of course he did - that was a mantra with him. "Should the foremen assign the jobs following the seniority clause"? Absolutely! He would have really screamed if someone did otherwise. "Did the foremen assign your jobs in accordance with the seniority clause"? They had. Finally, "doesn't the wool coat prevent your clothing from going up in flames if you are hit by a metal splash"? Leroy had to admit that they had done it all properly according to contract, and the coats did serve a very useful purpose. So one more question. "Now that you know the work was assigned fairly and in accordance with the contract, how do you feel about the Melt Shop people"? Leroy allowed that maybe they really were human beings and doing a good job. Then he looked down at the floor, gripped his cap in his hands, and exclaimed with emotion "Sven has always had it in for me!"

At last we were getting close to the real problem. Another thing you want to notice is that we have now gone from the general to the personal. Leroy started talking about how all of his co-workers were having problems, and he was simply speaking for all of them. Now, at last, we were going to talk about HIS problem.

It is always easier to talk about "them" than it is to speak about "me". People who always talk about what "other people" want or do, usually are expressing their own opinions. They do so for one of two reasons. They are either too emotional about the subject, or are afraid to express their own opinions.

LIFE'S DATA STACKERS

(Well all right, there IS a third reason for pretending to speak for others. The practice is most commonly found among a rather disgusting breed of double tongued, finger-crossed political vultures. These creatures constantly tell us what "the people" want so the vultures can justify their own self-serving spending programs - programs designed to wrest votes from the unwary or unconcerned. They are simply liars who dare not tell the truth.)

With his outburst Leroy finally began to voice his own deep-rooted personal hang-up. The "bogeyman" in his life was a man named Sven. Who was this horrible monster that caused poor Leroy so much mental anguish? In my opinion, he was probably one of the best supervisors I have ever run across. Totally honest, always consistent, dependable, clear in his communications and always fair in his dealings with his subordinates. Besides all these wonderful virtues, he also achieved high production at the lowest possible cost. At first it seemed inconceivable that Sven, of all people, could be the monster in Leroy's life. Of course that was MY perception, but obviously, not Leroy's. Time for those three questions again: What happened? What did he expect (or predict) to happen? Can you think of a reason for the difference? Again, I will shorten the many questions and answers down to the basics.

What had happened was that several years before, Leroy had received a disciplinary slip from Sven. According to Leroy it

RESOLVING PROBLEMS AND GRIEVANCES

was completely undeserved and proved that Sven was out to get him. Of course, since Leroy was perfectly innocent, he had not expected to be disciplined. At this point there was considerable discussion about the details of what had happened. It turned out that Sven had relied upon the testimony of a foreman and had in fact disciplined Leroy. To verify the story, I pulled Leroy's personnel file. There was no disciplinary slip. I showed this to him and asked why there was no slip in the file. Time for more discussion. "Leroy, did you go to Sven and complain about what you thought was unfair treatment"? Yes, he had. "Well, what happened? What did Sven do"? Leroy then had to admit that Sven had done a more thorough investigation and had subsequently torn up the disciplinary slip - therefore no slip in the file. "Leroy, if there is nothing against you in the file, and you say Sven tore up the slip, did you really get disciplined"? The answer was obvious, but Leroy had been so upset when the incident took place his mind apparently shut out the fact that Sven had corrected the mistake. Now, in my office he admitted that Sven had done the right thing in rechecking the facts. "Leroy, are there any other reasons why you think Sven has it in for you"? "No" "Do you still think Sven is unfair"? "No, I guess not".

I cannot help but feel that Leroy was as happy as I was to get this situation cleared up. He left my office in a good mood and a smile on his face. From then on he seemed to feel better about himself, his job, and Sven. Even his fellow workers

LIFE'S DATA STACKERS

noticed his more open and friendly attitude. The Company noticed a considerable reduction in grievances.

Recognizing the time and effort required by in-depth personal counseling, most organizations try to find ways to keep the problems from arising in the first place. In previous chapters we have already gone over some important rules for dealing in a reasonable and fair manner with others. All of these are important and will generally keep most complaints down to a dull roar. However, when a person perceives that they have suffered some kind of injustice, they search for a means to be heard and to have the inequity adjusted. The systems for resolving problems go by many names but most commonly they are referred to as a grievance or complaint system. The mechanisms are fairly standard whether in a union contract, an employee manual, or even a church policy statement. There are usually several meetings during which the complainant can discuss the situation with increasingly higher levels of management. These systems are as good as the people who operate them, and when operated in good faith, can be reasonably effective. Rather than bore you with the routine everyday methods, let me tell you about a different kind of procedure that incorporates many good human relations techniques.

RESOLVING PROBLEMS AND GRIEVANCES

A NEW SYSTEM FOR HANDLING COMPLAINTS

Picture, if you will, a pickup truck parked on a barren rocky slope. Nearby lie boring tools and other equipment used to take mineral samples from the remote mountainside. Nothing is happening. It's close to midnight. The freezing wind shrills incessantly around the truck. The truck's heater cannot completely overcome the intense cold, so the two occupants huddle close together for warmth. It is a man and a woman. The steamed up windows attest to their ability to maintain a satisfactory level of body heat, despite the frigid conditions.

The folks in the truck might applaud the side benefits from an equal employment opportunity policy, but their supervisor had a much different opinion. Work they were NOT doing was essential to the next day's production, and their little escapade would cost the Company thousands of dollars in lost time. This was not their first offense, but it was the last - they were fired. In most industrial settings this would result in a filing of a grievance protesting the discharge. A union representative might help them with the case and claim all sorts of extenuating circumstances. Eventually arbitration would follow. Too often the final decision would be based on sympathy, some obscure technicality, or how much the arbiter wanted to get future work from one of the parties. Like the roll of the dice in a Las Vegas crap game, the odds were usually stacked against the Company. You know how it is - the offender becomes a victim and we really shouldn't expect the culprit to be responsible for his or her

LIFE'S DATA STACKERS

own actions. However, in this organization, there was no union available to assist the fired "lovers".

Promising to provide representation to an employee is one of a union's major organizing tools. To blunt that tool, and more important, to provide a fair way to settle disputes over discharges, the corporate office developed a peer review system. This type of procedure is based upon the assumption that when you extend trust to employees, you can usually depend on them to respond in a trustworthy and responsible manner. Remember our earlier human relations rule? An action will result in an equal and similar reaction. Another basic human relations action required to make the system work is adequate and honest communications. And of course, management must be willing to accept any action of the review committee. That is one very important factor that most managements do not like. To be truly effective over a long period of time, it is necessary for management to "let go" of one of their sacred rights. The "right" to have the last word.

It was to this peer review system that our cold cuddling couple appealed. Briefly, the employee could proceed through his immediate supervisor, the department superintendent, the committee of his peers and finally Company-paid binding arbitration. The peer committee was exactly what the name implies, and included five other non-management employees chosen at random to hear the case. The department superintendent would present management's reasons for the

312

RESOLVING PROBLEMS AND GRIEVANCES

discharge. The employee, along with a co-worker, should he so desire, would present his own defense. The Personnel Manager served as moderator but had no vote. The five committee members made the final decision by secret ballot. (There are special precautions taken to insure honesty in committee selection and secrecy in voting.) Either party could then appeal the result to an arbitrator at Company expense. The "cool couple" went this route and lost. Their fellow employees decided against them.

Over several years of operation the employee review committees always did an excellent and responsible job. Decisions went both ways, but they always seemed to be correct. Communications, honesty, and consistency in actions did much to stack the work force's data banks. I am sure it contributed considerably to the mine's success in remaining union free. The payoff was overheard in a nearby restaurant. Someone asked a union organizer why he didn't go out and organize people at the mine. His response was simple but telling. "They (the employees) don't want us out there".

Some of you may think that this type of peer review isn't all that uncommon. You may have heard of peer review systems being used by a few companies, high schools, college student governments, and professional groups. In too many cases though, if not the majority, the participants get their data stacked to believe things will operate in one way, only to find it doesn't.

LIFE'S DATA STACKERS

Over and over again the implementation of peer review systems is compromised by major breakdowns in predictability.

Perhaps the most common fault in creating and implementing peer review systems is the failure to make them TRUE peer review systems. A "true" peer system is one that is not controlled or heavily influenced by a supervisory body or person. If it is, it's not able to solicit accurate or meaningful peer reviews and will fail over time.

We all have problems and complaints whether at home or at work. We would all like to have some reliable and reasonable way to resolve them. The systems and techniques vary widely and go by many names. However, they all serve to provide people with a chance to be heard and given recognition as worthwhile individuals.

When attempting to solve a person's grievance remember to use at least four of our basic rules: First, what is real is real - you must deal with the other person's perception of reality; second, every decision the person has made is, in their view, correct; third, any gap in communications will be filled by negative rumors or assumptions (how have the communications been with this person and do they have the true story?); and fourth, all grievances result from breakdowns in predictability. Applying these four basic rules will require you to ask a lot of questions with tact and patience, but it is a powerful form of communication. How you handle these situations will make a

RESOLVING PROBLEMS AND GRIEVANCES

strong statement to others as to your attitudes, principles, and integrity. It is up to you to decide if you want to create an atmosphere of trust and cooperation or one of suspicion and strife.

LIFE'S DATA STACKERS

CHAPTER ELEVEN

THOSE UNPREDICTABLE POLITICIANS - LARGE AND SMALL

Imagine, if you will, a quiet elementary school classroom in an upscale suburban community. It's located just outside a medium-sized city devoted to heavy industry. The teacher is doing what teachers have done for uncounted years: encouraging the children to participate in "show and tell" time. It's a lovely spring day outside, the birds are singing, vacation time is near and there isn't a foreboding cloud in the sky. Suddenly, into this otherwise congenial atmosphere comes a jarring note of discord. Having asked the children what their fathers did for a living, the teacher, having her data stacked to expect the usual run-of-the-mill answers, cannot believe the words coming from the mouth

LIFE'S DATA STACKERS

of the pretty little girl in the second row. "My daddy is a machine gunner".

Now *there's* a classic case of the unpredictable, the unexpected, the unforeseen - a real false teeth dropper. What restraint it must have taken for the teacher to regain her shaken composure. Asking about the children's favorite things, their vacations and what their parents do had always been useful - it enabled the children to have the experience of talking before a group and gave both teachers and class some insight into each student's life. Learning about a child's background and mental outlook also helps the teacher know how to interact and teach each student. It's also beneficial for classmates to learn more about one another. In teaching, as in any other occupation, it helps to know the data. This teacher quickly reached a conclusion that there was a whole bunch of information she needed to add to her own personal computer. But wait, could the little girl be serious? Did her answer make any sense? And most important, was it true? The answers are: yes, she was serious, yes, under the circumstances it did make sense, and lastly – yes, it was completely accurate.

So a little schoolgirl has a father who, though not in the Army, operates a machine gun. Does this have anything to do with politics, predictability, and data stacking? Absolutely! In the never-never land of crime and corruption, politicians and payoffs, citizen apathy and bureaucratic bungling, data stacking becomes essential and yet predictability perilous. You and I can easily predict where people work, can't we? Certainly we know that a bartender works in a bar, a doctor in a hospital, a pilot in an airplane, a U.S. Senator in Washington, D.C. and a machine gunner in - well uh, someplace that doesn't want any trouble - someplace like the Tumble Inn (Tumble Inn being a fictitious name to protect those concerned).

The Tumble Inn could perhaps be described as a very popular "roadhouse" which operated for years offering serious, if illegal, gambling, drinking and other divertissements (before the advent of the big Indian gambling casinos). It was located beyond the city limits of the industrial city but well within the reach of hordes of hopeful gamblers. Inside the building you could find all kinds of entertainments for your sybaritic pleasure. Completely illegal, all the dealers, equipment, girls, and booze were out in plain sight. Not so obvious to the patrons were the semi-hidden ceiling turrets and corner cubicles containing watchful armed men. The little girl's daddy was one of those men. He was, in fact, a machine gunner.

THE POLITICS OF RUNNING AN ILLEGAL OPERATION

The operators of the establishment showed no concern whatsoever about the authorities - they clearly did not expect to be raided. How could they accurately predict the ability to operate with seeming immunity for so many years? The location and activities of the establishment were well known throughout

LIFE'S DATA STACKERS

the area. Your first guess might be that they were paying hefty bribes to the local officials, since that seems to be the standard modus operandi for many criminal types. I am sure payments were made, but there were other very important considerations. The "smarter than the average bear" owners of the Tumble Inn could operate quite openly due to their political savvy - their intimate and intelligent use of their knowledge of the local political scene. Though not politicians in the sense of seeking elected office themselves, they were political enough to know how the various law enforcement agencies and elected officials had **their** data stacked, and how to keep their data stacked in a manner most favorable to the Tumble Inn operation. The Tumble Inn proprietors relied on predictable persons such as dishonest underpaid law officers, vote hungry office holders, and also on the usual turf battles among governmental departments.

The elected officials in the nearby city rationalized their lack of action with the excuse that the Inn was beyond the city limits and, besides, their constituents liked to gamble and would be unhappy if the Inn were shut down. Sounds like a predictable response, especially since the Tumble Inn went to considerable trouble to keep their patrons and dishonest politicians happy. First, the customers were allowed to win a reasonable amount of money, but more important, big winners were given an armed escort home. After all, if winners were robbed on the way home, that would scare off other possible customers. See what good data stackers the proprietors of the Tumble Inn were? At the

THOSE UNPREDICTABLE POLITICIANS – LARGE AND SMALL

same time, this type of benign treatment kept the citizens from pressuring the police to close the place down.

Finally, the owners of the Tumble Inn were politicians enough to understand and take advantage of how various governmental agencies characteristically defended their own "turf" from other agencies. Defending one's turf has always been an important part in local, state, and national politics - and of course in business corporations and even the local marching and chowder societies. In this case, it was the turf of area law enforcement agencies. Years and years of past law enforcement practice and procedure were well known to the Tumble Inn crew. They knew the city police could not go outside the city limits. The Sheriff took care of the county, and local protocol dictated that he not interfere within any community that had its own police force. The State Police concerned themselves mostly with crime on the highways, but even in the rare cases when they would deal with "off-highway" crime, they did not try to enforce laws inside city or village limits. How many of you can guess the simple, quite legal scheme the Inn crowd dreamed up to accomplish their seeming invulnerability? It was all based on knowing how the "law" had its data stacked. As I mentioned earlier, the Tumble Inn was located out in the country beyond the limits of any town or village. Many of the employees lived in houses, trailers etc. in the area immediately surrounding the roadhouse. Step one - they established their own town. Yep, it was all very legal and allowed them to operate within their own

LIFE'S DATA STACKERS

"city limits". Next, one of the Inn employees was "elected" Chief of Police. Once they had their own "police force" no other law enforcement group would take any action within that jurisdiction. The Tumble Inn folks thought they had it made - and for many years they did. Everything was going really great until some of the once predictable aspects of their world became unpredictable.

First, an almost unbelievable event occurred. An honest man was elected Mayor of the nearby city. No one would have predicted that turn of events. The Mayor then brought in an honest police chief who had been well trained in FBI schools. Now, in a town noted for its sin and corruption, that was really unpredictable! Then the new Mayor and police chief ignored the "turf" boundaries and began to seek the cooperation of other enforcement groups as well as the business community. As a result the Tumble Inn found itself being deprived of many services that would normally have come from the big city-such as telephone service. The real capper, and the final straw, was a raid and shutdown by State liquor agents. The State liquor agents' "turf" was statewide and not limited to any political boundaries. Bye bye Tumble Inn. Do you suppose laid-off machine gunners can collect unemployment?

POLITICIANS CAN BE SO EXASPERATING

After watching local, state, and federal government officials all over the country, we have to wonder why the politicians, once they get into office, are so frustrating. What is it they do that makes many of us so angry and distrustful? Why do we have "grievances" against them? Simply put, because they're unpredictable! Some are just plain liars, but even the most honest among them seem to be ignorant of how important it is to be consistent and for their actions to be predictable to their constituencies. Too often they just seem to zig and zag in response to the latest polling data. I guess that means we can at least predict that, as a result, they will be unpredictable. Some of this inconsistency may be intentional, so that the public never gets to concentrate on any one thing long enough to get really mad about it.

Another reason that politicians in office incite so much ire is that they too often ignore the other human relations rules I discussed earlier. They fail to communicate properly, or promptly, which encourages us to dream up negative assumptions about their motives and/or actions. They at least appear to have little or no regard for their constituent's abilities to make intelligent decisions and judgments. As a result the politicos feel compelled to make more rules and guidelines for us idiots.

OK, so they "feel our pain". But that doesn't mean that they should assume that we need or want more tax-increasing ill-considered legislation. This assumption of public ignorance or don't care attitude is not entirely their fault. Politicians receive a lot of help from some other well-known culprits in this scenario. We find these disinterested members of the public in homes all

LIFE'S DATA STACKERS

across America. Insomniacs ensconced in their womb-like recliners watching Leno, Letterman and How the World "Churns", on television, Ma and Pa reading newspapers at the breakfast table while the bread quietly incinerates in the toaster, plus a miscellaneous mélange of mindful minions dutifully listening to a gaggle of garrulous gurgling talk radio prognosticators. What do you suppose all these solid, and sometimes soft-headed, citizens have in common? What activity occurs regardless of their race, their age, their sex, or their national origin? Why, of course, in their semiconscious state they are "working hard" at getting their data stacked. Too lazy to learn for themselves, they placidly accept what is thrown at them from sources whose objectivity they do not question. Did I mention GIGO again - garbage in, garbage out? Do you see how sneaky these data stackers are? When you least expect it, when your defenses are down, they attack!!

THE GULLIBLE PUBLIC

Unfortunately it's quite difficult for the general public to sort out the truth from the lies or distortions disseminated by politicians and by popular media outlets reporting on politicians and their actions. Tangled syntax and mangled metaphors are too often combined to lead us down the proverbial garden path. In this sometimes Orwellian world of politics, lies frequently become perceived as "truth", either because they "fit" one's social agenda or world view, or revolve around the deceptively

THOSE UNPREDICTABLE POLITICIANS – LARGE AND SMALL

technical use or redefinition of common words such as the word "is". This sad situation is encouraged by the large number of people who will readily believe whatever they see on television, in the movies, or in newspapers and magazines. We hear comments like "it must be true or they wouldn't print it", or "show it on TV" or "say it on the radio". And then there are always a certain number of people who will apparently believe almost anything. As P.T. Barnum once put it, "there is a sucker born every minute". It's for these folks that the politicians thank their respective deities - if they have any.

How do we the public get that way? Why are we so indifferent and uncaring about how our data is stacked? Perhaps it's because we've become accustomed to it after years and years of indoctrination (ideological data stacking) not only from politicians and the news media, but also from educators, union bosses, social groups, the boss at work, and from other self-appointed "experts" who've been ready and willing to tell us what to think and believe.

Whether the source is a professional politician, a perceived authority in his or her field, or perhaps an author, or news commentator who, over the years has developed a faithful following - regardless of the source, those who will not learn to be more discerning are fated to collect dubious and often lopsided data in their internal computers. By now you should be an expert at recognizing those "always alert" propaganda input

LIFE'S DATA STACKERS

terminals called sight, sound, and smell. (Smell? Certainly! Haven't you seen those magazine advertisements with a scratch and sniff patch?) You can't always control the input, but you can certainly evaluate it. Now a brief look at two or three examples of those who trust "data stackers" too much.

When you were in school did you believe everything the teacher or professor told you? And do you still? Do you still know for certain that person was always correct? When you read a text book on American history did you accept everything at face value such as, for example, regarding the discovery of America? Did you learn that America was discovered Columbus, by Norwegians, by a bunch of Irishmen in a leather boat, or maybe a lost tribe of Israel? What you learned depended on what book you read. What is true may be something else entirely.

In school you probably had to accept whatever version the teacher gave you. At the very least you most likely had to parrot back the stuff as it was taught or you would get a bad grade.

The truth is that many professors and teachers, and the textbooks they select, are far more politically motivated and less interested in presenting a balanced view than you might expect. History books, in particular, are notorious for presenting information that is far from the truth, for presenting debatable historical theories as fact, and for being grossly affected by their authors' ignorance or personal, political, or social agenda. In these days of "political correctness" this problem has been

THOSE UNPREDICTABLE POLITICIANS – LARGE AND SMALL

magnified considerably as some authors struggle to reshape history to suit their own viewpoint. There are still some reliable history books available but you have to search for them – and know what to look for.

You need to be able to tell the good teachers from the closet politicians. A good professor or teacher will invite questioning and listen to other opinions. Sadly, that type of instructor has become much too rare – especially in the wake of the era of the "flower children" with left wing faculties increasingly running many American universities. The innocent lambs fresh from high school, and from homes where politics are seldom discussed, are often easily indoctrinated into dubious belief systems.

Most parents make little or no attempt to stack their children's political data, or to teach their children how to evaluate and question, before sending their little darlings off to the big time university and into the clutches of the eager, politically-motivated faculty. As a result, many of those trusting students become politically-motivated teachers and professors themselves, and continue to teach subjects from the same one-sided political, social, and philosophical perspective they were taught and accepted as objective truth.

Before you send your children off to do battle with our highly-politicized educational system, please do your best to teach them to question everything they see, read and hear. Teach them to always consider the source of such information and

LIFE'S DATA STACKERS

whether it's being stacked in a less-than-objective way - and to look into and honestly consider opposing opinions before reaching their own conclusions. This type of preparation may well be your most important job as a parent and a primary data stacker.

At the same time, as you teach them to spot politically-motivated instructors and to evaluate and question what they're taught, perhaps you should also teach them to do so with DISCRETION. After all, some instructors regard students who ask questions as being impolite or insolent at best, or worse, if there is an implication of a differing opinion, as being trouble makers or lacking in intelligence. There goes the scholarship and/or the grade point needed to get into graduate school!

Again, not all politicians are elected public officials or actively seeking political office. There are also politicians running for the presidency of high school classes, and for various elected positions with labor unions, fraternal groups, and home owners associations. And let's not forget that army of bureaucrats who, though unelected, think nothing of taking a simple legislative act and turning it into a tangle of incomprehensible, and frequently improper, rules and regulations favoring a political outcome never intended by the legislature.

Each such group has its social or political agenda that the group insists on promoting for its own benefit – and often at your expense. It's important, therefore, that you determine this

THOSE UNPREDICTABLE POLITICIANS – LARGE AND SMALL

sometimes hidden agenda before the group can stack your data with self-serving garbage.

I saw an example of this while serving on the Board of Directors of a vocational school system. There was well-organized lobbying by teachers and administrators who were seeking to "feather" their own individual nests. Political action? You bet it was. There were full time well-paid administrators who spent many months each year figuring out how to stack our (Board of Directors) data banks to get more money for some rather dubious projects, allegedly for "the good of the students", but actually more for the benefit of the administrators. The money, of course, came out of the pockets of taxpayers.

One day, much to the dismay of the administrators, our Board decided to start asking a lot of questions and even demanded proof that the administrators' requests were necessary. That simple approach resulted in many dollars being cut out of the administrator's proposed budget. "Sandlot" politicians such as these rely on their ability to stack your data in their favor and on your failure to ask questions and hold them to account. Don't let politicians' propaganda overload your rationality circuits!

To spend time in the world of local, state, or national politics is to step into a never never land of intrigue, greed, ambition, power, chicanery, and above all, data stacking. To succeed and survive in politics the practitioner must develop great skill in manipulating the minds of his or her constituents. Every form of communication and psychological technique is

LIFE'S DATA STACKERS

brought into play by politicians for the purpose of controlling your thoughts and actions. Those who've never learned to ask questions or examine the premises of politicians' plenteous propaganda are most likely to be deceived. They are, therefore, the politician's favorite target. The old expression, "the masses are asses", is most properly applied to these – the ones who will not think for themselves. Combine this with the scandalous degree of voter apathy in this country, and you have a recipe for, at best, political mediocrity. In the business world we say "we get what we inspect for" - a maxim that also applies in politics. You won't get good honest government unless voters inspect and demand it. If the politicos have successfully stacked your computer to expect low standards, they'll give you what you expect. I guess you could say that in this regard, we citizens deserve what we get.

Since fact is so often much better than fiction, I think it's time to discuss in more detail some of the hi-jinks of real life politicians - officials who were elected by people just like you and me! The following examples show what happens when we, the great unwashed masses, whose brains have been filled with "garbage in", now produce "garbage out" in the form of elected officials.

STATE AND LOCAL HI-JINKS

Did you hear the one about the Municipal Court judge who KEPT his pre-election promises? His was an elected

THOSE UNPREDICTABLE POLITICIANS – LARGE AND SMALL

position that made him responsible, among other things, for handling traffic cases. During his campaign he assured the voters that if elected, he would "fix" their traffic tickets. Wow! What an opportunity for the local scofflaws. Naturally the good citizens, having had their greedy self serving data stacked, and demonstrating their low expectations, elected him to office.

Does this sound unbelievable to you? It wouldn't if you knew the community. This was a town where the police chief had a criminal record, and relatives of police officers ran houses of prostitution. The "mob"- run numbers racket could be found in every bar and small retail establishment. Why, even little old ladies sold chances on the numbers. To them it was a means to earn some income when they had no pension program. In this town, almost anything illegal could and did happen. Looks like the Judge knew his voters pretty well.

After his election, that upstanding representative of law and order immediately began to live up to the voter's expectations. He took care of those nasty and inconvenient traffic tickets. In fact, he did this so well it eventually came to the attention of the State's higher courts. The higher court, having a bit more integrity, removed the judge from office. Anywhere else such a removal would have ended the Judge's career - but not in this town. The local citizens, smarting from this affront to their wishes and to their elected hero, turned around and elected him Mayor!

LIFE'S DATA STACKERS

Incidentally, if you think this is a rare occurrence, look around in your own city and state and see how many similar cases you can find. Sally Donnelly, reporting in the September 6, 1999 issue of Time Magazine on the Baltimore mayoral race, wrote that, "Of the 27 original candidates for mayor, six have criminal-arrest records, three have filed for bankruptcy, and one is a convict". For another outstanding example, political history buffs may also want to check the history of Boston and the career of its famous Mayor, James M. Curley. Nuff said!!

The distance between city politics and union politics is no great leap. In fact, they are often closely intertwined. Some years ago, in a certain large Midwestern city, only one brand of electrical conduit could be installed. There was no law specifying the use of that particular brand, it was a union thing. The steel company that manufactured the product had learned that, to do business in that city, it would have to meet the demands of a particular person: a man known as "Umbrella Mike". The steel company discovered that learning the local "facts of life" (or getting your data stacked) could be unpleasant. The steel company could make the conduit, sell it to a builder, but no union man would install it without an OK from Mike. City officials, who had learned how to get and keep the votes of the union members, looked the other way. Once the Company learned this they took whatever actions were necessary to get Mike on their side - and they did it so well that only **their** conduit could be used from then on.

THOSE UNPREDICTABLE POLITICIANS – LARGE AND SMALL

You may be wondering why the gentleman was called "Umbrella Mike". It's said that he would carry an umbrella into a bar, hang his umbrella on the bar rail, and visit with specific patrons. In an unobtrusive manner, those wanting favors would slip money into the top of the partially open umbrella. Mike was never seen to touch the "contributions". Once all of the participants in this little "game" had their data stacked as to how things were done, the wheels of commerce and city government ran smoothly.

Coincidentally, as I am writing this, the local TV station is reporting on the removal of a south Florida City Councilman from office following a conviction for trading political influence for sexual favors. He was sentenced to a long term of probation and many hours of community service. OK, at first glance it appears the law caught up with a bad guy. Well, maybe. The news report was telling about some local women who had gotten up a petition to have his sentence reduced so that he'll be able to run for office in the next election!

Why would anyone want to put a convicted crook or incompetent back into office? At first glance it doesn't seem to make sense. It does, however, if we ask how the misguided voters might benefit. Many may have money, power, notoriety, special favors, and/or preferred legislative actions to gain from a crook's reelection. Or, put into easily understood words, the voters' motivation is just plain old-fashioned greed.

LIFE'S DATA STACKERS

Similarly, self-interest is the obvious motive behind many welfare recipients' support for politicians who provide easy-to-obtain handouts. Over the years, welfare recipients have had their data stacked rather well by the legislators. "Vote for me and you will receive goodies". "You scratch my back and I'll scratch yours". This is not to pick on those receiving welfare - they are only one example of a pervasive evil in our system.

Other examples include the farmer who gets the highway crew to clean out his private road, the large chicken packing company that's allowed to dump its untreated effluent into a river, the building materials company that gets all of the city's business without bid, the insurance company whose contributions obtain favorable decisions from a state Supreme Court, or the police department that looks the other way when union members become violent on a picket line.

You, the voter, like to have "friends" in high places and tend not to vote for those who would take away your unearned benefits. Your internal computer has been well stacked over the years - first, by those who told you that this was a reasonable attitude, and second by the politicians who are happy to be "generous" with the taxpayer's money.

An old time candidate for President of the United States, Al Smith, is reputed to have said, "no one wants to kill Santa Claus". Al Smith, and the ancient Romans who provided "bread and circuses", knew that freebies would buy votes and/or power.

334

THOSE UNPREDICTABLE POLITICIANS – LARGE AND SMALL

However, the people whose data is stacked in this manner will eventually bring disaster on themselves. High taxes, armies of bureaucrats, burdensome regulations are all results of noninvolvement and the public's lack of interest. As Pogo, the famous cartoon character, has wisely observed, "we have met the enemy and they is us". See what I mean by emphasizing the importance of looking around you? I bet we could make a very long running TV series based on the ill-informed public and the miscreants who prey upon them. We could run it on the "Gotcha" channel.

STACKING MY OWN POLITICAL DATA

You'd be justified in thinking that I have a negative view of politicians in general, and that I have gone out of my way to present them in a bad light. (I did, however, mention one honest Mayor at the beginning of this chapter!) Could it possibly be, heaven forbid, that MY data has been stacked in an adverse or incorrect manner? Ok, it's only fair that I sit down and examine my own experiences to see where these opinions originated.

Upon reflection I recall that my data has been stacked by a combination of things I've done and that have been done to me, by people I've met, and by stuff I've read and observed. I was raised in a city of about 200,000 in population. I did the usual teen-age in-school things such as running for class and club offices. I first gained exposure to "real-world" politics by helping a city councilman run for office. What fun it was, handing out

LIFE'S DATA STACKERS

leaflets, door to door precinct work, putting up posters, and running errands for the local politicos. This brought me into contact with a lot of "interesting" characters and contrasting influences. The father of one good friend was the honest President of our City Council, while another friend's father ran the local numbers racket. These experiences led me to major in Political Science when I attended college.

Over the years I became acquainted and worked with a number of local, state, and national legislators - helping some in their campaigns. At one time I had to resist the self-serving demands, and wrath, of a powerful Southern Senator while staffing a new plant in his state. I have worked as a precinct chairman, been a delegate to a state convention, and spent interesting time with delegates on the floor at a Democratic Party national convention. Along the way I provided consulting services to city officials on compensation for city employees, served on Planning and Zoning Commissions, and appeared before legislative committees.

As you can imagine, I met an interesting assortment of players on the political scene. Too many were the usual run-of-the-mill individuals who were more interested in their own reelection than in the welfare of their constituents. There certainly wasn't an abundance of true "statesmen" in the crowd. This miscellaneous collection contributed mightily to my personal data bank – and perhaps will help explain why I may now seem jaundiced.

THOSE UNPREDICTABLE POLITICIANS – LARGE AND SMALL

But, there's always hope, and from time to time good people do emerge and manage to get elected to public office. One of my favorite people along those lines was the late Adlai Stevenson. Stevenson helped me unstack some of my negative assumptions as he demonstrated that a decent person could maintain his integrity and still run for office. His career, from educator to Governor, to Presidential candidate, and to United Nations Ambassador, is thoroughly documented in history books and need not be detailed here. But my first impression of the man came while working as a volunteer during his successful campaign as a reform candidate for Governor of Illinois. In accordance with one of the basic rules I now advocate, that listening is divine, I paid attention to whether the words and goals he expressed in public were the same as those he expressed in private. They were. Many hours spent riding buses from city to city, speech to speech, and in headquarters meetings gave ample time to learn more about this man.

I remember well the night he was elected Governor. I held his son on my lap while he and other staff members reviewed the campaign, and later, after closing campaign headquarters, two of us along with the newly elected States Attorney stood on a rainy Chicago street corner while Stevenson discussed his hopes for the future of the state. As he demonstrated later, the concerns he expressed that night for Illinois were genuine - not just campaign rhetoric. He was a refreshing change from the usual political hacks, and it

LIFE'S DATA STACKERS

demonstrated to me that an honest person COULD succeed in politics. So, although a lot of my data has a negative basis, I have not given up completely. However, these days the dominant communication media organizations, with their lop-sided attempts to find fault and scandal, sure make it tough to be positive or even know who the "good guys" are - especially at a national level. Shall we go there now?

TRUST AND DISTRUST AT THE NATIONAL LEVEL

Was it something the politician said? Something like:

Read my lips!

I did not have sex with that woman!

The era of big government is over!

Our troops will be home by Christmas!

I am sure any one of you can add many more such unreliable utterances. Politicians' inability, or desire, to deliver on their campaign promises is legendary. As a result, many of us have learned not to expect too much from those who claim to have our welfare close to their hearts.

In politics we find a miserable self-perpetuating symbiotic relationship between the public and politicians. Our "upstanding" elected leader conducts focus groups and studies opinion poll after opinion poll to determine the state of our collective minds. This tells him what he needs to do, or at least what he needs to **say** he's going to do, to be reelected and maintain the perks and power of his office. WE stack HIS data

THOSE UNPREDICTABLE POLITICIANS – LARGE AND SMALL

through our answers to the polls. Then our "leader" at least appears to give us what we said we wanted. But too often a politician delivering on a promise is like the old description of something gained in contract negotiations. "He gave me the sleeves out of his vest".

Of course, by cleverly wording the questions asked of focus groups or in opinion polls, our sneaky leader, or sympathetic pollsters, can get us to respond in a way that HE, the leader, wants. Some trusting souls really believe that polls conducted by the media and by political party consultants are truly accurate. "We surveyed 1000 people and now know what over 300 million people think - plus or minus 5%".

Hogwash!! First, it is well known that 45 to 50 percent of the people called in a telephone survey hang up without giving answers. It's a better than an even bet that the majority of those hanging up would have had a negative response. Why won't they answer the questions? Since I haven't taken a poll on that question, I can't say for sure, but I can make a few guesses:

Perhaps people refuse to answer because they're aware of pollsters' reputation for phrasing questions in such a way as to insure the responses they want - the old self-fulfilling prophecy trick. Or perhaps they're aware that pollsters, after hearing an unwanted answer, have been known to say "you aren't the type we want" and stop the interview.

And for those who do answer, why are their responses less than reliable? Again, I have no hard data to support this, but

LIFE'S DATA STACKERS

I suspect that, for one thing, where a question of "political correctness" is involved, many people will not tell the truth for fear of appearing bigoted or insensitive - especially to an unknown person on the phone who probably knows more than just your telephone number. There's also the additional fear of reprisal. Many of us have read or heard Congressional testimony about people who voiced opinions contrary to those of a President and found themselves investigated by the IRS, the FBI, the EEOC, the EPA or you name it. Combine that information with things like Caller ID, and/or the fact that those being polled know or suspect that the pollsters know whom they are calling, (yes, they have YOUR number). It's therefore easy to understand how calls can tend to generate either a lot of favorable answers or at least nothing controversial. It would be a welcome change if opinion polls were truly anonymous and properly constructed so that results would more accurately represent the voice of the people.

Time to get back to Big Brother. Having determined what course to take, our "leader" begins to manipulate the media, and the media, in turn, manipulates us. Between them, they stack OUR data to believe that Sir Boss is doing what is best for us and the country. We receive touchy feely make-us-feel-good flattery along with such mundane benefits as construction projects, recreation areas, or additional ways to underwrite our day-to-day living costs - hopefully at someone else's expense. In Congress they call these "ear marks". The fact that all of the latter benefits

THOSE UNPREDICTABLE POLITICIANS – LARGE AND SMALL

cost far more when the money first has to be routed through Washington, D.C., or that the new bridge was really needed much more in some other Congressional District, is conveniently overlooked in the constant search for votes.

Oh, what a heady combination they are: power and money, money and power. Republican, Democrat, Reform Party, Libertarian, Socialist or any other, the bottom line is money and power. Huge sums will be spent to indoctrinate you and me into their way of thinking.

With politicians, lying is a way of life. They know full well that any lie told often enough will eventually become "truth" as it is quoted and re-quoted by others who don't bother to question the source or accuracy of a statement or statistic. It's the "rule of three", well known to trial lawyers: if you can figure out a way to say it three times, a jury will believe it.

Various Presidents have readily taken credit for economic good times when the real credit lay with the independent actions of the Federal Reserve Board. Of course the Board may also get the "credit" when things go badly. It is a wonder that any of us withstand the onslaught of this unending avalanche of self-serving propaganda.

But wait a minute, fellow citizen, when did you last ask serious penetrating questions or do research on any of these political proposals? When was the last time you wrote or called your Congressman to voice your opinion? What have you done to restack your local politico's data banks? If you haven't done

LIFE'S DATA STACKERS

any of these things, guess whom you must blame for what happens?

Did I just mention propaganda? Now there's an interesting word. The "data stacker's" tool. During World War II, the word acquired a very bad reputation as Hitler's minions spewed falsehood after falsehood to Germany and the world. This has caused the term to become associated with distortion and/or deception. In fact, the proper definition of propaganda, from Webster's dictionary, is "any systematic, widespread dissemination or promotion of particular ideas, doctrines, practices, etc. to further one's own cause or to damage an opposing one". So, according to its definition, the word propaganda actually implies nothing regarding the accuracy of the information – only that it's disseminated or promoted in such a way as to further a cause (or damage an opposing cause). Come to think of it - that sounds exactly like what most members of our news media do. What they report, though generally not false or inaccurate, is tailored to promote a particular candidate, point of view, or world view. This, in itself, would not be deceptive or wrong if it weren't for the fact that the news media does this while pretending to be objective.

It's really a great shame that our primary news sources, while holding themselves out as sources of impartial information, are, in fact, slanting the news to suit their own agendas.

THOSE UNPREDICTABLE POLITICIANS – LARGE AND SMALL

Objective, balanced journalism has given way to ADVOCACY journalism.

If we are going to have our data stacked, it would be nice to have it done by honest reliable sources - even if they have a known bias. To a certain extent it's possible to do this now – if you know where to look: If I want to learn the Republican view I can read the Spectator. The Daily Worker will let me know what the Communists are thinking. ABC, NBC, CBS, but especially the CNN network and the New York Times, although claiming impartiality, can usually be counted on to extol Democratic candidates and a left-wing world view. However, deception occurs to the extent that these and other major newspapers and the broadcast networks are able to convince the public of their objectivity and impartiality while continuing to present information in a less-than-objective fashion.

This is in addition to the things they prefer not to report at all, or the stories that these news outlets have manufactured in order to convince us what we should think. While in his late teens, one of my sons was attending a Republican Convention. While he and some friends were walking back to their hotel from the convention center, a major network TV truck pulled up, and mistaking them for young leftist radicals, asked them to start a riot so they could get some good pictures. Fortunately, my son and his friends passed on that particular opportunity to be on the 11 o'clock news – but learned a very valuable lesson on how news is sometimes made.

LIFE'S DATA STACKERS

In another case, a dozen protesting students appeared at a minor entry gate to a very large university while 30,000 other students attended classes as usual. That night the national newscast made it look like the entire student body was enraged over the issue the dozen-or-so students were protesting about. And let us not forget the faked truck crash video that NBC's Dateline aired, and the apology that NBC was forced to make when their deception was exposed.

Could it be, though, that, in general, the dominant news media outlets are objective, and only appear to be biased to those whose data has already been stacked in a more conservative direction? It's interesting to note that in a 1992 survey of Washington D.C. journalists by the Freedom Forum, an independent foundation, and the Roper Center, a respected public opinion firm, 89% voted for the Clinton-Gore ticket. In 2007, another university study revealed that the three major news networks gave Democrat politicians about three or four times the positive coverage given Republicans. Please, those of you in the business, don't bother telling me how, in spite of this, you are really impartial in your presentation of the news. It isn't possible. Whether you are conservative or liberal, your stacked data will ultimately show through. All I would ask of you is that you simply admit your bias up front, and then go on with your programs.

There have been some glaring examples of poor, improper, or unfortunate "data stacking", which must be laid at

344

THOSE UNPREDICTABLE POLITICIANS – LARGE AND SMALL

the feet of our national leaders. In their unending quest for votes the political gurus often lead us down unnecessary, often dangerous, and sometimes ridiculous paths – like the Congressional committee that was convened to listen to the unscientific and ill-informed opinion of a movie star who was quite willing to talk way too much about things of which she knew way too little. Using incorrect data from the government, and eager to promote her own agenda, she testified about the use of a chemical called Alar on apples. This scare tactic resulted in a loss of millions of dollars in sales to apple growers while the public shied away from eating a beneficial fruit or drinking apple juice. A more careful study of the information, while proving that, in fact, Alar presented NO health risk, came out too late to save the growers from huge losses.

This was only one of many fiascos that can be laid at the feet of an administrative agency called the EPA - an organization known to shoot first and get the facts later - if ever. You may have noticed how the EPA uses "stars" and big news stories to convince us (stack our data) of this or that danger to our environment. Have you also noticed that when the science supporting the danger is discredited or disproven, retractions are seldom reported? Global warning anyone? On the other hand, where is the EPA when there is a real problem? Why does the agency sit back and ignore real cancer causing agents like MTBE in gasoline? The reason is that MTBE is an additive that the EPA has promoted heavily, claiming that it would make major

LIFE'S DATA STACKERS

reductions in carbon monoxide. The EPA continues to maintain that position in spite of research data that says the reduction is minor. MTBE is now appearing in our drinking water and may be causing cancer and aggravating other preexisting physical problems. Can the EPA's concern for minor reductions in carbon monoxide over serious physical injury be related to the money and pressure from various industry lobbyists - lobbyists who long ago learned (had their data stacked) that if they paid enough money to certain political campaigns they could get either favorable action or inaction from administrative agencies and you, the public, would not complain? In turn, our "esteemed" legislators and executives accept the payouts so that they can increase their personal fortunes and/or continue to buy YOUR vote.

One such situation is making the rounds of various "state houses" across the country as I am writing. It's an attempt by special interests to pass legislation to provide themselves with special protection from liability for the damage being caused by MTBE. They want this legislation passed NOW, before you have a chance to find out how serious the problem is. The situation is now bad enough that some of the media are being "forced" to tell the story. Sooner or later you will learn of this danger and will perhaps demand some action or institute law suits for damage to your health. Maybe it is time for you to stack the internal computers of your own local legislators. Be a STACKER!!!

THOSE UNPREDICTABLE POLITICIANS – LARGE AND SMALL

In the 70's the "Great Society" and social "scientists" helped create all kinds of unrest around the country by raising the expectations of inner city citizens as to what they could reasonably expect from their fellow citizens and government in the way of better living conditions. You have heard of the Watts riots haven't you? I observed somewhat similar events while I was living in Milwaukee, Wisconsin. We heard all kinds of things from our national "experts" about how these people should not be expected to wear hand-me-down clothing, how they all deserved or were "entitled" to a good living and good jobs etc etc. Worthwhile objectives, but those creating the expectation provided no real instruction on how to realistically achieve those goals other than to "spend" - to transfer wealth from workers to non-workers. When a mob surged into a major department store in Milwaukee and stole new merchandise from the racks, no one was prosecuted because they were "entitled" to it. Wonderful! This stacked the looter's data to believe that to achieve the goal of better living conditions, such actions were acceptable and would not be punished. The looter's internal computers now said, "great, let's do it again and again". The politicians taught them that they were entitled to all the goodies they wanted and government law enforcement agencies would be "understanding" if they had to steal them. You may also recall in an earlier chapter I mentioned that when a person has a breakdown in predictability, they have a grievance. These poor people were led to expect many things and a style of living that the government,

347

LIFE'S DATA STACKERS

social agencies and the taxpayers could not deliver - it is no wonder they had some rather large and serious grievances.

So we pay our money and expect to get results. Right? Big money big results, small money smaller results. It has been ever thus in political circles. If I am a big contributor I expect to at least get a night in the Lincoln Bedroom at the White House. My data has been stacked to believe and expect such things. Ah what a difference a "few" dollars will make. Not too many years ago, there was a lady who accumulated considerable wealth and a multitude of high level contacts as she went from wealthy husband to wealthy husband. Pamela Harriman is reputed to have contributed some twelve million dollars to Democratic Party coffers in exchange for the job of Ambassador to France. (A less desirable location could probably be bought for less.)

In considerable contrast to Pamela's patronage prize was the "big deal" some college friends and I received in Washington, D.C. The father of one friend had made a reasonable contribution to the party and had obtained a letter of introduction for us. Well, we did not get any big jobs, but we did get a personal visit with the Senate majority leader, lunch in the Senate dining room (complete with the famous Senate Bean Soup), and a head-of-the-line private elevator trip to the top of the Washington Monument. What I experienced was on a different scale, but the same basic principle applied. We have educated our elected officials in the ways of raising money for

THOSE UNPREDICTABLE POLITICIANS – LARGE AND SMALL

their reelection, and they have learned their lessons well. I suspect that we will find that things are not much different on the international level.

INTERNATIONAL PERILS OF PREDICTION

How many billions of dollars has the United States spent to either "buy" votes in the United Nations, or to promote the continuance and/or support of one political faction over another in a foreign country? Is it any wonder, then, that everyone from backwater dictators to world class powers have had their data stacked to expect a "payoff" of some kind in return for their promise to act in a manner suitable to our government? Past experience and observation has taught them that they can acquire funds in return for cooperation or compliance.

However, they've also learned that, when compliance fails or is politically unacceptable, a few simple threats will usually result in big payoffs from our country. A movie called "The Mouse that Roared" satirizes this phenomenon: The leaders of a small imaginary bankrupt country "roared" at the United States by declaring war – having learned from history that they would receive big-time "aid" money from the U.S. once their little country had lost that war – solving their financial crisis. A handful of "invading soldiers" arrived from the small country by ocean liner and wandered around Manhattan until someone finally noticed them. To simply ask for some help would not

LIFE'S DATA STACKERS

have brought sufficient aid, so they threatened the U.S. with this terrible, though tiny, invading force.

"Want to keep the Communists out of power in my country"? ask the leaders of small Latin American countries, "then send us some cash!". "Want us to promise not to make or use atomic weapons"? ask the leaders of North Korea, "Then promise never to attack us – and, by the way, send lots of free food - and build us a nuclear reactor for peaceful purposes". Hitler took a somewhat more negative approach toward achieving his goals: In effect, he said to the leaders of other nations, "Give me what I want or I will simply send my armies to destroy you" - or, put another way, "You smaller countries can predict that I will kill your people and destroy your buildings if you do not capitulate". With their data stacked from observing Hitler's devastation of countries that had resisted, they gave in without a fight.

In Teddy Roosevelt's day the United States stacked the data of other nations' leaders by acting consistently in accordance with the motto: "speak softly and carry a big stick". Foreign countries knew what to expect (predict) from Roosevelt if they harmed our citizens or otherwise acted contrary to U.S. interests. It's not surprising that, during the Roosevelt administration, conditions remained peaceful with respect to the United States in the world.

This state of international affairs was much like that of the early colonial days when Britain ruled the seas and had established "Pax Britanica". Other countries knew what would happen if they started trouble (data communicated). If they acted against the interests of Great Britain, the British navy, which was supreme in all the oceans, predictably followed through and reinforced the previous data entry. Everyone got the message, and it worked.

Today we may still talk loudly, but too often wave a toothpick and then fail to follow through (the two Gulf Wars being exceptions to this approach). "Garbage in and garbage out". "You Serbians had better be good or we'll conduct a few air strikes against you - well, next time you do it we'll be sure to act - OK, you came to a conference and said you'd be good from now on, and we believe you - gee, you murdered some more innocent civilians! This time we REALLY mean what we said we would do last time but didn't - well this time we DO mean it! Please come to the conference table again even if you didn't keep your last promise, O.K? We're definitely going to bomb you if you don't! This is your very last two week notice! And please promise not to hide any of your equipment in the meantime, O.K? You're making us really mad now! We're really really thinking of hurting you this time!", etc, etc, etc. Predictability? Oh yes, in spades. Of course, after the bombing finally started, we didn't want the opposition to be too mad at us, so we helpfully told them not to worry about our sending in troops.

It's also possible that the antiwar sentiment during and after the Viet Nam war was more than a little responsible for

LIFE'S DATA STACKERS

stacking Saddam Hussein's data in such a way as to embolden him to thumb his nose at the United States in the Middle East. He quite reasonably predicted that nothing would happen. He failed to perceive the shift in national sentiment in the U.S. following the post-Viet Nam era and the increased resolve of certain U.S. presidential administrations. His internal computer had not kept its data banks up to date. Remember, LISTENING IS DEVINE? Unfortunately, after our success in Desert Storm, the "Monday morning quarterbacks", the ever liberal media and opposing politicians began such a cacophony of criticism that it is small wonder that old Hussein felt safe again. This "garbage" data was then reinforced by our failure to move against the Serbs or take action when UN inspection teams in Iraq found violations etc. Later, after many years of violating UN sanctions with impunity, Saddam Hussein found it hard to believe that the U.S. would make any serious move to interfere with his murderous regime and his desire to obtain and use weapons of mass destruction. Of course, he made other mistakes as well: Out of his fear of Iran he allowed the world (and IRAN) to believe that he still actually had biological and chemical weapons. He also convinced the USA and the other western nations in the process, and, consequently, did much to start the second Gulf war. Another of Saddam's wrong predictions was that the second President Bush would never attack Baghdad - after all the first George Bush stopped short of that city. Once again, though, Saddam failed to realize and appreciate the differences between the policies of the two

THOSE UNPREDICTABLE POLITICIANS – LARGE AND SMALL

Presidents and the differences in the situations the two Presidents faced.

Another example of a tragedy that may have been averted but for a questionable assumption based on improper data accumulation is the Spanish American War. When the battleship Maine was sunk in Havana harbor American newspapers immediately assumed that Spain was responsible and called for war - an assumption that has since been shown to have most likely been incorrect. Not one major news outlet had sufficient restraint to say, "stop – let's first examine the facts and the wreckage". So, off to war we went in two oceans.

Also, in the early days of our country, King George III predicted that the colonists in New England would not resist his increased taxation - and that his kingly coffers would benefit from the increased income. The King's prediction was based on data obtained from his experience with other colonies around the world having been similarly mistreated for years without their having revolted. So why should the American Colonies be any different? The King's internal computer thus made a fateful decision. His miscalculation became apparent to him when he learned of the Boston Tea Party.

The history books are overflowing with stories of the astronomical costs suffered due to such miscalculations by heads of state. Millions of lives have been lost and billions of dollars have been spent because leaders have had their data improperly stacked. Rarely is it difficult, in retrospect, to trace the causes of

LIFE'S DATA STACKERS

international catastrophes to incorrect predictions or brutal actions conceived and executed on the basis of poor data - poor data that can often, in turn, be traced back to data stackers such as parents, living conditions, cultural environments etc.

Before World War II, the words of Neville Chamberlain illustrated one of history's biggest miscalculations. His words "peace in our time" have come to represent the failure to prudently control data input - to sort out the garbage information from a notoriously unreliable source (Hitler) from higher quality information obtainable from a reliable source (a review of Hitler and Germany's previous actions and the experiences of others in dealing with the Third Reich).

Consider also how many Russians died at the command of the brutal Joseph Stalin - a man who had learned about controlling others through brutality from a father who was a drunken child abuser. Oh yes, Stalin had his data stacked very early in life, and then practiced what he had learned on those around him. As the data is stacked, the tyrant will act.

It's so easy to get our data stacked without our even being aware of it. The first attack on the World Trade Center in New York City was traced to a Middle Eastern terrorist group. Later, when a terrible explosion took so many lives in the bombing of a federal center in Oklahoma City, it was almost a foregone conclusion that it was, like the World Trade Center bombing, the work of foreign terrorists. The press, many law

THOSE UNPREDICTABLE POLITICIANS – LARGE AND SMALL

enforcement agencies, and the public were certain it was the work of another Middle Eastern group. Once again, as in the Maine incident, few people proposed waiting to learn the facts. The careful investigative approach isn't dramatic enough to sell newspapers or improve TV ratings - especially since, as we all know; only foreign terrorists would do such a thing. Oh my how our data was stacked! At work, once again, was the rule about lack of information - that communication gaps will always be filled with negative assumptions and rumors. As we now know, this atrocity was perpetrated by American men. But lacking information, we did assume, didn't we?

I feel sure that our national politicians, when involved in formulating and executing foreign policy, do their best to carefully, and with great diligence, study the backgrounds of foreign leaders to learn the contents of those leaders' internal computers. Our elected officials almost certainly consider the information the various intelligence agencies collect, and hopefully give considerable weight to the psychological profiles and previous ACTIONS of various world leaders and their opponents. But it's not enough for our leaders to study how other leaders' data is stacked. Our leaders must strive to be predictable in the eyes of other national leaders.

Predictability can be difficult to achieve, however, in a government where the President and the entire executive branch can change completely – as often as every four years. About the

LIFE'S DATA STACKERS

time the rest of the world adjusts to one man's policies, another one takes his place and often implements a whole new agenda. It's tough to predict us Americans.

But then, sometimes when other world governments do act in predictable ways, our government fails to respond in ways that take that predictability into account. As we saw during the Cold War, the Russians never lived up to all of the conditions of any treaty they signed. Yet, despite that dismal record, our government continued to enter into treaties with the Soviet Union in the naïve hope that that nation would honor them. Somebody's data should have been stacked well enough to predict the results. What was that you said Mr. Chamberlain?

You may call it by several names; credibility, reliability, predictability, trustworthiness etc. but, by whatever term, it is essential in all successful human relations. A mistake in understanding between two people may cause a problem that affects only a few. However, in the fields of international and domestic politics, it becomes much more important since the potential consequences are of such a great magnitude. Here, in the larger arena, the failure to understand why someone thinks the way he does may cost billions of dollars – or worse, take millions of lives.

THOSE UNPREDICTABLE POLITICIANS – LARGE AND SMALL

CHAPTER TWELVE

C
O
D
A

Now we come to the last chapter - one headed by a word that is quite familiar to musicians but perhaps unknown to most others. In Webster's New World Dictionary the word "coda" is defined in the following manner: "a more or less independent passage added to the end of a section or composition so as to reinforce the sense of conclusion". Some would say it means to go back and repeat the main theme of the composition. We shall do so.

As any good student will tell you, when you reach the end of a book, it never hurts to go back and take a second look at the chapters you've already read, to gain a broader overall picture of what you've learned. This is particularly true of a textbook when an important test or final examination is in the offing.

CODA

The final exam on what you've learned in this book will be taken and graded every time you encounter another human being. Should you flunk this exam you will never reach your full potential nor realize the wonderful benefits to be derived from positive relations with others. Please be aware that, in this sense, you have been and will continue to be tested every day of your life. Although you may not have done too well on these exams in the past, there's absolutely no reason that you cannot improve your human relations performance in the future.

The time to prepare is now! Like most of us, you can probably use all of the help you can get to achieve at least a passing grade. It's my hope that the contents of these chapters will provide you with that needed help. You may well feel that one particular chapter, more than the others, applies to your personal situation while other chapters seem unnecessary. However, I believe you'll find that each chapter does apply to you to some degree and it's important that you review and see and appreciate the larger picture – and appreciate how the nine rules fit together. If you do, you'll soon discover that these basic "rules" have very broad application to every phase of your life, and to those around you. Having said that, I will do like the man said – "I told you, and now I am going to tell you what I've told you".

We've discussed gangsters and politicians, newlyweds and bar-hoppers, unions and management, bosses and "slaves", teachers and students, parents and children, steelworkers and

LIFE'S DATA STACKERS

soldiers, pilots and professors, and even one lonely guy out of gas in the Nevada desert. Certainly a miscellaneous mélange of characters, but one that includes characters who, like you, have something in common: Correctomundo oh brilliant disciple, it's that wildly voracious brain of yours that's constantly demanding more and more information - and those fantastic five senses constantly at work stacking your internal computer. Your brain is always gathering data so that it can make decisions for you and help you survive. Don't tell me that YOU control your brain - that YOU tell it what to think and do. When was the last time you had to tell your brain to make your body breathe? Heck, contrary to popular childhood mythology, it's almost impossible to hold your breath long enough to turn blue. Fortunately we're born with a brain that already has the necessary "blueprints" to get our basic bodily functions and movements off to a good start. Then comes an unending, until you die, learning period during which, through input from those "fantastic five" senses, you learn to cope with the universe around you.

It's imperative that we constantly acquire new data to add to, or correct, the old. We simply MUST do this if we are to survive and function at an acceptable level in an ever changing world. In fact, we can't even accomplish such simple things as walking and talking without data stacking. However, we must learn at as early an age as possible to be selective in what we stuff into the old brain case. This means being careful about whom we associate with, what books we read, what TV shows

CODA

we watch, what radio shows we listen to, where we take our vacations and even what music we buy. These are all "data stackers" and we can, to a large degree, select from among them only those that will provide the most beneficial information.

You probably are or have been acquainted with people who would commonly be described as "know-it-alls". You should pity, not hate them. Since they "know it all" they don't feel the need to input (learn) or monitor the quality of new data entering their internal computers and therefore end up becoming more and more ignorant - while at the same time remaining self-confident enough to be arrogant. Remember my warning: beware the arrogance of the incompetent and the ignorant. The person who realizes early on that he or she can never "know it all" and who actively continues to pursue knowledge and skills, will be far more successful in life.

For instance, it is generally believed, among Human Resource personnel, that a person cannot be taught how to use common sense or to be self motivated. But HR personnel have developed this "know-it-all" attitude based on limited data: their consistent inability to draw such qualities out of employees by the usual methods of providing better working conditions, offering more pay (number 5 in a list of 10 things employees considered most important), by offering bonuses, or using fear or coercion. To learn how to elicit self-motivated behavior from employees, managers and HR personnel must come to realize that employees need to first be made to see the value of such

LIFE'S DATA STACKERS

behavior by using their own internal computers to complete a bunch of calculations based on the totality of their past experiences. Such employees probably lack self-motivation because they never had a parent, teacher, or counselor provide their internal computers with some clues and information about the benefits that accrue when they gain the ability to motivate themselves to take positive actions. It's preferable that a person be taught this at a very early age. But, if not, even after a person has grown older and joined the work force without having learned to be self motivated, managers can still elicit such behavior by following the basic rules on human relations that I've presented here - and especially the one concerning recognition (all people want and deserve recognition!).

Alas and alack, although some Human Resource people understand that it's possible to draw self-motivation from unmotivated employees, such HR people are often frustrated by having to provide job candidates for managers who refuse to climb out of their ruts of poor leadership and would never even consider implementing solutions along the lines of the basic rules I've presented. Consequently, HR people who find themselves in this position may find that the only way left to them to develop a highly motivated work force is to hire those who already have a high energy level and a desire to work. Increased employee self-motivation that occurs after hiring can usually only be brought about by a "good" manager who has been able to make changes through some careful and well-thought out data stacking.

CODA

Similarly, motivating children into desired actions or character traits takes "good management" by parents. Let me mention here two cases of negative motivation imposed by parents and environment at an early age. I ran across the first case when I stopped in a small town while I was traveling through Oklahoma. Behind the reception desk of the small nondescript motel I stayed in was an attractive young lady with a good personality and obvious intelligence. During the course of conversation I asked how long she had lived in this town. Her answer was "forever". She obviously disliked the routine job she held and was frustrated with life in this out-of-the-way village. Oklahoma City was only 180 miles down the Interstate, but here she sat. Why? All of her life her parents and associates talked only of living in this town and staying near family etc. To go to the "big city" was not only unthinkable, but her data had been stacked in a way that caused her to believe that she probably could not be successful there. A waste of talent and a life brought about by negative data stacking.

SIDE COMMENT: While this young lady is yearning to get out of her small town there are increasing numbers of older folks moving out of the city and into those same towns. Yes, it may be a stage in life, but not all of them are retirees. Many have had their data well stacked about some of the disadvantages of the large cities. (The young lady may later decide, upon acquiring more data, that small town living is not so bad, but she

LIFE'S DATA STACKERS

needs to get out and stack her own data.) Now those people moving back are anxious to find a quieter and safer environment for themselves and their families. You see, everyone has a different viewpoint acquired through their own personal past experiences, and that keeps moving vans running up and down the highways.

The second case negative motivation imposed at a young age, concerns a young man who came into a factory personnel office one day to apply for an assembly line job in an appliance company factory. He came from a farm family with parents of limited education and was, at the time, working on the assembly line of a local cookie factory. Testing revealed an extremely high intelligence level and he presented a positive personality during the interview. It turned out that his parents saw no need for more than a high school education to enable their son to work on the farm or in a factory. They never taught their son that he could aspire to higher achievements and so he never considered himself capable of going into other than factory or farm work. When asked if he would be interested in data processing, he had no idea what that meant. A few years later he was the assistant manager of a data processing department controlling the production, finances, and administration of a major appliance manufacturer. You see, he had to get some new data into his internal computer. Data that told him he was intelligent and capable of achieving far

CODA

more in life. He had to overcome the old negative data from his home environment by inputting new information.

I hope that by now I've made it quite clear that to be happier and more effective in everyday life we all need to acquire and use the human relations skills and knowledge laid out in the preceding chapters. We must be selective in choosing our "data stackers" to the extent possible from amongst bosses, employees, friends, spouses, children, teachers, lovers, and enemies. They can all use help - and you too noble friend. As I said before:

Doctor, lawyer, merchant, chief
Use these rules or come to grief!

For those of you who weren't paying attention in class, let me now list again the nine Guidelines for good human relations and coincidently good data stacking.

1. WHAT IS REAL, IS REAL - OR - PERCEPTION IS REALITY

To Ted Bailey, the real world was a place where successful people never made a mistake. To others, mistakes are not only common but considered reasonable learning experiences. These different perceptions lead to radically different approaches to life. The "facts of life" are different for each person based upon the totality of his or her data stacking. The attitudes and actions of a child raised in an abusive

LIFE'S DATA STACKERS

atmosphere are far different from those of a person raised in a loving and supportive household. At work, employees' attitudes and their perception of the "facts" are shaped by their realities. Dr. Charles Hughes, on page 21 of his book, Making Unions Unnecessary, expresses it this way: "Discussions on whether employees should or should not feel "that way" are fruitless. Attitudes are facts as perceived by the employees". Your assignment: Take time to determine your own "reality" and decide if it needs changing and/or updating.

2. EACH ACTION WILL NORMALLY RESULT IN AN OPPOSITE (BACK TO YOU) AND EQUAL REACTION.

How many times have you seen a violent outburst between two people, brought on by an exchange of words that gradually increased in anger and intensity? If I say something insulting to you, you will most likely try to respond with something at least as bad as my comment. Many a husband and wife have started an argument speaking softly - only to end up shouting. In the Bible, it says that a soft word will turn away wrath. Someone apparently knew the value of this guideline long before I did.

CODA

3. AN ABSENCE OF COMMUNICATIONS WILL ALWAYS RESULT IN NEGATIVE RUMORS AND/OR ASSUMPTIONS.

You're right, no one tells you anything. No one seems to care whether you get the necessary information to make decisions or do your job right. Since the upper levels (or your parents) will not tell you anything, you tend to assume the worst. No one says they love me, so I guess they don't. The neighbors are driving a 10-year old car (and you don't know why) so you assume they must be short of money. Times are tough, but the Company refuses to tell us about its financial condition or plans - so I guess I'd better start looking for another job before I get laid off. My wife didn't answer the phone when I called from work, so she must be having an affair - or is lying dead on the bathroom floor. It goes on and on doesn't it? Not all people have a "duty" to share their personal lives with you, but don't let this lack of knowledge build up suspicious or negative thoughts about them. Give them the benefit of the doubt until you learn some facts. However, in a business environment, it's my opinion that companies *do* have an affirmative duty to communicate with their employees. Instead of telling employees only those things they MUST know, tell them EVERYTHING – except, of course, that which they must not know.

LIFE'S DATA STACKERS

4. THE HUMAN COMPUTER IS NEVER WRONG! EVERY DECISION YOU MAKE IS 100% CORRECT.

You saw it here first! Now you know there's at least one person who thinks you're always correct. Mind you, I didn't say you're necessarily always right. We covered this in chapter one. We're correct at any particular instant in time, but we can just as quickly gain new information (data) that tells us we were wrong and something else is right. A puny little kid approaches you and says he wants your money. Your computer quickly calculates that you can beat his brains out, if necessary, and you decide to tell him to get lost. The youngster pulls out a 357 magnum and shoves it in your face. Ah, how quickly your computer accepts this new data and makes an entirely different decision - but a correct one.

5. ALL GRIEVANCES, OR COMPLAINTS, RESULT FROM A BREAKDOWN IN PREDICTABILITY.

Consider for a moment what you read in Chapters Four and Ten. Isn't it frustrating when unexpected things happen? Even a surprise birthday party that's loads of fun can be dampened by the wish that, if you had only known ahead of time, you could have put on that new outfit or gotten a haircut. When the Russians unexpectedly put Sputnik into orbit around the earth it caused many grievances at high levels of our government. Chagrin at being excelled, and worse, fear of the military implications. Most of our problems are a little more prosaic: A

CODA

snowstorm in the middle of the night when you have an important meeting at 8 a.m. - the day care center closes without notice - the boss wants you to work overtime on the night you planned to go out. If you could have predicted these things, you could have made other arrangements or at least have been mentally prepared.

6. TO LISTEN IS DIVINE

Listen very carefully and you just might be able to predict events more accurately and avoid those grievances mentioned earlier. Knowing you had an important meeting in the morning; did you listen to the weatherman the night before as he warned of a heavy snowfall coming your way? Might have helped. Did you hear the day care owner talk about how they weren't doing too well financially? Did you listen to your child when he said one of his schoolmates was bragging about bringing a gun to school? Did you listen to your parents when they described the lessons they had learned in life? Have you asked questions and listened carefully to a friend's problems? Have you learned how those around you have their data stacked so that you can do a better job of predicting their actions? Did you listen when she said something about getting married? Nothing like a little listening to keep a person happy and out of trouble.

LIFE'S DATA STACKERS

7. EACH PERSON DESIRES, AND DESERVES, RECOGNITION.

Recognition - the cornerstone of human relations. It's more than simply telling people that you think they're worthwhile and have value. Your interest must be truly sincere. If not, it will become obvious and ruin your creditability. It means communicating with them on a regular basis and (again) listening to their joys and sorrows. When you ask questions to improve your predictability, you are showing interest in the person. That and the subsequent listening to their answers provide recognition of the highest order. Of course, you should communicate and pass along information - it shows that you consider them to be worthy of receiving it and that you think they deserve to know the facts. There are many forms of recognition: the sharing of information, listening to the opinions of others, an appreciative smile, the proverbial pat on the back, and even applying punishment when appropriate.

8. AS THE COMPUTER IS STACKED, THE PERSON WILL ACT.

As you embark on your program of learning more about people, you'll become much more aware of how an individual's actions are guided by the sum total of the information in his or her internal computer. Many leaders of industry and government have learned the need for hard work and the aggressive pursuit of a goal as they struggled to fight their way out of poverty. A

CODA

soldier back from battle may dive under a table at the sound of an explosion - his computer having been stacked to take that action in order to save his life. In alcoholic families bad habits are passed down through generations, creating the need for organizations like Adult Children of Alcoholics that try to unstack some of the harmful data. In a previous chapter I mentioned the example of spouses who are raised to expect one or the other to be in charge of finances based on their gender. And, of course, remember there was good old Joseph Stalin, raised by a drunken and abusive father and who, in turn, grew up to abuse and destroy those around him.

9.   BEWARE THE ARROGANCE OF THE INCOMPETENT

To me the "incompetent" fall into four basic categories. The first of these includes those persons who simply lack sufficient brain power. Through no fault of their own they do not have a high enough IQ to master the world they're in. I've seen persons so afflicted manage to hold decent jobs through good training and sometimes by means of a charming personality, but often the individual becomes overbearing in an attempt to hide his or her inadequacies.

Next there are those folks who've never gotten the word. They are what you might call the "under-informed" group. These types only read the newspaper headlines, watch the nightly news on TV, go to conventions just to play golf, sit in bars, or engage

LIFE'S DATA STACKERS

in "bull" sessions etc. Why bother to dig deeper than the surface information? Maybe they're just lazy - at least mentally. However their lack of in-depth knowledge of a subject never stops them from offering "expert" opinions on most any subject.

A third group includes those who may be well informed but lack experience. You've heard of them before - people who got all of their knowledge from a book. In earlier chapters I mentioned the professors who ran management training seminars without having had any practical management experience themselves. Then there are single newly graduated psychology majors who have the guts to do family counseling. Oh sure, these types can talk long and loud about what you should or should not do, but they haven't walked the walk.

The last group is the worst. They're well informed, have experience and enough brain power, but are terribly conceited. While you may argue that these persons should at least be regarded as competent despite their conceit, to me the fact of their conceit makes them incompetent. It prevents good relations with family and friends, makes them obnoxious at work, and causes considerable resentment among all persons they deal with. No one really wants to work with them. Conceit can really screw up a team approach to any project - be it a multimillion dollar deal or a family wedding. And people who screw things up that way are, to me, incompetent.

It is a shame isn't it? Often those who are the most incompetent and/or ignorant tend to go about acting superior and

CODA

obnoxious. Often for the purpose of overcoming or masking their inferiority complexes they must throw their weight around and puff and huff about how important they are. As one management consultant expressed it – they're so incompetent, they don't know they're ignorant. So often this type of person will come on so loud and strong about a subject that some listeners will think that he must be right - so the listeners keep quiet. This only allows the offender to continue browbeating others, and too often, move up in the world. Sometimes a few well thought out questions will pop their balloon and reveal the shallowness of their knowledge. If you ever have the opportunity, this approach is especially fun to use when some politician is espousing his latest cure - all for the people.

A FEW CONCLUDING THOUGHTS

You should use these nine guidelines to help you obtain a better understanding of why people do the things they do. The rules, when you use them in conjunction with each other, will assist you in all your endeavors. By implementing these rules you'll acquire a better understanding of the "human computer" concept and the importance of recognizing the impact of the various "data stackers" in your life. They are there. You cannot avoid them or shut them out. Learn to use the positive stackers while rejecting the damaging influence of the bad stackers.

It's my hope that through reading this book you'll become a better student of human nature. The observation and study of those you love, your enemies, strangers, business associates and all other persons, is a fascinating occupation. As you become more proficient in this skill you will begin to notice the little things that open the doors of understanding. Perhaps of greater importance is what you will learn about yourself. Try sitting down and asking yourself why you think a certain way, or why you took a particular action. Sometimes a close friend or family member can help by asking questions similar to those used in resolving grievances. Honest self-examination may lead to changes in your outlook on life and/or those around you. Author Jonathan Harr, on page 73 of his book, "A Civil Action" expresses it well. "You can never know enough about why someone acts the way they do".

I would like to finish by quoting the late distinguished humanitarian, physician, and philosopher Dr. Albert Schweitzer. He made a very important observation:

> "We wander through life, in a semi-darkness in which none of us can distinguish exactly the features of his neighbor; only from time to time, through some experience that we have with our companion, or through some remark that he passes, he stands for a moment, close to us, as though illumined by a flash of lightning".